NEVER FORGET NATIONAL HUMILIATION

CONTEMPORARY ASIA IN THE WORLD

CONTEMPORARY ASIA IN THE WORLD

DAVID C. KANG AND VICTOR D. CHA, EDITORS

This series aims to address a gap in the public-policy and scholarly discussion of Asia. It seeks to promote books and studies that are on the cutting edge of their respective disciplines or in the promotion of multidisciplinary or interdisciplinary research but that are also accessible to a wider readership. The editors seek to showcase the best scholarly and public-policy arguments on Asia from any field, including politics, history, economics, and cultural studies.

Beyond the Final Score: The Politics of Sport in Asia, Victor D. Cha, 2008

The Power of the Internet in China: Citizen Activism Online, Guobin Yang, 2009

China and India: Prospects for Peace, Jonathan Holslag, 2010

India, Pakistan, and the Bomb: Debating Nuclear Stability in South Asia, Šumit Ganguly and S. Paul Kapur, 2010

Living with the Dragon: How the American Public Views the Rise of China, Benjamin I. Page and Tao Xie, 2010

East Asia Before the West: Five Centuries of Trade and Tribute, David C. Kang, 2010

Harmony and War: Confucian Culture and Chinese Power Politics, Yuan-Kang Wang, 2011

Strong Society, Smart State: The Rise of Public Opinion in China's Japan Policy, James Reilly, 2012

Asia's Space Race: National Motivations, Regional Rivalries, and International Risks, James Clay Moltz, 2012

ZHENG WANG

NEVER FORGET NATIONAL HUMILIATION

HISTORICAL MEMORY in CHINESE POLITICS and FOREIGN RELATIONS

COLUMBIA UNIVERSITY PRESS / NEW YORK

Columbia University Press
Publishers Since 1893
New York Chichester, West Sussex
cup.columbia.edu

Paperback edition, 2014

Library of Congress Cataloging-in-Publication Data

Wang, Zheng, 1968–
Never forget national humiliation : historical memory in Chinese politics and foreign relations / Zheng Wang.
p. cm.—(Contemporary Asia in the world)
Includes bibliographical references and index.
ISBN 978-0-231-14890-0 (cloth : alk. paper)—
ISBN 978-0-231-14891-7 (pbk. : alk. paper)—
ISBN 978-0-231-52016-4 (e-book)
1. China—Foreign relations—1949– 2. China—Foreign relations—Psychological aspects. 3. China—Politics and government—1949– 4. Collective memory—China—Political aspects. I. Title.
JZ1734.W38 2012
327.51—dc23

2012015969

Columbia University Press books are printed on permanent and durable acid-free paper.
Printed in the United States of America

Cover image: Courtesy of Xinhua *Cover design: Angela Voulangas*
Book design: Lisa Hamm

FOR XIAOJUAN

CONTENTS

ILLUSTRATIONS

FIGURES

TABLES

PREFACE

I GREW UP in Kunming, the capital city of Yunnan Province in southwestern China. When I was a boy, China had ended its decades-long policy of being a closed society and had begun the process of reform and opening up. I remember the first time I saw Westerners. My friends and I were playing on the street when they passed by. We were so mesmerized by the presence of these strange new people that we could not help but follow them as they explored our city. Soon, we were joined by a large gathering of Chinese children and adults eventually blocking their path. For these Westerners, China was no doubt as much a mystery as they were to us. Certainly, none of us that day, Western or Chinese, could have anticipated what China would look like thirty years later.

Today, I am a professor teaching international relations at a university not far from New York City. In my university, there are more than ten professors just like me, raised in China and having received PhDs in the United States. There are even more students coming from China to attend school here. When my wife and I were buying birthday gifts for our young daughter, we found that most of the toys were labeled "Made in China." No longer separated from the rest of the world, China has become the world's factory. Never before in history have China, the United States, and the rest of the world become so closely linked together as they are today.

This past summer, I took a flight back to China to visit my family. The Boeing 777 on which I traveled did not have a single unoccupied seat among the three hundred available. This flight, and more than thirty others just like it, runs every single day of the year, shuttling thousands of people back and forth between the two nations.

A veteran of the State Department told me that thirty years ago, when the United States established relations with the People's Republic of China, there were less than fifty American diplomats and staff assigned to the embassy. In 2008, a new U.S. Embassy complex was formally opened in Beijing. Today, more than 1,100 U.S. federal officials work in this enormous new building, and there are four U.S. consulates in other cities in China.

When compared to thirty years ago, however, there is one thing that has not fundamentally changed; for most Westerners, China is still a mystery. Being a professor of international relations, my students often ask me about China's future, but I cannot always answer their questions; there are too many variables, too many perspectives, and too much uncertainty. I am reminded of an article Prof. David Shambaugh of George Washington University wrote for *Time* on the occasion of China's 60th anniversary. His article provides a comprehensive and thoughtful review of China's national experience since the founding of the People's Republic in 1949. Even with such a thorough review, however, Shambaugh concluded his article by saying: "One thing is certain: China will remain a country of complexity and contradictions—which will keep China watchers and Chinese alike guessing about its future indefinitely."[1]

The reason China is still a mystery is not a lack of data or statistics. Even if the Chinese government could adequately address people's complaints about its lack of transparency, the mystery of China would remain, because the roots of these questions lie in the lack of understanding about the inner world of the Chinese people. What are their motivations? What are their intentions?

But this is not a closely guarded secret of the Chinese. These questions do not have clear answers for many Chinese people, either. As Susan Shirk, an expert on Chinese politics and a former deputy assistant secretary of state, rightly put it, the central question in the debate about China is not about how to measure China's strength but how to understand Chinese intentions:

> The question of whether China is a threat to other countries cannot be answered just by projecting China's abilities—its growth rates,

> technological advances, or military spending—into the future as many forecasters do. Strength is only one part of the equation. Intentions—how China chooses to use its power—make the difference between peace and war.[2]

From a broad perspective, what I try to do in this book is to help people to better understand the Chinese people, their inner world, their motivations, and their intentions. China experts may have different perspectives on many issues, but they should agree on one point: One cannot understand China's current situation without knowing China's past. In this book, I propose the idea that historical memory is the most useful key to unlocking the inner mystery of the Chinese. Furthermore, I have an even bolder proposition to present: While many societies have "dominant ideas" or "national ideas"—defined by Jeffrey Legro as "the collective beliefs of societies and organizations about how to act"[3]—I believe that the Chinese people's historical consciousness and its complex of myth and trauma are the dominant ideas in China's public rhetoric. National ideas are difficult to change because, like all traditions that are institutionally entrenched, they become ingrained in public rhetoric and bureaucratic procedures. These ideas often unconsciously but profoundly influence people's perceptions and actions.

The research in this book identifies historical memory as the prime raw material for constructing China's national identity. Since national interests are constructed by national identity, and national interests in turn determine foreign policy and state action, a thorough understanding of Chinese historical consciousness is essential to understanding Chinese politics and foreign policy behavior. It is my hope that this book's portrayal of historical memory can be useful in decoding China's political transition, popular sentiment, and international behavior in the post-Tiananmen and post–Cold War eras.

NEVER FORGET NATIONAL HUMILIATION

INTRODUCTION

FROM "TANK MAN" TO CHINA'S NEW PATRIOTS

WHEN THINKING about China, many in the West tend to conjure up an image of the young Chinese man who stopped the advance of a column of tanks in Tiananmen Square on June 5, 1989, the day after the Chinese government began cracking down violently on protests in Beijing. This famous picture no doubt depicts a confrontational relationship between Chinese people and the Communist regime. Many, in fact, gained the view from the pro-democratic student movement in 1989 that the Chinese government was illegitimate and people wanted it to be overthrown.

However, some twenty years later, what shocks the world most in recent events—from the Tibet unrest of 2008 to the tragic earthquakes of 2008 and 2010, and from the 2008 Beijing Olympic Games to the 2010 Shanghai Expo—is the new relationship between the Chinese people (especially the younger generations) and the ruling party. Recent experiences seem to indicate that the current Beijing regime has a very patriotic and supporting populace that many governments would be envious to have. As a *New York Times* reporter observed in the disputes over the 2008 Olympic torch relays, educated young Chinese "rank among the most patriotic, establishment-supporting people you'll meet."[1]

But *why* is this young generation in China, many of whom attended elite schools in the United States or Europe, so patriotic and nationalistic? Certainly today's Chinese young people are no longer the Red Guards from the isolated country of forty years ago, but neither are they the antidictatorship "Tiananmen generation" of twenty years ago. They are the Internet generation, and many of them speak English. China's opening up and the international community's engagement with China in the last thirty years seems to have resulted in a new generation of anti-West patriots. But, assuming these young people are more than brainwashed xenophobes, how can we understand the genuine outrage toward the West apparent in China's youth today? What are the sources of China's new nationalism? All in all, what has happened during the last twenty years?

These questions about China's current affairs are actually closely related to two major questions that have puzzled observers of China since 1989. After the Tiananmen Square incident, many scholars predicted that the regime in Beijing would not last long because the official socialist ideology had already lost credibility. So, first, how did the Chinese Communist Party (CCP) survive and then regain popular support in the 1990s? Was it simply through prosperous economic development, or were there other influential factors? And second, how can we explain the rapid conversion of China's popular social movements—from the internal-oriented, anticorruption, and antidictatorship democratic movements of the 1980s to the external-oriented, anti-Western nationalism of the 1990s and 2000s?

The purpose of this book lies in explaining the relevance and importance of historical memory in understanding these questions. While it may not offer straightforward answers, the aim is to provide important background information, perspectives, and insight to consider these complicated multilayered questions. In particular, this book argues for the relevance and importance of historical memory in explaining China's political transition and international behavior during the recent two decades. It suggests that even though existing theories and literature illuminate certain aspects of China's political transition and foreign affairs behavior, a full explanatory picture emerges only after these phenomena and actions are analyzed through the lens of historical memory.

HISTORY AND MEMORY

The subject of this book is historical memory, but what exactly is that? Why does historical memory matter? And how could the study of a people's collective memory and history education answer questions about this country's political transition and foreign relations?

When I present my research, I always begin by showing four photographs to introduce what "historical memory" is. These photos (see figure I.1) show young people in China who are connected in various ways with four Chinese characters—*Wuwang guochi* (勿忘国耻)—meaning "never forget national humiliation." From a little girl painting those deeply emotional words on the back of a car to a group of schoolchildren pledging in front of the slogan written on their classroom blackboard, these four images demonstrate the pervasive correlation with the idea of actively remembering the historical events that happened a long time ago. While most of the people photographed are far too young to have actually experienced the national traumas of the so-called century of humiliation, the "one hundred years of national humiliation," they appear to acutely feel the emotions of its victims.

Anyone viewing these photos will feel compelled to examine the deep emotional bond of these young people with this phrase and to wonder where they might have cultivated these ideas. This book seeks to explain how and why these young people have become so engaged with this rallying cry. Through their family stories, history textbooks, and gatherings at government events, I will show how they have all developed a relationship with this national phrase and how this will inform their understanding of who they are and their perception of the rest of the world.

Historical memory can be linked to a single event. While only a fraction of Americans actually witnessed the fall of the Twin Towers on September 11, 2001, future generations of Americans will undoubtedly remain connected to this national trauma through its retelling in the news, family stories, and history education classes. Just as the national humiliation of China is used to teach the Chinese people who they are and how the world looks, so, too, will 9/11 inform future Americans about the world they are living in?

Often it is hard for us to see the forest for the trees. Our historical memory is intangible, and it is nearly impossible for us to cleanly divorce our own perceptions of history from the semiorchestrated construction of our national narrative. A society's elites often use the construction of national monuments to create symbols for its citizens to remember a nation's story. But the elites select which parts of a history to remember, and which parts to forget. The National Mall in Washington, D.C., reminds Americans of the glories and traumas of the United States. Each year, millions of students visit their nation's capital to see these grandiose symbols and hear the stories that define what it is to be an American.

(a)

(b)

FIGURE I.1. The same four Chinese characters appear in each of these photos: *Wuwang guochi*, "Never forget national humiliation." (a) A nine-year-old girl writes the characters on the trunk of her father's car during an anti-Japanese protest, Zhengzhou, 2005. (Photo courtesy of Asia News Photo.) (b) Policemen form the four characters during an educational ceremony for the seventy-seventh anniversary of the 1931 Japanese invasion, Shenyang, 2008. (Photo courtesy of Asia News Photo.)

(d)

(c) A victim of the Japanese invasion describes her story to children in front of the four characters engraved on the big bronze bell at the September 18 Museum, Shenyang, 2002. (Photo courtesy of Xinhua News Agency.) (d) Primary schoolchildren pledge in front of the slogan written on the blackboard, "Never Forget National Humiliation, Strengthen Our National Defense," Changchun, 2009. (Photo courtesy of Xinhua News Agency.)

Chapter 4 of this book provides a detailed account of how and why the Chinese government constructed and remodeled more than ten thousand memory sites nationwide as a central component of its patriotic education campaign that started in 1991.

National holidays and anniversaries are always more than just an extra day of rest; rather, the significance of these dates and the special attention given to them are used by elites to remind the citizenry repeatedly of their history as a people. Every year, each of these holidays retells the story of why it is a day of celebration, with each holiday serving as a reminder of part of the national story. The selection of which days to celebrate, however, also reveals which stories a nation may wish to forget.

For example, 2009 was a significant year in China, with many important anniversaries. The world witnessed an enormous celebration of the 60th anniversary of the founding of the People's Republic of China. The government designed every detail of this ceremony to remind its people about the national experience. To begin the ceremony, China's elite color guard began by marching in perfect lockstep exactly 169 strides from the center of Tiananmen Square to the flagpole to raise the national colors. Each of these literal steps forward was meant to represent one year since the beginning of the Opium War in 1840. This symbolism highlights something very deep within the Chinese culture, and by understanding simple events like the marching of the color guard we can learn a lot about China's perception of itself and inform our understanding of where China hopes to march into the future.

Equally instructive are "dark anniversaries"—events like the 1959 Tibetan uprising, the closing down of the Xidan Democracy Wall in 1979, and the Tiananmen Square tragedy of 1989—that have been formally ignored by the Chinese government.[2] When planning which anniversaries to celebrate, the Chinese government turns a blind eye to certain parts of China's history. Beijing has even gone so far as to ban the mere discussion of specific events it would choose to forget.

Choosing what to remember and what to forget is not a simple sorting process for history education. Historical memory is more than an understanding of history. How the government defines history is a deeply political issue that is closely related to the legitimacy of the government and rightly shapes the national identity of China. While historical events themselves have been viewed and reviewed in scholarly works around the world, the government's portrayal of these events is not adequately analyzed.

As Anthony D. Smith has argued, "no memory, no identity; no identity, no nation."[3] It is this collective memory of the past that binds a group of people together. On the national level, identity determines national interests, which in turn determine policy and state action.[4] Understanding a people's collective memory can help us to better understand their national interests and political actions. Powerful collective memories—whether real or concocted—can also be at the root of prejudice, nationalism, and even conflicts and wars.[5]

Historical memory is still an understudied field because it does not fit neatly into one specific academic discipline. Both the subject and its implications are so scattered throughout many fields that few scholars have attempted to tackle it through comprehensive analysis. As a scholar of international relations, I have chosen to study this subject in a different way than a historian, anthropologist, sociologist, or psychologist might. I am exploring this concept because without understanding how the Chinese people see themselves, it is impossible to know their national interests. National interests are the fundamental building blocks in any discussion of foreign policy, and historical memory is the prime "raw material" for constructing ethnicity and national identity.[6] That is the reason why I believe historical memory is the key to understanding Chinese politics and foreign relations.

To understand a country, the orthodox research approach focuses on collecting political, socioeconomic, and security data and then conducting a macroanalysis of institutions, policies, and decision making. Such an approach, however, has critical limitations for comprehending the deep structure and dynamics of the country. In this book, I argue that to understand a country, one should visit the country's primary schools and high schools and read their history textbooks. A nation's history is not merely a recounting of its past; what individuals and countries remember and what they choose to forget are telling indicators of their current values, perceptions, and even aspirations.[7] Studies about history and memory in China can answer such basic questions as, What is China? and Who are the Chinese?

CHINESE HISTORICAL CONSCIOUSNESS

Modern historical consciousness in China is powerfully influenced by the "century of humiliation" from the mid-1800s to the mid-1900s. Chinese remember this period as a time when China was attacked, bullied, and torn asunder by imperialists. Many authorities on Chinese affairs have highlighted the special significance of this period to Chinese history and memory. For example, political scientist Peter Hays Gries writes: "It is certainly undeniable that in China the past lives in the present to a degree unmatched in most other countries. . . . Chinese often, however, seem to be slaves to their history."[8] Similarly, sociologist Jonathan Unger argues, "More than in most other countries, history was and is considered a mirror through which ethical standards and moral transgressions pertinent to the present day could be viewed."[9] Adding another dimension to the picture, we can look to Anne F. Thurston's comments about national psychology, which tell us, "Everything we know about individual psychology suggests that the traumas so many Chinese have suffered in the past dozen, 30, 50, 100, 150 years are both exceptionally painful and exceedingly difficult to overcome."[10]

Although most scholars readily acknowledge the prominence of history and memory in Chinese politics, the bulk of research touching on their relationship to Chinese foreign affairs behavior does so only indirectly and tangentially. The insights that do exist are scattered among diverse bodies of literature on history, politics, culture, and communication. Given the abundance of works directly exploring the role of history and memory in politics in other parts of the world, the absence of similar studies in China's case is surprising.

The few direct discussions about this topic are found in short policy articles written by China experts from think tanks. For example, in a newspaper opinion article, Minxin Pei states that "China's national experience and collective memory constitute a powerful force in foreign-policy decisionmaking."[11] However, such insights need the support of empirical research. Moreover, systematic research exploring the deep structures and implications of history and memory in Chinese politics and foreign policy decision making is still lacking. This book represents an attempt to systematically link the domestic politics surrounding history and memory in China to its international behavior.

The fields of international relations and political science have developed within a framework of Euro-American intellectual traditions—the expectations, values, and rationality that are embedded in Western culture. However, people often fail to question the validity and applicability of Western theories and models in non-Western cultures. Each specific cultural framework has its own intellectual and cultural heritage. For understanding a country like China, one of the world's oldest civilizations, it should be common sense that we need to study the country's indigenous attitudes, resources, and motivations that drive its foreign policy behavior. This will help us to bridge the gap in understanding between people in the West and China.

China certainly has its own intellectual and cultural heritage on peace and conflict, and more importantly, this heritage includes both pro-conflict and pro-peace discourses. For example, does the legacy of memories from the past wars that China has suffered—there are estimates of 35 million casualties at the hands of the Japanese alone, according to China's national history textbooks[12]—lead to a great realization of the destruction of war and a commitment to more peaceful methods of resolving conflicts? Or does this powerful historical memory fan the flames of current animosities and serve as the root of new prejudices, nationalism, and even war? In this book, I attempt to decode China's indigenous attitudes, resources, and motivation. The exploration of these questions can provide a unique and important approach to the study of China's rise and the related opportunities and challenges.

This book describes how the legitimacy-challenged Chinese Communist Party has used history education as an instrument for the glorification of the party, for the consolidation of national identity, and for the justification of the political system of the CCP's one-party rule in the post-Tiananmen and post–Cold War eras. The campaign for patriotic education has greatly contributed to the rise of nationalism in China in recent decades. There is actually a feedback loop in today's China whereby the nationalistic history education stimulates the rise of nationalism, and the rise of nationalism provides a bigger market for nationalistic messages.

Furthermore, it is not necessarily true that democratization will naturally "disinfect" nationalist myths from China's marketplace of ideas and pave the way for more conciliatory views on historical issues. Remembrance in democratic states can prove to be more chauvinist than conciliatory.[13] Without liberating the country from the compelling complex of historical myth and trauma, nationalist leaders could employ history and memory issues as tools of mobilization. Many maintain that China's one-party rule and its emergent military capability are growing threats to peace in the world, but I argue that the real problem that must be addressed is identity education and understanding of the world within China.

Historical memory also provides new perspectives to understand Beijing's foreign policy behavior, especially during international conflicts. In this book, I argue that the Chinese people's collective historical consciousness about the country's traumatic national experiences and the state's political use of the past constitute a powerful force in the way the Chinese conceptualize, manage, and resolve external conflict. One of the important findings of this research is how the content of history and memory has defined China's national interests and national objections. For the ruling party, some nonmaterial interests that are defined by the content of historical memory, such as national dignity and face and respect from other countries, are equally important or even more important than China's material interests such as trade, security, and territory.

DOES TIME HEAL?

Throughout the long process of writing this book, many common questions have surfaced concerning why I chose to tackle this topic. As part of this introduction, it is appropriate and important to address these questions directly.

Question 1: So much time has passed since the national humiliation. Hasn't time healed China?

In general, yes, time heals wounds everywhere. But in all societies, there are always some people—educators, elites, state leaders—who hope that the younger generation of society will not forget what happened to their people in the past. In every nation, people tell stories about how they, as a group, got to where they are. A central element to the creation of this narrative is selecting what the people will remember and what they choose to forget. This is how a state constructs its national identity; education systems are in a way a system designed to create a mold of the idealized citizen from this national identity. One of the objectives of this book is to unveil how historical memory, history education, and the state's ideological education campaign were used to rebuild and recreate a new Chinese identity following the end of the Cold War and China's political change in 1989. This book demonstrates the role of historical memory in China's nation building.

It has been a puzzle for China watchers to try to understand why Chinese youths are becoming increasingly nationalistic based on events that took place in an increasingly distant past. It was Francis Fukuyama who observed that the upsurge in nationalism in East Asia appears to be associated with generational changes. Surprisingly, it is the young—and not the old—who seem to be at the vanguard of this growing nationalism, even though the younger generation did not directly experience the military conflicts upon which many nationalist narratives are constructed.[14] This phenomenon has yet to be explored and could serve to create a new understanding of China's national identity.

Question 2: China is now a rising power. Shouldn't its success provide healing?

Chinese sentiment of past humiliation has been so powerful in shaping the Chinese national identity only because this group of people has also been so proud of their ancient civilization and the other past and recent glories. This book explains how new accomplishments and growing confidence have often served to strengthen the myth/trauma complex. They have, at times, served to activate, not assuage, people's historical memory of past humiliation. This is why it is very important for today's people to understand the Chinese historical consciousness, even though China is now ascendant and people have begun to talk about the "G2" (the United States and China as the "Group of Two" in global issues). China's rise should not be understood through a single lens like economics or military growth, but rather viewed through a more comprehensive lens that takes national identity into account.

So much time is spent in the West worrying about these intentions and the sometimes puzzling behaviors of China's foreign policy. Looking at historical memory is not just a look at the past; instead, uncovering historical memory is a progressive look forward in understanding where China is trying to go. If we want to figure out China's intentions, we must first appreciate the building blocks of Chinese intentions. Who we think we are defines what we think we want. Understanding Chinese national identity from this perspective can give insight into who China is seeking to become as it makes its rapid rise compared to the rest of the world.

Question 3: I know what you are doing—isn't this book simply using historical trauma to explain China's anti-Western nationalism?

This book does not seek to explain the simple notion of why the Chinese are unhappy with the West; that is far too simple a usage of the rich knowledge that can come from an understanding of historical memory. In many countries in Asia, Africa, and Latin America, particularly postcolonial states, historical grievances are indeed an important source of anti-Western nationalism. However, the implications of historical memory are not that simple. In many societies, especially in China, historical memory has already become a constructed social norm in the national "deep culture" and will influence people's thoughts and actions. Compared with "surface culture," which constitutes things such as food, dress, and customs that we can see, hear, and touch, deep culture refers to the unconscious frameworks of meaning, values, norms, and hidden assumptions that we use to interpret our experiences.[15]

This book explores the power of historical memory in Chinese identity formation and political discourse. It uses historical memory to explain the cultural and historical foundation of Chinese nationalism, China's intentions, and China's rise, and it presents the postulate that historical memory is one of the biggest factors shaping the exercise of Chinese power and is the key to understanding Chinese politics and foreign relations. However, historical memory is still one of the most misunderstood and least addressed elements in Chinese politics today.

Question 4: How can a book written about historical memory be researched scientifically?

I can understand why people ask this question and would like to respond by quoting from Andrei Markovits and Simon Reich. In their research about how Germany's past continues to influence its present policies, they considered collective memory to be "the biggest factor mitigating the exercise of German power," and noted that it is "an element many political scientists usually avoid but any journalist working in Germany regularly sees in action":

> The politics of collective memory—impossible to quantify, hard to measure with the methods of survey research, yet still very real—is a major ingredient of the political arena, the public discourse, and the policy setting in every country. It circumscribes the acceptable. It defines such key ingredients as pride, shame, fear, revenge, and comfort for a large number of a country's citizens. It is central to an understanding of the forces of nationalism.[16]

This research can contribute to methodological discussions concerning the use of identity as a variable to explain political action. To conduct this research, this study uses an in-depth qualitative and historical approach. Evidence has been gathered from a large volume of history textbooks, official documents, memoirs, and interviews. In an effort to solve the puzzle of how to deal with ideational factors in politics, I have created two frameworks for the analysis of empirical data, and I use these two frameworks as a way to prove that historical memory is not just an epiphenomenal, explanatory model for China's domestic politics and foreign relations.

Although we would never expect a chemist or mathematician to include their personal experiences to supplement their research, my experiences should serve to provide context for this specific and otherwise methodologically proper work. As Paul Cohen notes, many of the most important components of historical memory are so subtle that it requires a sort of "insider cultural knowledge."

> It is not a form of knowledge that Chinese deliberately conceal from non-Chinese. It tends to be hidden, rather, mainly because the ways in which it is acquired—transmission within the family setting, early school lessons, popular operatic arias heard on the radio, and the like—are not generally available to people who have not had the experience of growing up in a Chinese cultural milieu.[17]

This book is not written from the outside looking in. As a boy, I learned from the history textbooks I will discuss. At Peking University, I took part in the Patriotic Education Campaign and later worked in the Chinese government. I am a product of this education. I hope to provide an insider's understanding that can contextualize China's historical memory.

Given that the focus is on examining the state use of history and the politics of memory in Chinese political transformation and foreign policy, this book frequently features direct translations of Chinese official documents, political leaders' articles, and history textbooks. Throughout this book, I examine a wide range of data, such as the words or the texts (e.g., official documents, transcripts of press conferences), the narratives of past conflict and national humiliation in history textbooks, and the historical analogies that the leaders have used to draw parallels between current times and historical events. I have also included discussions about the selection of data and literature in several chapters of this book. As a person who has been educated in both China and the West, I hope that I can interpret one culture to another in meaningful and actionable ways.

ORGANIZATION

This book primarily focuses on two aspects of historical memory: the Chinese people's collective historical consciousness about the country's traumatic national experiences, and the state's political use of the past. In general, this book explores what happens to politics when historical grievances and national humiliation come to the center of political discourse. It examines how the Chinese historical consciousness about the country's traumatic national experience, combined with the state's political use of the past, have become powerful forces in China's national identity formation and in the way China conceptualizes, manages, and resolves external conflict. It focuses on two major questions:

1. How have the Chinese Communist leaders used history and memory to reshape national identity so as to strengthen their legitimacy for ruling China after the end of the Cold War?
2. How has this reconstruction of identity influenced China's political transformation and international behavior?

The book has nine chapters. The first, "Historical Memory, Identity, and Politics," provides the theoretical and analytical frameworks for the study of historical memory in domestic politics and foreign relations. The literature and theories presented will help relate the Chinese case to global contexts and will also introduce general theoretical frameworks for the analysis of empirical data.

Chapter 2, "Chosen Glory, Chosen Trauma," sets the stage for the rest of the book by providing the reader with an overview of China's century of humiliation. In particular, it highlights historical events that still loom large in the Chinese psyche today and, in so doing, investigates China's Chosenness-Myth-Trauma Complex.

Chapter 3, "From 'All-Under-Heaven' to a Nation-State: Humiliation and Nation Building," examines how the discourse of national humiliation became an integral part of the construction of national identity and nation building in three different periods: the late Qing, the Republican, and the Maoist eras.

The subsequent three chapters examine the state's political use of the past and the function of historical memory in political transformation in the post-Tiananmen and post–Cold War eras. Chapter 4, "From Victor to Victim: The Patriotic Education Campaign," focuses on how China's humiliating modern history has been used by the government to conduct ideological education through the national Patriotic Education Campaign after 1991. Chapter 5, "From Vanguard to Patriot: Reconstructing the Chinese Communist Party," then examines how the Communist government uses the content of history and memory to construct the rules and norms of the ruling party. The following chapter, "From Earthquake to Olympics: New Trauma, New Glory," explains Chinese behavior during the Olympic Games and the Sichuan earthquake relief effort in 2008 through an examination of historical memory and national humiliation.

The next two chapters explore the impact of China's institutionalized historical consciousness on its foreign relations, especially in relations with the United States and Japan. Chapter 7, "Memory, Crises, and Foreign Relations," uses the historical memory variable to explain China's conflict behavior in recent crises with the United States. The findings in this chapter indicate that historical memory often serves as a major motivating factor in international conflict, especially when the confrontation is perceived by the Chinese as an assault on the nation's fundamental identity, face, and authority. Chapter 8, "Memory, Textbooks, and Sino-Japanese Reconciliation," then provides a case study on the controversy surrounding history and the adoption of history textbooks between China and Japan. It addresses this issue from the perspective of conflict resolution, with particular attention being given to the discussion of how joint history writing can be used as a tool for peace building and reconciliation in East Asia.

The last chapter, "Memory, Nationalism, and China's Rise," attempts to integrate the main points of the book, especially regarding the notion of how the lenses of history and memory facilitate a better understanding of China's rise, intentions, and nationalism.

While reading this book, it is important to keep in mind that we must be sensitive to the difference between history and historical memory. The focus of this book is on questions relating to the formation and strategic use of historical consciousness. Historical consciousness is defined here as the area in which collective memory, the writing of history, and other modes of shaping images of the past merge in the public mind.[18]

There is no doubt that a delineation can be made between history and memory. History is the reconstruction of the past from a critical distance, while collective memory is recollections and representations of past historical events shared by a particular group. It must be clear that this book is about historical *memory* and not history—it is not about "what actually happened" in history, but rather about the Chinese understanding of history and elite history making. Collective memories are very often imaginary or constructed, rather than based on actual facts and events.

We cannot hope to bridge the divide between what actually happened and the constructed narrative without possessing a degree of sensitivity for these differences.

As this book will show, specific events do not necessarily define historical memory. Staring too closely at the arguments posited for what actually happened can blind us to the larger picture of the formation of collective memory and its function in nation building. This larger picture of historical memory is the gateway to understanding China's worldview, interests, and intentions.

1

HISTORICAL MEMORY, IDENTITY, AND POLITICS

IN THE workings of social life, the past does not always exist as a hard, objective, or factual reality—something "out there" to be grasped and appropriated.[1] The past is not solid, immutable, or even measureable; rather, it is a fluid set of ideas, able to be shaped by time, emotion, and the politically savvy. Furthermore, we seldom step back from our own cultures to assess their components—the stories that shape our thinking. We therefore often overlook the role that history and memory play in the present. However, in many societies, including China's, collective memory and the political use of history serve very important functions both inside the social group and in the group's interactions with other groups.

While exploring the sources, dynamics, and structures of contemporary conflict, some scholars have paid special attention to the power of historical memory over human thoughts, feelings, and actions. This is especially apparent in studies relating to the remarkable proliferation of deadly conflicts between ethnic groups after the end of the Cold War. For example, Irish historian Ian McBride writes that "in Ireland, the interpretation of the past has always been at the heart of national conflict."[2] Victor Roudometof of the University of Cyprus believes that "the conflicting ethnocentric national narratives of the different sides have generated the Greek-Bulgarian-Macedonian dispute of 1990s."[3] According to Gerrit W. Gong, remembering and forgetting issues have come to shape international relations in East Asia.[4] For Polish historian Jerzy Jedlicki,

"The twentieth-century history of Eastern Europe is a perfect laboratory to observe how the genuine or apparent remembrances of the past may aggravate current conflicts and how they themselves are modified in the process."[5] From Eastern Europe to the Middle East and East Asia, these case studies illustrate that many intractable conflicts are deeply rooted in the history and memory of the involved parties. Without paying close attention to history and memory, any conflict resolution process is bound to fail.

Although many world conflicts have their genesis in the history and memory of various factions, the role this concept plays in national politics and international relations remains a decidedly understudied field. The insights into the theories of historical memory are scattered among diverse bodies of literature on history, politics, culture, philosophy, and communication. The reasons for this relative lack of attention to historical memory vary widely across different disciplines. In history, Roudometof argues that the long-standing tradition of seeking "scientific objectivity" has not allowed the examination of historical writing in relation to the articulation of collective memory until recently.[6] In sociology and anthropology, the legacy of pioneers such as Emile Durkheim and Maurice Halbwachs "was eclipsed in mid-twentieth century by the more empirically oriented and positivist tradition of U.S. mainstream sociology."[7]

Ideas (including historical memory and other ideational factors) have been underestimated—if not entirely ignored—in the field of international relations. This is because the most current and widely accepted systemic approaches to the study of international relations are realism and liberal institutionalism. Both of these approaches take rationalist models as their starting points and focus on how structures affect the instrumental rationality of actors. In such models, the preferences and causal beliefs of actors are a given. Most analysts who rely on such approaches have relegated ideas to only a minor role.[8]

In fact, how ideational factors affect international relations has been one of the most bewildering puzzles for scholars. Progress in incorporating cognitive variables into empirical research on decision making has been relatively slow and uneven.[9] Scholars who have struggled with this question list three factors that may pose difficulties to research that uses identity as a variable. First, the existence of identity as a universal but largely implicit concept makes it difficult to isolate and understand.[10] This is because identities and perceptions may *influence* decision-making behavior but do not unilaterally *determine* such behavior. They are only one variable cluster within a rich and complex causal framework for explaining decision making.[11] Second, it is extremely difficult to find a one-to-one correlation between perceptions and behavior.[12] And third, when identities are measured, the techniques used (large-*N* surveys, interviews with policy makers, ethnographic fieldwork) are typically not available to social scientists who study elites in closed or semiclosed states.

In this chapter, I will review the major studies that make up the theoretical framework for understanding the politics of historical memory and will present an assessment of the current state of the field. I focus here on understanding the function of historical memory in group identity formation and how historical memory influences people's perceptions, interpretations, and decision-making processes, especially in a conflict or crisis situation. The literature and theories presented will help relate the Chinese cases to global contexts and will also introduce general theoretical frameworks for the analysis of empirical data.

In an effort to meet the challenge of conducting systematic research on historical memory, I have created two frameworks for research, based on the existing literature on historical memory and theories of identity and beliefs. The first is a method of measuring historical memory as a collective identity. A set of research questions is presented to measure whether and how the content of historical memory serves as four types of identity content:

1. Constitutive norms (norms or rules that define group membership)
2. Relational content (references and comparisons to other identities or groups)
3. Cognitive models (content that affects the way group members interpret and understand the world)
4. Social purpose (content that provides the group socially appropriate roles to perform)

Each of these four types of identity content implies an alternate causal pathway between this collective identity and policy behaviors or practices.

The second framework is a set of questions examining the function of historical memory in people's perceptions, interpretations, and decision-making processes. According to this framework, there are three causal pathways in which the beliefs or ideas of historical memory can serve to influence political actions:

1. As road maps that increase actors' clarity about goals or ends-means relationships
2. As focal points, by facilitating the cohesion of particular groups or by causing conflict and constituting difficulties to the settlement of the conflict
3. As institutionalized ideas and beliefs that constrain policy when embedded in political institutions and in patterns of political discourse

With these two frameworks for research, I hope to provide a model by which researchers can conduct a more rigorous study of historical memory. These frameworks can help categorize and subsequently demonstrate the effects of historical memory. They have been used throughout this book as a way to prove that historical memory is not just a post hoc rationalization of behavior motivated by national interests but rather a direct source of policy behavior motivation. It is my hope that these frameworks will be useful not only for those interested in historical memory but also for those interested in China's foreign relations specifically.

HISTORICAL MEMORY AND IDENTITY FORMATION

With the rise of sociological constructivism in the 1990s, historical memory and identity have received more attention because national identity is seen as determining national interests, which in turn determines policy and state action.[13] A significant amount of literature on the politics of memory is centered on the role of historical memory in the formation of group membership and identity. Collective memory binds a group of people together, and the prime raw material for constructing ethnicity is history.[14] According to Anthony D. Smith, ethnic, national, and religious identities are built on historical myths that define who a group member is, what it means to be a group member, and typically who the group's enemies are.[15] These myths are usually based on truth, but are selective or exaggerated in their presentation of history.

Group identity is also shaped in large part by certain struggles that a group has endured. These struggles can be classified as "chosen traumas" and "chosen glories."[16] According to Norwegian scholar Johan Galtung, key historical events are critical in defining a group's identity and determining how that group behaves in conflict situations. Galtung identifies the categories of "chosenness" (the idea of being a people chosen by transcendental forces), trauma, and myths, which together form a syndrome: the Chosenness-Myths-Trauma (CMT) complex or, to use a more evocative term, the collective megalo-paranoia syndrome.[17] Similarly, Vamik Volkan, a psychoanalyst at the University of Virginia, examines how individual identity is inextricably intertwined with one's large-group (i.e., ethnic) identity and how mental representations of historical events shape this identity. Volkan identifies chosen traumas (the horrors of the past that cast shadows onto the future) and chosen glories (myths about a glorious future, often seen as a reenactment of a glorious past) as elements in the development of group identity.[18]

Chosen traumas and glories are passed on to succeeding generations by parents and teachers and through participation in ritualistic ceremonies recalling past successful or traumatic events.[19] A group incorporates the memory of traumatic events into its identity, which leads one generation to pass enmity to the next. In other words, later generations share the suffering of past generations even though they did not take part in the actual traumatic events themselves.[20] Like chosen traumas, chosen glories become heavily mythologized over time.[21] This is because they have the effect of forming bonds and connecting group members with their larger group, which increases members' self-esteem by being associated with such glories.[22]

There are three main approaches to looking at historical memory in identity formation: primordialist, constructivist, and instrumentalist. Following the first approach, some scholars assert that collective memory and identity are formed on the basis of the primordial ties of blood, kinship, language, and common history. These are objective cultural criteria that distinguish one group from another.[23] As Gong writes, "Transferring from generation to generation, history and memory issues tell grandparents and grandchildren who they are, give countries national identity, and channel the values and purposes that chart the future in the name of the past."[24] Through the lens of primordialism, people often suggest that ethnic conflicts from many years ago and the "centuries of accumulated hatreds" are behind much present-day violence, such as the case of the China-Japan relationship.

Constructivists, on the other hand, view identity as manufactured rather than given and emphasize that ethnicity and identity are socially constructed. People choose a history and common ancestry and create, just as much as discover, differences from others. In *The Past Is a Foreign Country*, David Lowenthal argues that it is we, the contemporaries, who construct our past selectively and for a variety of reasons. According to Halbwachs, who conducted pathbreaking work on the subject, collective memory reconstructs its various recollections to align itself with contemporary ideas and preoccupations; in other words, the past is reconstructed with regard to the concerns and needs of the present.[25] Benedict Anderson argues that print languages laid the foundation for national consciousness by creating unified fields of exchange and communication.[26] According to him, print capitalism (the book market, mass media, etc.) linked people in disparate regions to a larger, imagined national community. People learn their group's history not only from their parents or grandparents but from history books, mass media, and formal schooling as well.

In the third approach, history and memory can also be used instrumentally to promote the individual or collective interests of leaders. In their struggle for power, competing elites often use history as a tool to mobilize popular support. Ethnic categories can also be manipulated to maintain the power of a dominant group and justify discrimination against other groups. The manipulation of the past provides the opportunity to mold the present and the future. The instrumentalist approach treats ethnicity primarily as an ad hoc element of a political strategy, used as a resource by interest groups for achieving such goals as an increase in wealth, power, or status.[27] In his book *Modern Hatreds: The Symbolic Politics of Ethnic War*, Stuart J. Kaufman argues that people are *taught* ethnic hatred, not born into it. The notion that ethnic groups in conflict have hated each other for hundreds of years is not always true; rather, powerful people in these countries take real events in their history and exaggerate them to create hostilities and as a means for mobilizing. War occurs as a result of symbolic politics in which ethnic leaders or activists use emotional cultural symbols to promote hostility toward other groups and pursue ethnic domination.[28]

Disagreements over how to remember the past—both about what actually occurred and how to articulate such events—are a nearly universal phenomenon. Often, the stories that are chosen and subsequently told for decades to come are the ones that have the backing of the people in power. Politicians and other authority figures can manipulate memories to tell a certain story or encourage people to think a certain way, and powerful groups can promote versions of events that reflect well on them and meet their needs, even if they are not completely accurate.[29]

Some scholars have examined the politics of history textbooks and how political powers influence their content. According to Michael Apple and Linda Christian-Smith, for example, though textbooks claim to teach neutral and objective facts, they are often used as "ideological tools to promote a certain belief system and legitimize an established political and social order."[30] The selection and organization of knowledge for use in educational systems is an ideological process that serves the interests of particular classes and social groups. Ever since the rise of the nation-state, history textbooks have been used by states as instruments for "glorifying the nation, consolidating its national identity, and justifying particular forms of social and political systems."[31]

Additionally, conflict itself shapes a group's identity. The more conflict there is between groups, the more likely individuals are to judge one another on their group affiliation rather than on personal characteristics.[32] Conflict can play an important role in generating and sustaining social identity. In other words, deep-rooted social identity may be a product of conflict at least as much as deep-rooted conflict is a product of clashing social identities. The widespread blindness to this reverse process is largely due to the assumption that social identities are inherent and primordial, coded in a group's proverbial DNA.

Whether through intergenerational indoctrination, the print media, education systems, or conflict itself, historical memory plays a major role in identity formation. Identity is formed by the experiences of both the individual and the society. It is important to know how these identities are formed in order to understand how they shape ethnic groups' or societies' understanding of the world.

HISTORICAL MEMORY, FRAMES, AND PERCEPTION

Humans have a limited capacity to organize and analyze data.[33] Consequently, we must rely on a simplifying mechanism to process the massive amounts of information we encounter in our daily lives. *Frames* are shortcuts that people use to help make sense of complex information. Often, these frames are built on underlying structures of beliefs, values, and experiences, which can differ across cultures and nationalities. In addition, frames often exist prior to conscious decision making and can affect subsequent decisions. Thus, by the nature of how and when frames are formed, factions are separated not only by differences in interests, beliefs, and values but also in how they perceive and understand the world, both at the conscious and subconscious levels.

Framing and reframing are vital to the negotiation and conflict management processes.[34] Knowing what frames are used and how they are constructed allows negotiators to draw conclusions about the development of conflict. In other words, understanding framing can influence the future of a conflict. Analyzing the frames people use in a given conflict provides fresh insight and better comprehension of the conflict dynamics and development.

One way people make sense of new situations is by comparing them to older situations already stored in their memories. The history of a people profoundly influences the perception they have of the world around them, as historical memories are important information processors. Thus, historical memory influences an actor's interpretation and understanding of the external world and specific situations, and it often leads actors to endow a group with certain motives and to interpret the world through frames defined in part by those motives. Like culture, history and memory are rarely the *causes* of conflict, but they do provide the lens through which we view and bring our world into focus, and through this lens differences are magnified and conflicts are pursued.[35] Historical memory helps both the masses and the elites interpret the present and decide on future policies.[36]

Through their lenses of historical memory, each party to a conflict or dispute has its own understanding and interpretation of the conflict situation. They often make comparisons between the current situation and their past experience, and the lens of historical memory influences the group's perception and attitude toward this situation. Through these lenses, conflicting parties view the conflict and thereby form the basis of their actions.

In his book *Analogies at War*, Yuen Foong Khong argues that leaders use historical analogies not merely to justify policies but also to perform specific cognitive and information-processing tasks essential to political decision making. The term *historical analogy* signifies an inference that if two or more events separated in time agree in one respect, then they may also agree in others. Because event A resembles event B in having characteristic X, and knowing that A also has characteristic Y, it can be inferred that B also has characteristic Y; in logical shorthand, AX:BX::AY:BY.[37] These historical analogies often form foreign policy and political propaganda.

Scholars have discussed how U.S. policy makers routinely resort to historical analogies. According to Khong, from World War I to Operation Desert Storm, American policy makers repeatedly invoked the "lessons of history" as they contemplated taking their nation to war.[38] In recent years, historical analogies between Iraq and Vietnam have been utilized by historians, pundits, and politicians.[39] Many discussions have also taken place about how differently America reacted to the 9/11 attack in comparison to the attack on Pearl Harbor.[40]

Differences in cultural context, national experiences, political ideology, and thinking patterns among nations of the world unquestionably lead them to have a divergent "sense of history." For each nation, the issues, structures, and implications of history and memory are varied. According to Gong, for example, the American tradition of immigration gives the United States an ever-changing "new-world identity," instead of a single "old-world identity."[41] By this, Gong means that Americans look forward in ways that emphasize the future more than the past, assuming the past has little bearing on the future. However, in many societies, particularly in some parts of Asia, people often look backward and use their past to define contemporary relations and future orientations. Gong contends that the difference between the U.S. sense of history and that of other countries can create divergent perspectives on issues of importance and eventually cause misunderstandings and misinterpretations during interstate dialogue. Using the 1999 U.S.–China embassy bombing crisis as an example, Gong makes an interesting comment: "The accidental U.S. bombing of the [Chinese] embassy in Belgrade forcibly demonstrated that in some matters of history, Chinese memory is too long while U.S. memory is too short."[42]

Minxin Pei echoes Gong's argument in his *Foreign Policy* article "The Paradoxes of American Nationalism." Pei believes that the forward-looking and universalistic perspective of the United States unavoidably clashes with the backward-looking and particularistic perspectives of ethnonationalism in other countries. These different approaches to history and memory can generate a "clash of histories." Pei also suggests that the relative lack of awareness of these differerent perspectives and worldviews creates a huge communication barrier between Americans and other societies. Whether consciously or unconsciously, the American sense of history makes Americans generally insensitive to other people's historical grievances.

HISTORICAL MEMORY, MOTIVATION, AND CONFLICT BEHAVIOR

Socially shared images of the past allow a group to foster social cohesion, to develop and defend social identification, and to justify current attitudes and needs. During conflicts, leaders often try to evoke memories of past traumas to spur people to action and make the group more cohesive. Historical enmity thus acts like an amplifier in an electrical circuit.[43]

Collective memory of past events can provide leaders with the basis for the mobilization of mass support. Scholars have particularly discussed how states and elites have used history and memory as instruments to conduct political mobilization. According to Volkan, once a painful event becomes a chosen trauma, the historical truth behind it does not really matter. Thus, the chosen trauma is used for the sole purpose of realizing the goals of the political elites. In moments of crisis, people turn back to the past with increased intensity. And when identity itself becomes challenged, undermined, and even shattered, memories emerge and are reshaped to defend unity and reinforce a sense of self and community.[44] Jedlicki discusses two ways in which "a vivid historical memory fans the flame of current animosities":

> First, it does so through the process of sanctification of some historical events that transforms their dates, places, actors and relics into powerful symbols, and the stories into unifying myths. Secondly, a memory of collective wrongs and losses suffered in the past from another nation, but also an awareness, however dim, of one's own nation's responsibility for wrongs done to other peoples, burden the present conflict with strong resentments and make it appear to be either a historical repetition, or a historical redress.[45]

The link between historical memory and the rise of nationalism is essential to note because myths, memories, traditions, and symbols of ethnic heritage are what gives nationalism its power. Perhaps even more important is the way these idealizations of the past can be rediscovered and reinterpreted by modern nationalist intellectual elites.[46] Nationalist (or religious) myths justifying hostility against another group are a key indicator that violence may occur. These myths are evident in national media, school curricula, official government documents and speeches, popular literature, and history. The more hostile the myths or ideology, the more likely violence will occur.[47]

A significant link also exists between historical memory and political legitimacy. This link is best evidenced by the attempt of nationalist movements to create a master commemorative narrative that emphasizes a common past and ensures a common destiny.[48] Political leaders often use historical memory to bolster their own legitimacy, promote their own interests, encourage a nationalistic spirit, and mobilize mass support for social conflicts.

The politics of memory has proven to be central in the transition to democracy throughout the world.[49] Perceptions of the past are essential in both delegitimating previous regimes and grounding new claims to political legitimacy. For example, the collapse of communism in Russia in 1991 necessitated, among other things, the rewriting of history textbooks.[50] By shaping collective memory, governments can uphold their own legitimacy and find reasons to topple that of others.

Collective memory is especially important during a seemingly irresolvable conflict. It influences people's approaches to conflict management in several ways. First, it can justify the outbreak of the conflict and the course of its development. If you believe you have been historically wronged, then you are more likely to engage in conflict. Second, in intractable conflicts, a group's beliefs, through collective memory, present positive images of the group itself as it engages in intense self-justification, self-glorification, and self-praise. A history of victimization and endurance can help build a group's self-esteem as the group members begin to see themselves as the progeny of a long line of survivors. Third, collective memory delegitimates the opponent. A group's memory of previous wrongs will keep the members from seeing the conflict through their opponents' eyes. Finally, a group's beliefs and collective memory present the group as a victim of the opponent.[51] These four influences create an inextricable web that often keeps groups engaged in conflict.

HISTORICAL MEMORY AS A COLLECTIVE IDENTITY: THE FIRST FRAMEWORK

A noteworthy study about the use of identity as a variable in helping to explain political action was conducted by the Harvard Identity Project.[52] According to this study, definition and measurement are two barriers to the more systematic incorporation of identity as a variable in helping to explain political action.

> There is not much consensus on how to define identity; nor is there consistency in the procedures used for determining the content and scope of identity; nor is there agreement on where to look for evidence that identity indeed affects knowledge, interpretations, beliefs, preferences, and strategies; nor is there agreement on how identity affects these components of action.[53]

TABLE 1.1 TYPES OF IDENTITY CONTENT

Constitutive norms (normative content)	The constitutive content of an identity specifies norms or rules that define group membership, the interests of groups, and/or group goals or purposes.
Relational content	The relational content of an identity provides comparisons and references to other identities or groups.
Cognitive models	The cognitive content of an identity affects the way group members interpret and understand the world.
Social purposes (purposive content)	The purposive content of an identity provides the group socially appropriate roles to perform.

A collective identity is defined as a social category that varies along two dimensions: content and contestation. This definition is based on theories of actions, such as social identity theory and role theory, as well as past research in this area.

The *content* of identity may take the form of four, nonmutually exclusive types: constitutive norms, relational content, cognitive models, and social purpose[54] (see table 1.1). When constitutive norms are present, the norms of a collective identity specify rules for group membership (categorization) and accepted attributes (identification). Constitutive norms organize actions in ways that help to define the interests of groups. This identity provides actors with socially appropriate roles to perform. In this conceptualization, the reasons to act in a particular way are found in a decision to perform a role, not in a decision to choose between paths to a preferred outcome.

Relational content, on the other hand, focuses on the relationships people have with others. Collective identities are always partly relational, composed of comparisons and references to other collective identities from which they are distinguished. The relational characteristics of collective identities include exclusivity, status, and hostility. Relational content determines the extent to which one social identity excludes another (exclusivity). For example, if you are member of group X, you are not allowed to be a member of group Y. Relational characteristics also create the relative status of one identity compared to others, so that group X is identified as superior to group Y. This superiority/inferiority dichotomy raises the level of hostility presented by other identities. The creation of in-group identity will tend to produce competitive behavior with out-groups or at least lead to the devaluation of out-groups.[55]

The content of a collective identity can be cognitive, meaning that it explains the way group membership is associated with conceptions of how the world works—specific cause-and-effect relationships—as well as descriptions of the social reality of the group. This model implies that a collective identity affects the way individual actors understand the world. In other words, the material or social incentives for a particular action will take different values according to one's identity. Thus, actions still flow from material or social incentives, but it is identity that affects the evaluation of these incentives.

Last, the content of a collective identity may be purposive, especially when the group attaches specific meanings and goals to its identity. This purposive content is similar to the commonsense notion that what groups want depends on who they think they are. Hence, identities can lead actors to endow practices with group purposes and to interpret the world through lenses related to those purposes.

In summary, each of these four types of identity *content* implies an alternate causal pathway between this collective identity and policy behaviors or practices. Every collective identity includes at least one of these types of content, and many collective identities comprise all four types.[56]

The content of identities is neither fixed nor predetermined. Rather, content is the outcome of a process of social *contestation*. Much of what we think of as identity discourse is controversy over the meaning of a particular collective identity. Specific interpretations of the meaning of an identity are sometimes widely shared among members of a group and sometimes less widely shared. Contestation can be thought of as a matter of degree—the content of collective identities can be more or less contested. When a society experiences certain circumstances, such as an external threat, contestation over identity may drop dramatically.

Social identity theory is another influential contemporary theory of group behavior and provides a useful supplement to the model of the Harvard Identity Project. It explains how identity emerges from the processes of social categorization and comparison and how it influences intergroup relations. Social identity theory is based on three central ideas about intergroup behavior: categorization, identification, and comparison.[57]

We categorize objects to understand them, and we categorize people in order to understand our social environment, thus identifying with groups to which we think we belong. In this way we can understand how people in a group think of themselves in terms of us versus them, or in-group versus out-group. It seems obvious that a positive self-concept is part of normal psychological functioning. As a way of maintaining positive self-esteem, we engage in intergroup comparisons that allow us to conceive of our groups as both different from and superior to groups to which we do not belong.

Social identity theory emphasizes the impact of collective identity and esteem on the individual. Instead of examining the individual in the group, social identity theorists focus on the group in the individual. Individuals seek positive self-identity and self-esteem, which is gained by group membership and the development of consensual, in-group identities. Individuals see themselves more as group members than as individuals, and they act accordingly via collective action. People who share the same collective identity think of themselves as having a common interest and a common fate. However, there is a cultural difference in people's in-group identities. Normally, the more collectivist the culture, the more people identify with their group and the more people will differentiate one's own group from other groups.[58]

Social identity theory also addresses how individuals respond to a negative social identity. Henri Tajfel and John Turner emphasize two important belief systems that shape people's thinking.[59] The first system, *social mobility*, is based on the general assumption that the society in which the individuals live is flexible and permeable. Through social mobility, individuals can attempt to leave a negatively distinct in-group and gain membership in a more favorable group. Therefore if one is not satisfied with one's life in a particular group, a person believes that it is possible—through talent, hard work, immigration, and so on—to move to another group. At the other extreme, *social change* is based on the belief that group boundaries are *impermeable*, meaning that individuals attempt to change certain aspects of their comparative situation in order to achieve favorable in-group comparisons. Social change strategies include social creativity (such as finding new dimensions of comparison and redefining the value attached to attributes), social competition (direct competition with an out-group to achieve actual changes in the status of the groups), and social action (such as social protest, social movement, and revolution). The desire of group members for positive social identity can also provide contending leaders with the basis for social mobilization of mass support.

Both the Harvard Identity Project model and social identity theory serve as useful guides for a more rigorous study of identity. On the basis of these two theories, I have created table 1.2 as an analytical framework for research. Particular questions are posed in an effort to measure the content and contestation of historical memory as a collective identity. This table also includes aspects of categorization, identification, and competition based on the ideas of social identity theory.

Based on the analytic framework shown in table 1.2, when a collective identity serves as a set of constitutive norms, this identity should have the following characteristics: it specifies rules for group membership (categorization) and accepted attributes (identification), contains an element of group self-esteem and myth, provides members with socially appropriate roles for them to perform, and organizes actions in ways that help to define the interests of the group. When examining the role of historical memory in a given group's identity construction, the following questions can help measure the content of historical memory as constitutive norms:

1. Does the content of historical memory specify rules that determine group membership and attributes? For example, who is a group member? What does it mean to be a group member?
2. Does the content of historical memory help to define the interests of groups?
3. Does the content of historical memory constitute the basis of the group's self-esteem, pride, and dignity?
4. Does the content of historical memory provide actors socially appropriate roles to perform?

A set of other questions is asked to measure whether and how the content of historical memory serves as the other three types of identity content—relational, cognitive, and purposive. Finally, the framework measures to what extent the content of historical memory has been shared or contested by the group. This conceptualization provides an analytic framework for systematic research of the function of historical memory. When exploring the impact of historical memory, group dynamics, or ethnic unity, these questions are useful as a guide to categorizing and measuring the effects of historical memory.

Using this framework, when examining the role of historical memory in a given group's policy behaviors or practices (such as foreign policy and conflict behavior), we are able to first find out what role historical memory

TABLE 1.2 HISTORICAL MEMORY AS COLLECTIVE IDENTITY

Content	**Constitutive norms**	Categorization	Does the content of historical memory specify rules that determine group membership and attributes? For example, who is a group member? What does it mean to be a group member?
		Identification	Does the content of historical memory help to define the interests of groups?
		Pride and self-esteem	Does the content of historical memory constitute the basis of the group's self-esteem, pride, and dignity?
		Role identity	Does the content of historical memory provide actors socially appropriate roles to perform?
	Relational content	Social comparison and competition	Does the content of historical memory help specify to whom this social group should compare itself and who the group's enemies are?
			Does the content of historical memory at some time lead to a more cooperative relationship with groups that are socially recognized as similar?
		Social mobility and change	Is the content of historical memory a source of group members' social mobility and social change?
			Does the content of historical memory provide political leaders with the basis for mobilizing mass support?
	Cognitive models	Interpretation	Does the cognitive content of historical memory describe how group membership is associated with explanations of how the world works—specific cause-and-effect relationships—as well as descriptions of the social reality of the group?
		Frames and analogies	Does the content of historical memory provide a source of frames, lenses, and analogies to interpret the world?
	Social purpose		Does the content of historical memory define group purpose?
Contestation			To what extent has the content of historical memory been shared or contested by the group?

plays in the formation of group identity. It is particularly important to examine what role historical memory plays in the process of this group's categorization, identification, and comparison of identity. In chapter 5, this framework will be employed to examine how history and memory define the Chinese Communist Party's identity and worldviews.

THREE CAUSAL PATHWAYS OF BELIEFS: THE SECOND FRAMEWORK

Another important work on the role of ideas in foreign policy was conducted by Judith Goldstein, Robert Keohane, and their colleagues. In their book, *Ideas and Foreign Policy: Beliefs, Institutions, and Political Change*, they propose a system for studying how ideas (defined as "beliefs held by individuals") help to explain political outcomes.[60] Ideas in this sense can also be considered the cognitive content of a collective identity. Using the previous framework it is evident that historical memory forms this collective identity and solidifies the ideas a group holds about its members and its adversaries. Goldstein and Keohane identify three "causal pathways" in which ideas, including those constituting historical memory, can influence policy behavior: ideas as road maps, ideas as focal points and glue, and institutionalization.

Even the most rational analysts agree that people have incomplete information when they select the strategies by which to pursue their preferred outcomes. Therefore the ideas and belief systems that individuals hold become important elements in the explanation of policy choices. Under conditions of uncertainty, beliefs and ideas may act as road maps in three ways. First, ideas influence actors' interpretations and judgments regarding certain situations, whereby they limit policy choices by excluding other variables, as well as rejecting contrary interpretations that might suggest alternative choices in that particular situation. In this way, ideas function as filters that limit policy choices. Second, beliefs and ideas can also provide compelling ethical or moral motivations for actions. Third, ideas and beliefs guide behavior by stipulating causal patterns. Ideas become important when actors believe in the causal links they identify or the normative principles that they reflect.

Ideas can also contribute to outcomes in the absence of unique equilibrium. They may serve as focal points that define cooperative solutions or act as coalitional glue to facilitate the cohesion of particular groups.

When political actors must choose between outcomes with no "objective" criteria on which to base choice, ideas focus expectations and strategies. Political elites may settle on courses of action on the basis of shared cultural, normative, religious, ethnic, or causal beliefs. Other policies may be ignored. Ideas or identities can act as causal factors in influencing policy behavior by coordinating cooperation and group cohesion; however, they can also contribute to outcomes in the opposite way—causing conflict and disorder.

Finally, once ideas become embedded in rules and norms—that is, once they become institutionalized—they constrain public policy. A policy choice leads to the creation of reinforcing organizational and normative structures, which then affect the incentives of political entrepreneurs long after the interests of its initial proponents have changed. In general, when institutions intervene, the impact of ideas may be prolonged for decades or even generations. In this sense, ideas can have an impact even when people no longer genuinely believe in them as a principled or causal statement.

In summary, ideas influence policy when the principled or causal beliefs they embody provide road maps that increase actors' clarity about goals or ends-means relationships, when they affect outcomes of strategic situations in which there is no unique equilibrium, and when they become embedded in political institutions. In order to discern whether the ideas of historical memory act as road maps and/or focal points in a group's policy and practice behavior, specific questions concerning the three aspects must be explored. These questions are outlined in table 1.3.

The first group of questions identifies whether the particular beliefs of historical memory play the role of road maps for response and behavior in conflict and uncertain situations. Given the conceptual framework presented previously, ideas and beliefs play the role of road maps in three ways:

1. Influencing actors' interpretation and judgment regarding the situations
2. Providing compelling ethical or moral motivations for actions
3. Guiding behavior by stipulating causal patterns

The accompanying research questions were designed to examine these three aspects. For example, the initial questions focus on how the beliefs of historical memory influence actors' interpretation and judgment regarding conflicts and policy options for response to them.

TABLE 1.3 THREE CAUSAL PATHWAYS OF BELIEFS

Road maps	Information processing and decision making	Do beliefs of historical memory influence actors' interpretation and judgment regarding conflict situations? Do beliefs of historical memory function as filters that limit choices by excluding other variables and contrary interpretations that might suggest other choices? Do beliefs of historical memory play any role in limiting, curtailing, and creating policy options for response?
	Motivation and mobilization	Do beliefs of historical memory provide ethical or moral motivations for actions? Do political leaders use people's particular beliefs of historical memory to mobilize mass support and/or justify hostility against another group? Does this usage affect the escalation and deescalation of the conflict?
	Guideline	Do beliefs of historical memory stipulate causal patterns to guide behavior under conditions of uncertainty?
Coordination	Cooperation	Do beliefs of historical memory serve as focal points that define cooperative solutions? Do beliefs of historical memory act as coalitional glue to facilitate the cohesion of particular groups?
	Conflict	Do beliefs of historical memory cause any conflict or constitute any difficulties to the settlement and resolution of the conflict?
Institutionalization		Have beliefs of historical memory become embedded in political institutions? Have the beliefs of history and memory been institutionalized?

The second group of questions examines whether and how the beliefs of historical memory serve as focal points and glue that coordinate cooperation and group cohesion or, to the contrary, whether they contribute to outcomes by causing conflict and disorder. The last set of questions considers whether the beliefs of historical memory have become embedded in political institutions and have been institutionalized.

HISTORICAL MEMORY AS A VARIABLE

Historical memory is indeed a very special subject of research. Because it functions at a preconscious or subconscious level, collective memory is very often our "collective unconscious." As a people's national "deep culture," historical memory is not objective knowledge and very often cannot be explicitly learned. While the idea of historical memory shaping identity is generally acknowledged, scholars have not found effective means of measuring or analyzing its effects. Models such as that of the Harvard Identity Project have made strides in addressing identity as a causal factor behind action. However, these theories have yet to be organized into a functional framework for studying historical memory as a variable. This chapter has outlined the existing literature on historical memory and has provided two analytic and theoretic frameworks for studying historical memory and its effects.

I hope that these two frameworks can act as road maps for conducting research on historical memory, as this book aims to contribute to methodological discussions concerning the use of historical memory as a variable to explain political action. As Peter J. Katzenstein suggests, national identities must be investigated empirically in concrete historical settings.[61] These two frameworks provide researchers with tools for analyzing empirical data and can be used to generate research questions measuring the effects of historical memory. This, in turn, will help researchers determine which aspects of an event or a conflict are worth considering. Researchers can use these two frameworks as guides to categorizing and measuring the effects of historical memory. Furthermore, even though this research focuses on using historical memory as a collective identity, it could be used for researching many other types of social identity.

Each of the frameworks can be used as an integral whole for more systematic research or can be divided into several components to focus on particular aspects of historical memory issues. The first framework, for example, addresses four types of identity content. Even though many collective identities have elements of all four types, a research project may choose to focus only on one of them. As previously mentioned, I will focus on the first types of identity content of constitutive norms in chapter 5, using this part of the first framework to explore the role of historical memory in the Chinese Communist Party's identity reconstruction. In particular, the chapter will explore how the elites use the content of history and memory to construct the rules and norms of the ruling party. In the next five chapters, I examine the role of historical memory in national identity formation, with each chapter addressing a different aspect of historical memory issues.

The second framework can be particularly useful in examining how memories of past injustices influence a people's interpretation and judgment regarding a current conflict situation. In chapter 7, this concept provides an analytic framework for examining how history and memory, as beliefs and ideas, have acted as road maps and focal points in the way China conceptualized, managed, and resolved three recent crises with the United States. In addition, in chapters 4 and 5, I address how historical memory has become embedded in political institutions and in patterns of political discourse in China—the processes of institutionalization.

:::

In the next chapter, I use the concepts of chosen glory and chosen trauma to discuss how China's unique national experiences—most significantly, pride over its ancient civilization, as well as a collective memory resulting from the century of humiliation vis-à-vis Western powers—have played a crucial role in shaping the Chinese national identity.

2

CHOSEN GLORY, CHOSEN TRAUMA

On January 15, 1840, Lin Zexu, the Qing commissioner on opium trade, wrote a letter to Queen Victoria.

> Our Celestial Dynasty rules over and supervises the myriad states, and surely possesses unfathomable spiritual dignity. Yet the Emperor cannot bear to execute people without having first tried to reform them by instruction. Therefore he especially promulgates these fixed regulations. The barbarian merchants of your country, if they wish to do business for a long period, are required to obey our statutes respectfully and to cut off permanently the source of opium. They must, by no means, try to test the effectiveness of the law with their lives. May you check your wicked and sift out your vicious people before they come to China, in order to guarantee the peace of your nation, to show further the sincerity of your politeness and submissiveness, and to let the two countries enjoy together the blessings of peace.[1]

Lin's "Letter of Advice to Queen Victoria" was written before the outbreak of the Opium Wars. This letter was read and approved by Emperor Daoguang before Lin published it in Guangzhou. However, it is still unknown whether it ever reached Queen Victoria. To this day, the letter stands as a haunting reminder of the self-assuredness and pride of the Chinese people before the brutal Opium Wars.

The arrival of the British army and the outbreak of war in June 1840 awakened Lin; he realized his level of ignorance about the outside world. In a letter to a friend written in February 1842, Lin discussed the reasons why his Celestial Empire was defeated:

> The British cannons were ten *li* [about 3 miles] away from us, our cannons cannot reach them but theirs can reach us. Our weaponry was inferior. Their cannons fired as repeating guns, one after another without stopping; ours had to wait for some time after we fired one cannonball and then could fire again. Our technology was backward. Many of our generals and soldiers were experienced servicemen, but a battle like this in which the two sides engaged in a war without seeing each other, that was what they have never experienced before.[2]

Lin became one of the few people in China to recognize that the Celestial Empire had already been left behind. From his 1840 letter, full of Chinese pride and superiority, to this one, written with obvious frustration over Chinese backwardness, Lin's two letters tell us how the Opium War quickly changed the Chinese people's view of themselves and the world.

As Rana Mitter comments, the Chinese had chosen the worst moment to fall behind in military technology.[3] Western Europe had undergone dramatic changes between the mid-Ming and mid-Qing dynasties—moving from the Renaissance and age of Columbus, through the Reformation and the rise and fall of the Spanish empire, to the Enlightenment, the French Revolution, and the Industrial Revolution.[4] In comparison, China was at a relative disadvantage in almost every area, from political organization to economic management to military thought. Jiang Tingfu concluded in his seminal book *Modern History of China* (*Zhongguo Jindaishi*):

> The fundamental reason for the Chinese failure in the Opium Wars was because of our backwardness. Our weaponry and our army were the defenses of medieval times, our government was a medieval government, our people, including the scholar-elite class, were people of medieval times. We fought hard, but failed even so. It was a natural and unavoidable outcome.[5]

As introduced in the previous chapter, key historical events—both traumas and glories—are powerful ethnic or large-group markers. When a group has suffered past losses, defeat, and severe humiliation, the mental trauma of these events may become part of its identity and bind its members more closely together. Similarly, the mental representation of a historical event that induces feelings of success and triumph can also bring members of a large group together.[6] As Johan Galtung suggests, in order to understand the workings of large-group (e.g., ethnic) identity and how that group behaves in conflict situations, it is important to know and understand that group's chosenness and myths of past glories and traumas. The Chosenness-Myths-Trauma (CMT) complex plays a critical role in defining national identity.[7]

Although my emphasis in this book is the idea that much of contemporary Chinese politics and thinking is heavily shaped by what happened during the "century of humiliation," it is important to put this period in context and understand that one century is a very short span of time in China's long history of civilization. It is impossible to fully understand the Chinese people's chosen traumas without a thorough understanding of their chosen glories. The three parts of the CMT complex reinforce each other socially.[8] Examining China's CMT complex can help us place the century of humiliation in the context of China's overall historical experience, thereby defining its function from a more comprehensive historical perspective.

This chapter reviews China's CMT complex, highlighting those historical events that still affect the Chinese psyche today. It is imperative that we know what happened in history before we can analyze and examine the formation of a group's historical consciousness. The purpose of this chapter is not to recount history, but rather to focus on how the Chinese remember history. For this purpose, I draw considerably from China's history textbooks and other official narratives. While we cannot count on these official narratives' objectivity, they do undoubtedly offer invaluable evidence toward a deeper comprehension of the Chinese understanding of history and elite history making in China. We turn now to understanding Chinese chosenness.

CHOSENNESS

Chosenness—the belief in being selected by some transpersonal force such as God, Allah, or History—is not unique to China. Many groups and cultures believe they are chosen by transcendental forces and elevated above all others. In China, this chosenness is ingrained even in their language. The way ancient Chinese referred to themselves, their country, and outsiders provides insight into their notion of the Chinese as chosen people.

For the ancient Chinese, their strong sense of chosenness is evident in the many names they gave to their country. China is called *Zhongguo* (中国) in Mandarin Chinese. The first character *zhong* means "central" or "middle," while *guo* means "kingdom" or "nation." People believed that they lived in the central kingdom of *tianxia* (天下), the "realm under heaven." According to Chiang Kai-shek, the name Central Kingdom was not just a geographical and cultural concept but was also loaded with political meaning. It was believed that whoever controlled Zhongguo, the Central Kingdom, would be the legitimate ruler over *tianxia*.[9]

China is also called *Zhonghua* (中华). In ancient Chinese, *hua* means "splendid" and "prosperous" and could also be used to refer to a beautiful dress or rich ornament. Ancient Chinese called themselves *Hua* and used the term *Yi* to refer to cultural or ethnic outsiders; *Yi* is often translated as "barbarian."[10] According to Lothar von Falkenhausen, the contrast between "Chinese" (self-designated as *Zhonghua* or *Huaxia*) and "barbarians" (*Yi*) was accentuated during the Eastern Zhou period (770–256 b.c.), when adherence to Zhou rituals was increasingly recognized as a "barometer of civilization."[11] The ruling elite, infused with a sense of Chinese cultural superiority, measured alien groups according to a yardstick by which those who did not follow the "Chinese way" were considered barbarians.[12]

While the *Hua-Yi* distinction is no doubt Sinocentric and could take on ethnic or racist overtones, especially in times of war, it is important to understand that the Chinese welcomed the assimilation of *Yi*. As Frank Dikötter discussed in his book *The Discourse of Race in Modern China*, ancient Chinese also believed that outsiders could be culturally absorbed and become Chinese (*Hanhua*) by adopting Chinese culture and customs. The theory of "using the Chinese ways to transform the barbarians" (*Yongxiabianyi*) was strongly advocated.[13]

Another common name for China is *Shenzhou*, which can literally be translated as the "sacred land" or "divine land." It was thought that the world was divided into nine major states, one of which is Shenzhou, the sacred land. This word originated during the middle of the Warring States Period (476–221 b.c.). Some Chinese like to call China *Tianchao*, the "Celestial Empire" or "Heavenly Dynasty." The idea is that China is the kingdom ruled by the dynasty appointed by heaven. In today's Internet discussion forums, Tianchao is still a favorite name that many young people use to refer to China.

The Chinese also refer to themselves as the "descendants of the dragon" (*Long de chuanren*). This legend also contributed to the use of the Chinese dragon as a symbol of imperial power. In contrast to European dragons, which are considered evil, Chinese dragons traditionally symbolize potent and auspicious powers, with control over water, rainfall, and floods.

Ancient Chinese believed their group was the chosen people who lived in a sacred land at the center of the world. They were proud of their own beautiful dress and high culture and considered ethnic outsiders to be "uncultured" and "uncivilized." But anyone belonging to one of China's neighbors who embraced the Chinese culture could be transformed and assimilated into an integral part of the Zhonghua nation, thereby becoming "Chinese." Historically, China's cultural sphere has extended across East Asia, with Chinese philosophy, customs, and writing systems being adopted to varying degrees by such neighbors as Japan, Korea, and Vietnam. In the eyes of the Chinese people, the successful assimilation of outsiders and the teacher-student relationship with several neighbors reinforced a view of Chinese civilization as universal and superior.

MYTH

Past victories in battle and great accomplishments of a technical or artistic nature frequently act as a group's chosen glories, as virtually every large group has tales of grandeur associated with it. The shared importance of such events, whether recent or ancient, real or mythologized, helps to bind the individuals in a large group together.[14] Myths about past and present glories usually lie at the center of each country's identity education, and China is not an exception. From primary school textbooks to literature, film, and popular arts, narratives about China's glamorous past and recent achievements are everywhere. There are several four-character "idioms" that have been frequently used to present China's myths:

- *Wenming guguo* (文明古国), "a civilized ancient nation"
- *Liyizhibang* (礼仪之邦), "a nation of ritual and etiquette"
- *Didawubo* (地大物博), "the vast land and bountiful goods"
- *Sidafaming* (四大发明), "the four great inventions of ancient China"
- *Canlanwenming* (灿烂文明), "a splendid civilization"

Four-character idioms often intimately linked with the myth, story, or historical fact from which they were derived. Understanding these Chinese idioms will enhance our study of Chinese historic memory and, in particular, our understanding of the CMT complex.

China's chosen myths and glories were showcased at the opening ceremony of the Beijing Olympic Games in 2008. Featuring more than 15,000 performers, the ceremony lasted over four hours and was reported to have cost more than $100 million to produce.[15] The hosts seized every opportunity to demonstrate China's glorious past and promising future and to recount its earlier attempts to integrate with the world. Elements of Chinese civilization, from major inventions to music and the arts, were carefully woven into the opening performances as the highlight of China's glories. Zhang Yimou, the famous filmmaker who became the chief artistic director for the opening ceremony, once said: "This is a job one hundred times more demanding than directing a blockbuster movie, because I am responsible for celebrating the realization of a century-old dream and showcasing a 5,000-year-old civilization."[16] Beijing spent more than two years preparing for this event. From the overall design to each individual performance piece, every detail of the 2008 Olympic opening ceremony was reviewed and revised based on the top leaders' opinions. It portrayed an official narrative of China's myths and glories.

The ceremony began with a *fou* drum sequence by 2,008 drummers. The *fou* is a 4,000-year-old Chinese drum that dates back to the Xia dynasty (ca. 2070–1600 b.c.), where it was used in rituals and later became a standard of Confucian ensembles.[17] The use of *fou* represented China's long history and provided a timeline for the night's performances. One of the chosen glories for the Chinese people is that the Chinese civilization is perceived as the oldest continuous civilization in the world. Chinese civilization has archaeological evidence dating back more than 5,000 years, and its recorded history extends in an unbroken chain over 4,000 years. As an element of ritual music, *fou* also represented China as a "nation of ritual and etiquette," or *liyizhibang*. Most Chinese share an intense pride in their complex systems of etiquette and hospitality. This pride is reflected in the use of such phrases as *liyizhibang* to refer to China.

China's pride in its country's many significant inventions was featured as a major theme in the Olympic opening ceremony. The "Four Great Inventions"—paper, the compass, gunpowder, and printing (both wood block and movable type)—had an enormous impact on the development of Chinese civilization and the world. The ceremony's artistic selections highlighted these four inventions—and thereby glorified China's myths.

The first part of the ceremony comprised the artistic section, "Splendid Civilization," and started with a short film. The film described the process of making paper and the art of calligraphy, representing the first great Chinese invention. Papermaking was represented with a dance and an ink drawing on a huge Chinese painting scroll, reminiscent of Chinese ink and wash art.

In the next segment, the giant scroll was moved aside to show a fluid array of hundreds of movable type blocks that formed three variations of the Chinese character *He* (和), meaning "harmony," which showcased the second invention: movable-type printing. Movable type formed from baked clay characters was developed in China in the Song dynasty (960–1276).

Next there was a celebration of the Chinese invention of the compass. Hundreds of oarsmen, with oars forming pictures of junks, created a performance that symbolized the voyages of Zheng He. Zheng was a Chinese mariner, explorer, diplomat, and fleet admiral who made voyages during the fifteenth century to Southeast Asia, South Asia, and East Africa, collectively referred to as *Zheng He Xia Xiyang*, meaning "Zheng He to the Western Ocean."

One of the great inventions, gunpowder, was demonstrated throughout the opening ceremony with extensive fireworks displays. Almost each section of the ceremony performances began with the explosion of hundreds of fireworks above the stadium.

The four great inventions represented ancient China's advanced science and technology, but Beijing also wanted to use the ceremony to highlight China's high culture and moral quality. This theme was represented in the opening ceremony through the dedication of several minutes to display the Silk Road and Zheng's voyages. Highly regarded as two of China's most important exchanges and encounters with the outside world during ancient times, these two instances are viewed by the Chinese as not only showcases of China's ancient civilization and strength but also, more importantly, as demonstrations of its high culture and moral quality.

Between 1405 and 1433, the Ming government sponsored a series of seven naval expeditions. Zheng He was placed as the admiral in control of the huge fleet and armed forces that undertook these expeditions. Zheng's first voyage consisted of a fleet of around 300 ships holding almost 28,000 crewmen.[18] The fleets visited Arabia, East Africa, India, Indonesia, and

Thailand, dispensing and receiving goods along the way. Upon returning from his fourth voyage, Zheng brought envoys from thirty states who traveled to China to pay their respects at the Ming Court. For the Chinese hosts, the Silk Road and Zheng's voyages also demonstrated that the Chinese had been open-minded and that China's culture is all-embracing.

In China's standard history textbooks, Zheng's voyages are praised as "voyages of peace and friendship."[19] People believe that Zheng generally sought to attain his goals through diplomacy and that his large army awed most would-be enemies into submission. In the Chinese narrative, Zheng's voyages have always been used as a good example of "winning respect through virtue" (*yidefuren*) rather than using force. Many Chinese believe that China has never bullied the weak and small. Some scholars consider that during the periods of Ming and Qing dynasties the Chinese had a strong "sense of moral superiority."[20]

However, Zheng He's voyages also provide an example of how Chinese historical memory very often engages in "selective remembering" and "selective forgetting." According to some recent scholarship, Zheng's voyages were often accompanied by violent behavior toward local populations. His soldiers invaded places like Palembang in Sumatra, Java, and Ayutthaya in modern-day Thailand.[21] It is also not true that China never invaded its neighboring countries. The rulers of many Chinese dynasties, from Tang to Qing, undertook numerous military campaigns to expand their territory and become one of the world's great land empires. Still, the image of China as a "peace-loving country" has been a myth and a common rhetoric, frequently appearing in China's official documents and school textbooks. In his speech at Harvard University in 2003, Premier Wen Jiabao said directly: "Peace-loving has been a time-honored quality of the Chinese nation." He also quoted Russian writer Leo Tolstoy saying that China is "the most peace-loving nation in the world."[22]

Many of China's other glories also appeared in the opening ceremony. In one segment, performers wore feathered headdresses and carried bamboo slips, representing the disciples of Confucius. They recited excerpts from *Lunyu*, or *Analects of Confucius*. Even though most of the events presented in the opening ceremony were of China's ancient civilization, China's new glory was celebrated by highlighting the space walk of Chinese astronauts, symbolizing China's successful space exploration and manned spaceflight program.

Looking back at history, we can see how the Chinese—the citizens of the Central Kingdom, the Divine Land, and the Celestial Empire and the descendants of the dragon—looked at the world and themselves. By going back to the time before 1840, the year the Opium War broke out, we can imagine how proud the Chinese were of their homeland, with its vast lands and bountiful resources. Throughout thousands of years of history, the Chinese people have been instrumental in developing technologies and advancing the knowledge of mankind. China has been the source of many significant inventions, including the Four Great Inventions. Over the course of history, science and the arts flourished, and the government developed into a sophisticated system of control run by bureaucrats chosen by competitive examination. Although China, like all societies, went through periods of war and decline, a new dynasty always emerged to bring the society back to a new peak of splendor.[23] As the Olympic opening ceremony clearly suggests, there is no doubt that the Chinese view themselves as possessing both a strong sense of both cultural and moral superiority.

Without a clear understanding of Chinese chosenness and myths, we would not be able to understand what the history of the hundred years after the Opium War means to these proud Chinese. We would also not be able to understand the shock of the century of humiliation, which still affects Chinese thought today and forms the national trauma attached to the Chinese people's collective memory. Over China's long history, the country has experienced many dynastic transitions, which often came with massive violence and war. Natural disasters, disease, and famine also frequently plagued the country. However, for many Chinese, these events bear no comparison to what China suffered during the period from 1840 to 1945.

TRAUMA

Many scholars have discussed the importance of the national humiliation discourse in Chinese identity politics. For example, William Callahan believes that humiliation is a key component of modern Chinese subjectivity. He also argues that the discourse of the century of humiliation is the "master narrative" of modern Chinese history.[24] Billy Wireman takes the view that "the most misunderstood and least discussed element in the Chinese situation today is the Humiliation Factor," adding that the United States does little to understand this "deep seated part of the Chinese psyche."[25] Peter Gries also argues that contemporary Chinese nationalism must be understood in the historical context of the "100 years of national humiliation," as its legacy makes the Chinese very sensitive to perceived slights to China's dignity.[26] Hu Ping, a famous Chinese writer, once said: "For Chinese people, history is our religion. . . . We don't have a supernatural standard of right and wrong, good and bad, so we view History as the ultimate Judge. . . . Each Chinese is a born nationalist."[27] These statements help to demonstrate the relationship between China's national experiences and the Chinese psyche.

While large groups may have experienced any number of traumas in their history, only certain instances remain alive many years later. A group's "chosen traumas" consist of experiences that come "to symbolize this group's deepest threats and fears through feelings of hopelessness and victimization."[28] It reflects the traumatized past generation's incapacity for mourning losses, connected to the shared traumatic event, as well as its failure to reverse the injury to the group's self-esteem and humiliation. A group does not really choose to be victimized and subsequently lose self-esteem, but it does choose to psychologize and mythologize—to dwell on and exaggerate—the event. In Chinese historical narrative, people often use the following three four-character idioms to summarize China's national humiliation during its century of humiliation:

- *Lü zhan lü bai* (屡战屡败), "repeatedly fought and lost"
- *Ge di pei kuan* (割地赔款), "to cede territory and pay indemnities"
- *Sang quan ru guo* (丧权辱国), "to surrender sovereign rights and bring humiliation to the country"

Foreign invasions and lost wars often become important sources of an ethnic group's chosen trauma. The major foreign invasions that China faced during its century of humiliation include the First Opium War (1839–1842), the Second Opium War (1856–1860), the Sino-Japanese War (1894–1895), the invasion of the allied forces of eight countries (1900), the Japanese invasion of Manchuria (1931), and the Anti-Japanese War (1937–1945).

Ceding territory, paying indemnities, and surrendering sovereign rights were all related to the "unequal treaties," *bupingdeng tiaoyue* (不平等条约). The century of humiliation is also referred to as the "treaty century," because many foreign powers forcibly required China to sign a series of devastating agreements following military defeats.[29] Chinese considered these treaties unequal because, in most cases, China was forced to pay large amounts of reparations, to open up ports, to cede lands, or to make various concessions to foreign spheres of influence. For example, in just a single treaty—the Boxer Protocol of 1901—China was required to pay a huge indemnity of about twice the annual income of the entire Qing government.[30]

FOREIGN INVASIONS AND LOST WARS

Prior to the First Opium War, China had a very different relationship with the Western powers than it had after the war. Until 1840, the only port available to foreign merchants was Guangzhou. Foreigners were also limited to doing business with only thirteen officially approved trade agencies, and local officials exacted high "protection fees" for their services. Furthermore, business was limited to the summer and autumn seasons, with foreigners required to retreat to Macao during the rest of the year. Foreigner merchants were not even allowed to learn Chinese, which further hindered their bargaining position.[31] All of these imposed limitations stemmed from a strong sense of Chinese cultural superiority. As Jiang Tingfu commented on the change in relationship, "We treated them unequally before the war, but they began to treat us unequally after the war."[32]

The outbreak of the Opium War was the result of a long-standing conflict between China and Great Britain over trade issues. Through her analysis, Patricia Ebrey considered that the rise of Britain as a great naval power dependent on foreign trade made conflict with China inevitable; China had no desire to organize trade on the European model, but Britain had the power to force acceptance of its terms.[33]

In June 1839, Chinese opium trade high commissioner Lin Zexu confiscated all British opium in China (approximately 2.6 million pounds) and openly destroyed all of it at the beach of Humen in Guandong. He also imposed a trade embargo on Britain until it ceased all opium trade. When word of Lin's destruction of the opium and imposition of this trade embargo got back to London, the British Indian Army was sent to China in 1840. The ensuing war between China and the British wreaked havoc on China's coast.[34] The British had superior weaponry and more advanced ships that were faster and armed with larger quantities of firepower. Moreover, British troops carried the latest and most advanced muskets of the time, which severely overpowered outdated Chinese artillery. By 1841, the British occupied several strategic coastal cities, including Shanghai. Eventually the British sailed up the Yangtze River and took up positions outside the walls of Nanjing, effectively forcing the Chinese to surrender.[35] On August 29, 1842, aboard HMS *Cornwallis*, the Treaty of Nanjing between China and Great Britain was signed.

The Chinese see the Opium War as a critical turning point in their history. In the official history narrative, the Opium War was the starting point from which China began to "degenerate from an independent country into a semi-colonial country."[36] Sun Yat-sen and Mao Zedong both used the appellation "semicolonial" to distinguish China from some other countries, such as India, which was entirely colonial under direct British rule.[37]

It is interesting to note the way the Chinese memorialize this event as a chosen trauma. In the same site that Lin Zexu confiscated the British opium, the Chinese government built the Opium War Museum in 1985. Museums and public monuments have played a crucial role in the formation of a national memory and identity throughout many societies, especially in China. These museums and monuments provide rich information to understand how a group of people remembers past events. They are used all over the world as reminders of trauma and glory, as statements of historical facts, and as tools for citizenship and identity education. The pictures and captions presented in this chapter illustrate the special narrative of Chinese historical memory.

These ideals are reflected in the construction of the Opium War Museum and can be referenced in the various monuments on the museum grounds. Before entering the museum, visitors first see a very special sculpture—two mighty hands breaking a huge metal opium pipe (see figure 2.1). Smoking opium required a particular type of pipe called a *yen tsiang* (or *yanqiang*), a "smoking pistol." The museum brochure explains the design of the sculpture:

> The big hands are symbolic of the power of Chinese people to resist the foreign invasions and the spirit that the Chinese people cannot be insulted. The broken opium pipe is symbolic of the ultimate failure of the imperialists' invasion crimes. The sculpture is telling us not to forget this part of history and the Chinese nation cannot be insulted.[38]

Though Lin later remarked on China's "inferior weaponry" and "backward technology" compared with the British cannons, the Chinese in 1985 nevertheless glorified the military through the erection of a huge sculpture of an artillery piece surrounded by three Chinese warriors in the entrance of the Opium War Museum (see figure 2.2). According to the

FIGURE 2.1. Broken opium smoking pistol, Humen, Guangdong. (Photo courtesy of Zheng Wang.)

FIGURE 2.2. Entrance to the Opium War Museum, built in 1985, Humen, Guangdong. (Photo courtesy of Zheng Wang.)

brochure, since the museum opened in 1985, more than fifty state leaders and 15 million people have visited it. The Opium War Museum became a national "patriotic education base" in 1996.

Since the Treaty of Nanjing had not directly addressed the issue of the opium trade, the British continued smuggling the drug into China. The Qing government's unwillingness to adhere to treaty provisions or renegotiate new treaties angered the West. A few events, such as the Father Chapdelaine Incident, provided enough tension between the Qing and the West to ignite the Second Opium War in 1856.[39] The French agreed to join the British invasion against the Qing. In December 1857, the joint forces took Guangzhou. In 1860, an Anglo-French expedition occupied Beijing for a month, and they set out to destroy the Yuanming Yuan (圆明园) royal palace, just outside the city.[40]

Groups have important symbols that represent or recall their glories and traumas. As the Great Wall and the Four Great Inventions are symbols of China's glories, Yuanming Yuan has become a symbol of China's chosen trauma. Yuanming Yuan, meaning "Garden of Perfect Brightness," is situated in the northwest of Beijing. Considered China's most beautiful royal garden, it was constructed in the early eighteenth century during the reign of Emperor Kangxi of the Qing dynasty. At the height of its existence, the palace was a repository of the best Chinese art and literature the country had to offer. Its interior was resplendent in a variety of precious antiques, jewelry, and art crafts.[41] However, the garden was burned, desecrated, and looted by the Anglo-French Expeditionary Force in 1860.

After 1949, the Chinese government decided to leave the ruined garden "as is" to remind future generations about Chinese suffering under imperialist aggression. Although most buildings in this garden were destroyed, the marble structures encompassing the pavilion and fountains of Yuanying Guan ("View of Distant Seas") survived the burnings and plunder to become the most famous symbol of the site and its ruination. As depicted in figure 2.3, the image of Yuanying Guan, standing steadfast among the surrounding ruins and debris, came to be known as the "national ruin" of China. By leaving the garden as is with no restoration efforts, it is reminiscent of the idiom "Never Forget National Humiliation."

Yuanying Guan is widely copied by builders, digital designers, and craftsmen.[42] Pictures of the ruin grace book covers, commercial brands, posters, calendars, and T-shirts.[43] The ruined park was elevated to the status of a national patriotic education base in 1994 and has become one of

FIGURE 2.3. The National Ruin, Beijing. (Photo courtesy of Zheng Wang.)

the most popular places for various ceremonies, anniversaries, and activities. The site is an icon of national humiliation that is a testament to both the Chinese civilization and foreign barbarism.[44] The editors of a national high school history textbook used a particularly bold font and brighter colors to highlight a question for class discussion: "Why did troops from countries who referred to themselves as civilized Westerners destroy the essences of the Eastern [Chinese] civilization?"[45] In choosing to leave this burned garden as it was, the ruins have become a physical reminder of what the Chinese historical memory remembers as Western hostility and the "rape" of China. Through facilitating such discussions and organizing youth groups to visit the ruin, today's educators can easily mold students to feel this national compassion for something that happened a century and a half ago.

After 150 years of sporadic warfare, the ruined park today is still the center of attention and discourse. While people have continuously debated whether this imperial garden should be restored and rebuilt or left as it stands, the appearance of looted Chinese relics from Yuanming Yuan in recent years on international auction markets has attracted wide attention and a strong response in China.[46] Through various film projects, television documentaries, and constant discussions on Internet forums, the garden has retained its influence over the years with increasing popularity in the Chinese imagination.

Many Chinese consider the greatest humiliation during the century of humiliation to be China's defeat by Japan, a former tributary and vassal state. Over several decades, Japan had begun modernizing and expanding its influence in Korea, which had long paid tribute to China and had been one of Qing China's most loyal vassals, sending four tribute missions a year.[47] In 1894, the first Sino-Japanese War broke out over the conflicting positions China and Japan held in Korea. On July 23, Japanese troops entered Seoul and overthrew the Korean emperor, replacing him with a pro-Japanese government. China's first modern naval battle took place off the mouth of the Yalu River on September 17, with the Japanese navy destroying eight warships of the Chinese Beiyang Fleet; the Chinese fleet subsequently retreated behind the Weihaiwei fortifications. However, incompetent Chinese leadership conducted some rather ignominious withdrawals, including the abandonment of the very well-fortified and defensible Weihaiwei fort.[48] As a result, the Beiyang Fleet was destroyed and its chief general committed suicide.

On October 24, 1894, Japanese troops crossed the Yalu River and entered China. In November, Port Arthur (Lushunkou) was seized by the Japanese, and troops pillaged the city, killing thousands of civilians in what is known in China as the Port Arthur Massacre.[49] By March 1895, the Japanese had successfully invaded Shandong Province and Manchuria and had taken the fortified posts that controlled the sea lanes to Beijing. The Chinese sued for peace. The war ended in 1895 with the Treaty of Shimonoseki, which changed the Sino-Japanese relationship from one of equal footing to Japanese superiority.

Figure 2.4 is a Japanese wood-block print from the Meiji era (1868–1912). During this time, a large volume of war prints depicting battle scenes was produced in Japan and used as wartime propaganda during the Sino-Japanese War. This print portrays the surrender of Qing officials to the Japanese navy after the Battle of Weihaiwei. The Japanese wearing military uniforms were intentionally depicted as much taller than the Chinese.

In April 2006, some of these Meiji images were posted on the Massachusetts Institute of Technology (MIT) website as part of a research project entitled "Visualizing Cultures." In response to these historical images, a large number of Chinese students at MIT and in the surrounding Boston area coordinated strong protests, as these propaganda images

FIGURE 2.4. Surrender of Chinese forces after the Battle of Weihaiwei (1895), Shandong, China. Japanese woodblock print from the Meiji era.

were deemed to humiliate China.[50] Even today, more than 115 years later, anything related to this part of history is still very sensitive, even among China's overseas intellectuals.

According to Chinese historical memory, by the end of the nineteenth century, China had been invaded and plundered by foreign powers for almost sixty years. We can use today's theories of globalization to understand the emergence of local resistance against the rapid expansion of Western influence in China. The Boxer Rebellion was one of these extreme grassroots responses to this opening.

Between 1898 and 1901, a violent, anti-imperialist, anti-Christian movement by the Yihe Tuan ("Righteous Fists of Harmony") emerged. "Boxers," as the radicals were called, operated under the slogan "Support the Qing, Destroy the Foreign" (*Fuqing mieyang*). Boxers across northern China took to the streets, and violence broke out against foreigners and Chinese Christians.[51] In response to this situation, eight powers—Austria-Hungary, France, Germany, Italy, Japan, Russia, the United Kingdom, and the United States—formed an alliance to send joint troops to Beijing in August 1900. On August 14, troops of the Eight Nation Alliance entered Beijing and the Empress Dowager and her high officials fled for Xi'an.[52] Once again, China's capital and its imperial palaces were occupied by foreign troops. The Forbidden City and Yuanming Yuan were ransacked, and priceless artifacts were taken away.

Further concessions by the Qing dynasty came just four years after the Boxer Rebellion. From 1904 to 1905, Russia and Japan fought a war over Manchuria, a piece of Chinese territory. Although the war was being fought on Chinese soil, neither Japan nor Russia ever consulted the Chinese government, and the Chinese could do nothing to stop it. The Chinese felt, as Rana Mitter commented, that this was proof that China's destiny now lay in the hands of foreigners who bore it little goodwill.[53]

Japan gained a dominant position in southern Manchuria after a victory over Russia in 1905. In the decades that followed, Japan's desire to command Manchuria's massive amounts of raw materials drove it to seek war with China. As China weakened due to civil infighting and Japan strengthened from further modernization, war became inevitable.

September 18, 1931, is an important date in the Chinese collective memory; it marks the beginning of the darkest period in the nation's modern history. On that day, a bridge at a Japanese-owned and -operated railroad crossing was bombed. The Japanese army, which had been occupying part of Manchuria since the first Sino-Japanese War, was allegedly responsible, but the Japanese blamed the attack on Chinese rebels and used it as justification for its army to begin its invasion of China. Following the "September 18th Incident," or the "Mukden Incident," as it came to be called, the Japanese launched a full-scale surprise attack on Shenyang, easily conquering the city. Zhang Xueliang, the local warlord and the effective ruler of Manchuria, withdrew his armies from the front lines without significant engagements. Within a week, the Japanese conquered most of Manchuria. According to Chinese historical narrative, the next fourteen years, from 1931 to 1945, under Japanese occupation were the bleakest chapter in the history of China and the most painful memory for many Chinese.

To commemorate the Mukden Incident, the Chinese constructed the September 18th Historical Museum, located on the exact site where the incident occurred in 1931. Built in 1991, the exterior of the museum depicts a large, very impressive sculpture designed to look like an open calendar, inscribed with the date September 18, 1931 (see figure 2.5). The Chinese intended that through this particular construction, future generations would forever remember this historic, humiliating date. The other side of the calendar page explains how the Japanese invaded the city and the particular events of this grim day in Chinese history. On the other side of the museum, a huge bronze bell is engraved with the four Chinese characters *Wuwang guochi* (勿忘国耻), meaning "Never Forget National Humiliation."

FIGURE 2.5. The Open Calendar, September 18 Historical Museum, Shenyang. (Photo courtesy of Zheng Wang.)

Six years after the Japanese occupied Manchuria, war broke out as the Japanese crossed the Marco Polo Bridge and marched toward Beijing on July 7, 1937. Beijing and Tianjin were easily taken by the Imperial Japanese Army, while Chiang Kai-shek managed to hold off the Japanese at Shanghai for three months. The Nationalist troops persisted despite heavy shelling and bombing, suffering almost 250,000 casualties. After the campaign against Shanghai, the Japanese kept on fighting all the way to China's capital of Nanjing.[54]

Another important date in Chinese historical memory is December 13, 1937, when Nanjing fell to the Japanese. In the following six weeks, Japanese soldiers raped and murdered the Chinese citizens of Nanjing and looted the city. It was reported in two Japanese newspapers that members of the Japanese army engaged in "killing competitions" to see who could kill more Chinese, and that at least 20,000 women were raped.[55] The estimates of the number of deaths in the Nanjing Massacre varies widely: the Chinese claim that 300,000 people died in the massacre, while the International Military Tribunal of the Far East estimates 260,000. Japanese scholars generally put the number somewhere between 100,000 and 200,000,[56] although some maintain that the widespread massacre was fabricated by the Chinese government for political reasons after the capture of Nanjing and that the battle was not inordinately violent.[57] Yet for many Chinese people, the "Rape of Nanjing" is incomparable and unforgettable. The memory of the Nanjing Massacre still sits unsettled in the minds of both the Chinese and Japanese. As David Askew has commented, this incident is a fundamental keystone in the construction of the modern Chinese national identity.[58]

Today, anybody visiting the Memorial Hall for Compatriots Killed in the Nanjing Massacre by Japanese Forces of Aggression will see a huge stone wall at the entrance with the death toll inscribed as "Victims 300,000" (see figure 2.6). The word *victim* is engraved in Chinese, English, and Japanese. Elsewhere at the memorial, another monument depicts the same number of 300,000 fatalities in eleven different languages (see figure 2.7). The decision to make this figure recognizable in so many different languages illustrates the Chinese insistence on the number of casualties, highlighting the role of historical memory and conceptualizing the notion of how a group of people chooses to remember its historical narrative. Built in 1985, Memorial Hall is located in the southwestern corner of Nanjing known as Jiangdongmen, near a site referred to as a "pit of ten thousand corpses." Many believe thousands of bodies are buried there.

By 1941, Japan controlled most major cities in the north and along the eastern coast of China, as well as the railroads connecting them. The Chinese Nationalists had retreated to the western regions and the Chinese Communists firmly held control in northern Shaanxi Province.[59] This was still largely the case when, on August 6, 1945, an American B-29 bomber dropped the first atomic bomb on Hiroshima, Japan; a second one was dropped on Nagasaki on August 9. That same day, the Soviet Union renounced its nonaggression pact with Japan and attacked the Japanese in Manchuria. Emperor Hirohito officially capitulated to the Allies on August 15, 1945.[60]

The Chinese celebrated their victory and the recovery of the lost lands. However, their happiness also came with a bit of bitterness, as they knew their victory was not their own doing. Without the nuclear attacks by the United States and the Soviet offensive in Manchuria, the Japanese surrender would not have come so quickly.

The second Sino-Japanese War, also known as the Anti-Japanese War or the War of Resistance, fought between 1937 and 1945, was the most destructive war in Asia during the twentieth century, with millions killed, wounded, or displaced on both sides. Chinese official history textbooks

FIGURE 2.6. "Victims 300,000," Nanjing Massacre Memorial Hall, Nanjing. (Photo courtesy of Zheng Wang.)

FIGURE 2.7. "Victims 300,000" in eleven languages, Nanjing Massacre Memorial Hall, Nanjing. (Photo courtesy of Zheng Wang.)

claim the total number of Chinese military and nonmilitary casualties to be 35 million. It is estimated that of 4.3 million Japanese troops, 1.5 million were killed or wounded in battle.[61]

"UNEQUAL TREATIES"

In his book *China's Destiny,* Chiang Kai-shek divides China's international relations during the century of humiliation into three chronological periods, punctuated by major conflicts and defining agreements.[62] The first period was from the First Opium War (1840–1842) to the Sino-Japanese War (1894–1895). The second began with the Treaty of Shimonoseki (1895) and lasted until the joint expedition of the Eight Powers (1901). The third phase lasted from the Boxer Protocol (1901) to the end of World War II (1945).

Chiang chose these major events as classification tools because they denote key shifts in how he believed Western powers treated China. The first period, from 1842 to 1895, can be characterized by "parallel competition in China."[63] Treaties were generally bilateral and included most-favored nation provisions, which indicate the competing powers vying for trade, property rights, and special concessions. The second classification period, from 1895 to 1901, saw the competition between the industrializing powers escalate into intense rivalry. Alliances were formed between Western powers, such as the British teaming with the Japanese and the French allying with the Russians.[64] After the Boxer Protocol of 1901, rivalries led to a violent struggle between Russia and Japan over Chinese territory. This final period can be characterized by Japan's push for consolidating power in its own hands and the other powers' inaction on the partition of China. In 1943, the United States and Britain signed new treaties with the Nationalist government for relinquishment of their extraterritorial rights in China. The Chinese century of humiliation finally ended with the conclusion of World War II and Japan's expulsion from China in 1945.

The first of the despised unequal treaties, the Treaty of Nanjing, ended the First Opium War and was seen as a turning point in Chinese history, as it marked the transition of China's international relations from a tributary to a treaty system. This treaty, along with its two annexes, created a new framework for China's foreign relations. Over the course of the next sixty years, ceding land and paying indemnities, what the Chinese referred to as "*Gedi Peikuan,*" became the basic model that the Qing government used to appease Western powers. The Treaty of Nanjing had six main provisions:

1. Extraterritoriality (foreign consular jurisdiction over foreign nationals)
2. Indemnities (a total sum of $21 million)
3. A moderate tariff and direct foreign contract with the customs collectors
4. Most-favored nation treatment
5. The opening of five new ports for trade
6. Ceding Hong Kong to the British[65]

As one historian notes, a "most ironic point was that opium, the immediate cause of the war, was not even mentioned."[66]

Perhaps the most far-reaching provision was the ceding of Hong Kong to the British. The colony was later extended to include the land just across from the island. Hong Kong became a lasting reminder for the Chinese of the one hundred years of humiliation, as the colony was not returned to Chinese territory until 1997.

One may wonder why China agreed to such demands in 1842, but it must be remembered that China still had relatively little international interaction. At that time, Hong Kong was a barren island unknown to people in Beijing; the top Manchu negotiator of the treaty even visited Hong Kong for the first time on a British gunboat.[67] In the eyes of the Chinese, the tariff rate requested seemed like an increase rather than a decrease. And extraterritoriality seemed to put the burden on foreigners to police themselves. The Chinese were not familiar with such tactics, and therefore they were not prepared for the long-term consequences. Emperor Daoguang and his senior officials did not even see these treaties as legal documents that they had to implement after signing. Signing the treaties was simply a nonmilitary means to relieve the Qing Empire of an immediate nuisance—the presence of British forces in the lower Yangtze area.[68]

The Second Opium War ended with the Treaty of Tianjin (Tientsin), which further exacted enormous concessions from the Qing government. Nine foreign powers—Denmark, France, Germany, Great Britain, the Netherlands, Portugal, Russia, Spain, and the United States—signed bilateral agreements with China.[69] The contents of each bilateral treaty included extended consular jurisdiction, with provisions for the supervision of trials and joint trials, meaning that foreign consular officers could monitor trials of Chinese nationals in all civil and criminal cases involving foreigners.[70] The treaties also fixed boundaries on foreign consular jurisdiction, effectively creating mini-states within China's borders. Foreign ships, both military and commercial, were allowed to be stationed in Chinese waters. The control of China's customs was turned over to foreign powers, and the nonreciprocal conventional tariff was expanded in the foreign powers' favor.

The Treaty of Shimonoseki ending the Sino-Japanese War in 1895 was another example of an unequal treaty. Article 1 of this treaty read:

> China recognizes definitively the full and complete independence and autonomy of Korea, and, in consequence, the payment of tribute and the performance of ceremonies and formalities by Korea to China, that are in derogation of such independence and autonomy, shall wholly cease for the future.[71]

Articles 2 and 3 ceded to Japan in perpetuity full sovereignty over the Penghu group, Taiwan, and the eastern portion of the bay of Liaodong Peninsula "together with all fortifications, arsenals and public property." In this treaty, China had to pay a war indemnity of 200 million silver kuping taels (7.45 million kilograms of silver) to Japan and open four cities to Japanese trade. Moreover, China granted Japan most-favored nation status.[72]

Taking advantage of China's weakness following the Sino-Japanese War, foreign powers vied with one another to secure leased territories from China and carve out their respective spheres of influence. The foreign concessions granted during this period include the German concession in Tianjin and Hankou in 1895; the Russian and French concessions in Hankou in 1896; and the Japanese concessions in Hangzhou in 1896, in Tianjin, Shashi, and Hankou in 1898, and in Xiamen and Fuzhou in 1899.[73] Western powers also proceeded to construct barracks and military bases, as well as obtaining the right to build railways and to work mines. It was in this period that Russia forcibly stationed troops along the Chinese Eastern Railway (Manchurian Railway), which the Russians helped to construct from 1897 to 1901. From that point on, the Western powers had the right to station troops in China.[74]

While the discussion thus far on unequal treaties provides some insight to the national trauma felt by the Chinese at the hands of foreign powers, none was more devastating than the conditions imposed by the Protocol of 1901, also known as the Boxer Protocol or Xinchou Treaty. The

Protocol of 1901 included provisions for China to pay a huge indemnity of 450 million taels of silver over a period of thirty-nine years to the eight nations involved.[75] With interest, this equated to more than 982 million taels. Based on the exchange rates at the time, 450 million taels equaled $335 million. The Qing government's annual income was only about 250 million taels at the time, making these payments almost twice the annual earnings of the entire government.[76]

The Boxer Protocol also granted the eight powers the "Legation Quarter," an area of Beijing, which would be administered and defended by the foreign powers themselves. Troops were stationed not only in the quarter but also along the route from Beijing to the sea, in order to protect the corridor.[77] The foreign powers were further given the right to set up navigational systems in China's coastal waters and inland waterways—a provision that effectively destroyed the last vestiges of China's coastal defense.[78]

The impact of Western imperialism in China from the 1840s onward helped to stimulate the internal collapse of the ruling Qing dynasty. As the French political cartoons in figures 2.8 and 2.9 suggest, the Chinese government was powerless to defend against these foreign powers. A revolution deposed the last emperor, and a Chinese republic was declared in 1911.

Although World War I provided a temporary distraction for the Western powers, the Japanese saw the war as an opportunity to expand their influence in China. In 1915, the Japanese government put forward its "Twenty-One Demands" to Yuan Shikai's warlord government, insisting on extensive economic and commercial rights throughout Chinese territory, as well as the right to station Japanese police in northern China. These demands aimed to consolidate the special rights previously held by different powers. With just one treaty, Japan attempted to sweep away all of these concessions.[79]

In the face of intense international pressure and extreme Chinese opposition, the Japanese withdrew several of the most controversial demands. The Chinese believed these demands would essentially transfer Chinese sovereignty to the Japanese. As a result, a reduced set of thirteen demands was transmitted on May 7, 1915, in the form of an ultimatum, with a two-day deadline for response.[80] On May 9, even with its humiliating language and extreme demands, Yuan's government accepted the treaty. The final form of the treaty was signed by both parties on May 25.[81]

It was this final treaty that shocked the world and outraged the Chinese people, strengthening the animosity between the two Asian countries

FIGURE 2.8. This political cartoon, "Dissecting the Chinese Monster," a poster of the French colonial period (1902), was used in a Chinese national history textbook to illustrate the extent to which foreign powers each forcibly "took a piece" of China.

and laying the foundations for the second Sino-Japanese War. From 1927 to 1940, May 9 became an official holiday in China called "National Humiliation Day."[82] The Twenty-One Demands effectively generated the first wave of intellectual nationalism in China. The phrase "Never Forget National Humiliation" (*Wuwang guochi*) first became popularized in Chinese newspapers and social discourse in 1915.[83]

FIGURE 2.9. This French political cartoon from the late 1890s, "Cutting the Pie," depicts caricatures of several powers. The pie they are cutting represents China being divided between Queen Victoria of the United Kingdom, Kaiser Wilhelm II of Germany, Tsar Nicholas II of Russia, the French Marianne, and the Meiji Emperor of Japan.

FOREIGN DEVILS

It was the Opium Wars that first forced China to open up its doors to foreign invading traders. Then, in the period between 1842 and 1860, China was forced to sign a series of treaties. With the Treaty of Nanjing and the

Treaty of Tianjin as the milestones, these accords constituted an unequal treaty system that strangled the development of China. A further humiliation came when China was defeated in 1895 by Japan, a country that for so long had been considered by China as its cultural inferior. Just five years later, in 1900, the Eight Nation Alliance marched into the Forbidden City. Following the Boxer Protocol and the Twenty-One Demands, weakened Chinese troops could not stop the Japanese full-scale invasion. These events all contributed to the "century of humiliation," which left profound impacts on Chinese politics, society, culture, and psychology. In doing so, these events left long-lasting scars on the nation.

For today's researchers, the foreign invasions and unequal treaties during the hundred years are merely events recorded in history books and people's memory. However, these treaties and wars had a direct effect on China, and these ideas have lasted in the Chinese psyche for a very long time. As Chiang Kai-shek wrote in 1943:

> China's political integrity, her laws, military affairs, police, taxation, communications, mining enterprises, salt administration, religion, education—indeed, everything vital to her culture, national defense and economy—had already been flagrantly violated, both in spirit and in substance, by the foreign powers by virtue of their unequal treaties with China.[84]

China's official history textbooks stress that the treaty system forced China to gradually "sink" from an independent agricultural society into a semicolonial society.[85]

The Chinese economic system had been based on agriculture since ancient times, when the center of the economy was the Yellow River basin and later the Yangtze River Valley. As China began trading with foreign powers, economic activity sprang up in the southeastern and coastal areas. The concession system thus damaged the country's total economic system, as poor areas became poorer and interior regions deteriorated rapidly. To some extent, the economic effects of the unequal treaties are still felt in China today. The severe changes to the economic system of the country and the separation of the port cities from the interior still affect China's economy and pattern of development.

Another direct consequence of the unequal treaties, especially as a result of the concession system and the spheres of influence, was the emergence of warlordism in China. After the fall of the Qing dynasty, battles between rival warlords raged. The foreign powers saw their influence in the region as a way to affect who would eventually take control of the country, and they used agents in their respective spheres of influence to incite warfare and harbor criminals. Foreign powers sold arms and ammunition to warlords and used the railroads to assist those warlords in their favor. Coups and countercoups were fostered in foreign concessions and assisted by foreign powers. Warlords allowed themselves to become the puppets of foreign governments in an effort to gain money, power, and favor.[86]

For centuries, Chinese society had been based on community, as people were dedicated to their families, then their clans, and also to their villages and communities. Confucianism dictated a strict social hierarchy, which was rarely broken. Relying on family rites and community regulations, the society was governed through high-level community self-government rather than control through law. Collectivist interdependence and family harmony were the societal glue for Chinese culture, dictating daily life and ordering communities for thousands of years.

However, this all changed during the treaty century, which ushered in the first wave of "globalization" for the agricultural society; rural life declined, and migrants headed to the cities to find work and fortune. The organization of the family, clan, village, and community also began to disintegrate following this move. China was no longer a unified nation with an effective central government and a strong grassroots community. In 1924, Sun Yat-sen described China as "a heap of loose sand." As leader, Chiang Kai-shek tried to build on that sand the foundations of a modern and united country; however, under his rule the country remained beset by outside aggression, deep internal divisions, corruption, and inefficiency among Chiang's ruling party.[87]

Before the Opium Wars, China had often been invaded and even occupied by its neighbors. The Manchurians were the last example in which the invaders became the rulers of China. Even so, the Chinese were proud of their successful assimilation of outsiders. The strong ability to culturally integrate outsiders was indeed a chosen glory of the Chinese people, but the invaders during the century of humiliation were different. The Chinese believed that these invaders wanted to assimilate China rather than be assimilated. As Peter Gries comments, the Central Kingdom was not only defeated militarily but also confronted by a civilization with universalist pretensions of its own.[88] For the Chinese, their resistance to the foreign invasions during this period was not only in defense of their territory but also to preserve Chinese culture and tradition.

While the ancient Chinese referred to cultural or ethnic outsiders as *Yi* ("barbarians"), during the century of humiliation foreigners were given a more negative term—*guizi* (鬼子), meaning "devils." It was only members of the imperialist invading powers, though, those involved in the century of humiliation, who were scorned—in some cases even to this day—with the title of *guizi*, such as *yingguo guizi* ("British devils") or *riben guizi* ("Japanese devils"). Rarely are Indians or Vietnamese classified as devils, even though China also fought wars against them. This distinction between barbarians and devils illustrates how the Chinese have incorporated the treaty century into the country's mythology.

The Chinese master narrative of the century of humiliation defines the national trauma China uses to identify itself. Before 1840, China considered itself the center of the world, the only true civilization. But with each new humiliation, the Chinese lost a bit of their national myth of greatness. Both chosen glory and chosen trauma are important ethnic or large-group markers. However, as Vamik Volkan has argued, whereas chosen glories merely raise the self-esteem of group members, generational transmission of chosen traumas provokes complicated tasks of mourning and/or reversing humiliation. Such traumas initiate much more profound psychological processes, as chosen traumas bind group members together more powerfully.[89] Understanding chosen trauma is crucial to discerning the process of generational transmission of past historical events and the formation of group identity.

In recent history, China has experienced a great deal of pain in its search for a modern identity, and its revolutions over the twentieth century—in 1911, 1927, 1949, and 1966—brought great suffering in their wake.[90] Patricia Ebrey has thoughtful observations on these Chinese revolutions:

> Those who look on the twentieth century as just as tragic as the nineteenth have reason to feel that the Chinese people might have been spared much suffering if China had managed to muddle through this stage of its encounter with the west without suffering so much humiliation, for then revolutionary change might not have come to seem absolutely necessary to so many thinking Chinese.[91]

It is no exaggeration to say that almost all of the important changes, revolutions, and reforms in China after 1840 are somehow related—if not a direct response—to the national humiliation during those subsequent hundred years. As John King Fairbank and Merle Goldman suggest, the

Chinese patriots' "understandable urge" is to create and process their own history, minimizing "foreign participation in the life of the Chinese people."[92] It is impossible, therefore, to reimagine the recent history of China without the implications of the century of humiliation; it is an integral part of the Chinese Chosenness-Myths-Trauma complex.

:::

In this chapter, I have reviewed the historical events that form the basis of the Chinese CMT complex. The rest of this book now explores how this complex has bound millions of Chinese together; how the state, the political parties, and the social elites have used these national traumas and glories to conduct identity education for their own political purposes; and how this CMT complex has complicated China's foreign relations in recent years.

3

FROM "ALL-UNDER-HEAVEN" TO A NATION-STATE: NATIONAL HUMILIATION AND NATION BUILDING

FROM *TIANXIA* TO *GUOJIA*

In March 1839, Charles Elliot, the British superintendent of trade, wrote a letter to Lin Zexu, the Qing commissioner on opium trade, regarding the trade issues between the two countries. In this letter, he referenced Britain and China as "two countries." This angered the commissioner so much that he returned the letter, saying, "no place under heaven can be referred to as equal to our celestial empire."[1] Merely by mentioning the two countries in the same sentence, the British official had sparked Chinese anger. This story has been used by historians as a good example of Qing officials' ignorance of the outside world before the Opium War. However, Lin's response should also be understood from the Chinese unique *tianxia* ("all-under-heaven") worldview.

In traditional Chinese thought, there was no modern concept of the nation-state (*guojia*), only of dynasty (*wangchao*) and of all-under-heaven (*tianxia*). Due to its special geography, Chinese civilization developed in a rather isolated environment prior to the Opium War, even though it was not completely closed to foreign influences (the introduction of Buddhism being an example) throughout its long history. Samuel Kim described how the natural geographical barriers shaped the formation of the Chinese worldview:

> China is guarded on the west by almost endless deserts, on the southwest by the Himalayan range, and on the east by vast oceans. Admired but often attacked by the "barbarians" of the semiarid plateau lands on the north and west, and cut off from the other centers of civilization by oceans, deserts, and mountains, China gradually developed a unique sense of its place under heaven.[2]

The Chinese believed that they lived in the central kingdom of *tianxia*. There are several major differences between the Chinese *tianxia* concept and the Western concept of world system. First, *tianxia* is a *culturally* defined community, which is different from the ethnically defined or politically defined world of nation-states. As Xu Guoqi asserts, "Civilization, rather than nation-state, was the basic unit of *tianxia*."[3] Basically, *tianxia* is not a political or legal concept, nor even a geographical realm with fixed national sovereignty and territory. Some scholars view the *tianxia* concept as "Chinese culturalism."[4] A specific culture of the imperial state and Confucian orthodoxy were used as criteria defining a community. Ancient Chinese believed that their Central Kingdom was the center of high culture and superior morality. More importantly, under the *tianxia* system, outsiders could be culturally absorbed and become Chinese by adopting Chinese culture and customs. In other words, Chinese culture and morality were superior but not exclusive.

Second, while a nation-state is bounded, *tianxia* is boundless. As James Townsend has suggested, ancient China was a cultural community whose boundaries were determined by the knowledge and practice of principles expressed through China's elite cultural tradition, drawn mainly from the Confucian philosophical and moral tradition.[5] The national community was established on Confucian cultural principles that would include ethnically non-Han peoples—such as the Manchurians—as long as they accepted Chinese cultural principles.[6] Over the last three millennia, many previously distinct ethnic groups in China have been assimilated into a Han identity, which over time dramatically expanded the size of the Han population.

Third, the *tianxia* system refused to acknowledge the world of formally equal states. One of the prime elements of the *tianxia* concept is the notion that China was the only true civilization, its cultural superiority unchallenged.[7] *Tianxia* represented a Chinese universalism. For ancient Chinese, China is the world, not "a country in the world." That was why Lin Zexu rejected Elliot's reference to Britain and China as "two countries."

The dialogue between Lin and Elliot was doomed to fail, as they spoke from two totally different systems.

Fourth, unlike the Western system of international relations, the *tianxia* system focused on soft power such as culture, morality, and harmony; it downplayed the role of military and economic power in maintaining the world order. Maintaining the *tianxia* system was based on a common historical heritage and acceptance of shared beliefs, not nationalism based on the modern concept of the nation-state. Membership in this community was defined by participation in ritual order that embodied allegiance to Chinese ideas and ethics centered around the Chinese emperor. Supreme loyalty to the culture itself, not to the state, was paramount. Contrary to the Chinese *tianxia* system, the Western international system was based on hard power such as military and economic strength, territorial expansion, and cutthroat competition.[8]

There were fundamental differences between a traditional empire and a modern nation-state, as well. Most Sinologists view the Chinese nation-state as a relatively recent development, one that made the transition from empire to nation only around the turn of the twentieth century.[9] Except for dynasty names, the Chinese nation did not even have an official name or a real national flag. As Immanuel C. Y. Hsu states, "Doubtless, imperial China was not a nation-state,"[10] and Lucian Pye argues that "China is a civilization pretending to be a nation-state."[11] The primary traditional Chinese self-image or identity was cultural. Having long been obsessed with a false conception of superiority and self-imposed isolation, the Chinese did not really possess the modern concept of the nation-state.[12]

If there was no nation-state, how could there be nationalism? According to Hans Kohn's definition, nationalism is "first and foremost a state of mind . . . which recognizes the nation-state as the ideal form of political organization and the nationality as the source of all creative cultural energy and of economic well-being."[13] Many researchers of Chinese nationalism agree that the concept of modern nationalism did not enter the Chinese mind until the end of nineteenth century. According to Xu Guoqi, China's special "Middle Kingdom syndrome" made it difficult for China to adapt psychologically to the new reality of international affairs. China was not prepared to join the family of nations as an equal member, even after the West forcefully compelled it to open to the world following the Opium War.[14]

In the Western world, the first great manifestation of nationalism was the French Revolution, which gave the new movement an increased dynamic force.[15] However, what awakened China and Chinese consciousness of nation-statehood was China's traumatic encounter with the Western powers—the defeats in wars and the ensuing unequal treaties. Chinese nationalism was in many ways a result of Western imperialism. Indeed, nothing could be more powerful than foreign invasions and coercive treaties to awaken a country's national identity and nationalist feelings.

Many scholars suggest that the first Sino-Japanese War (1894–1895) was a turning point. In the words of Liang Qichao (1873–1929), the foremost intellectual leader of China in the first two decades of the twentieth century, the Sino-Japanese War "awakened my country from the long dream of four thousand years."[16] According to Liang, the military defeat by Japan finally compelled many Chinese to think seriously about the fate of their nation. In 1915, Chen Duxiu, an influential scholar and one of the founders of the Chinese Communist Party, said, "If it had not been for China's military defeats in 1894 and 1900, we might still be writing our 'eight-legged essays' and be wearing pigtails."[17] (The "eight-legged essay" was the classical essay-writing form that scholars had to master to pass the imperial examinations in Ming and Qing China.)

The failures and humiliation in the second part of the nineteenth century made the Chinese gradually realize that their *tianxia* system had collapsed. Sadly, China was no longer the center of the world; even worse, it had fallen to the status of semicolonial country and would have to fight for its basic survival among the world's nations. It is not difficult for us to imagine the huge cognitive dissonance the Chinese—especially the intellectuals who understood what was happening early on—suffered during that time.

As we can see, consciousness of the nation-state was aroused in China only after the Sino-Japanese War, but the Chinese soon found that their nation had been forced into a competitive world order in which the law of the jungle prevailed and their heavenly empire was actually a weak state in danger of collapse. Not unreasonably, the great dread of early Chinese nationalists at the turn of the twentieth century was the collapse and disappearance of the unitary state—a fear well captured in the phrases *wang guo* ("the death of the state") and *wang guo nu* ("slaves of a country that has died").[18] The cruel reality and the dissonance between being citizens of a celestial empire and being *wang guo nu* became the powerful motor for China's first nationalist movement. Xu Jilin calls this period of time "an age of extreme jingoism":

> In such perilous dog-eat-dog circumstances, the late-Qing period witnessed a paroxysm of nationalism, of patriotism, and of education for military citizenship. The period between 1895 to the early years of the Republic proved to be an age of extreme jingoism.[19]

The arrival of foreigners, as well as their products, religions, and gunboats, gradually helped the Chinese understand and accept the modern concept of the nation-state. As Joseph Levenson noted, the intellectual history of modern China in large part has been the process of making *guojia* (a nation-state) of *tianxia*.[20] The new concept provided an intellectual and political basis for China's nationalism and its quest for renewal and a new national identity. Townsend is right to say that the history of modern China after the first Sino-Japanese War was "one in which nationalism replaces culturalism as the dominant Chinese view of their identity and place in the world."[21]

AWAKENING CHINA

The emergence of nationalism in China was not a grassroots movement. On the contrary, as Paul Cohen observes, in the late Qing period the complaint most often heard was that Chinese, unlike other peoples, were somehow impervious to feelings of national shame.[22] Many people at the bottom of the society were struggling for their daily survival and were unable to comprehend the deep reasons for their suffering. They also did not know what they could do to make changes. But China's early nationalist movement was not a top-down phenomenon, either. China's national humiliation was in many ways directly caused by the Qing Court itself, due to its corruption and incompetency. During the late Qing, when the issue of national humiliation first began to emerge in public discussion, the Qing government tended to be a silent bystander.[23]

The Chinese nationalist discourse during the late Qing had what can more accurately be called a "middle-out" approach. Early awakened intellectuals, business leaders, and professionals—midlevel but influential members of the society—were the leaders of the movement. They reached out to influence people at both the bottom and the top of Chinese society. Many who had received a modern education were familiar with both national and world affairs and were deeply concerned about the national fate. As Cohen finds, the Chinese who were most vocal in leading the charge against their compatriots' propensity to ignore or forget were the intellectuals who happened to feel very strongly about the repeated humiliation China had sustained.[24]

One of the intellectual leaders during this period of time was Lu Xun, China's most influential modern writer and essayist. Lu named the first collection of his short stories *Nahan*, which is literally translated as "shouting." Lu believed that China's new intellectuals should shout out to wake up their compatriots. The collection's English title is *Call to Arms*. The story of Lu himself is a good example of this middle-out nationalist movement.

Lu Xun was born in 1881 in Shaoxing. In 1904, he went to Japan to study medicine, but did not complete his medical education there. Lu explained why in the famous preface of his book. One day after class, a Japanese instructor showed a lantern slide about the Russo-Japanese War (1904–1905), which documented an imminent public execution of an alleged Chinese spy by Japanese soldiers, surrounded by his Chinese compatriots.

> At the time, I had not seen any of my fellow Chinese in a long time, but one day some of them showed up in a slide. One, with his hands tied behind him, was in the middle of the picture; the others were gathered around him. Physically, they were as strong and healthy as anyone could ask, but their expressions revealed all too clearly that spiritually they were calloused and numb. According to the caption, the Chinese whose hands were bound had been spying on the Japanese military for the Russians. He was about to be decapitated as a "public example." The other Chinese gathered around him had come to enjoy the spectacle.[25]

Lu was shocked by the apathy of the Chinese at the execution and decided that it was more important to cure his compatriots of their spiritual ills rather than their physical diseases.

Quitting his studies and returning to China in 1909, Lu started a new career as a writer. Today, there are dozens of his novels, essays, and poems being selected for inclusion in primary and secondary school textbooks. A major theme of Lu Xun's works was to expose the weaknesses of the traditional culture—the slavish mentality, selfishness, mendacity, timidity, and passivity. He was referred to as the "banner" of the New Culture Movement. At one point, Sun Yat-sen, the first provisional president of the Republic of China, made the same decision to give up the pursuit of a medical career, but Sun chose to lead a revolution to make changes. Walking along different paths, both of them hoped to awaken the nation.

During the late Qing period, patriotic intellectuals conducted a lot of consciousness-raising activities. National humiliation, especially the history of the unequal treaties, was used by these educators as the main topic of the awakening movement. They made clear connections between the treaties and China's problem. Historical events of national humiliation, such as the first Sino-Japanese War and the Twenty-One Demands, soon became the symbols of China's national awakening and identity building.[26]

With the rise of nationalism, China had completed the transformation from the cultural *tianxia* system to a political *guojia*. As Geremie Barmé notes, patriotism and protectionism evolved in China from the late nineteenth century in tandem with the transformation from imperial dynasty to modern nation-state.[27] The awakening of the Chinese people was not just a historical narrative or an education campaign; it was also a political technique for building a sovereign and independent state.

The discourse of national humiliation thus became a Chinese repository of techniques for achieving national salvation and national development, as Dong Wang suggests.[28] The very essence of the unequal treaty has come to define what it means to be Chinese—to be both a victim and vanquisher. On the one hand, China was a victim of Western imperialism, forced to abandon the high culture of the *tianxia* system for the base survival-driven nation-state worldview. On the other hand, these humiliations provided the all-consuming fire needed for China to rise like a phoenix from the ashes and overcome the West on its quest for glory.

After giving up his medical career, Sun Yat-sen founded Xingzhonghui—translated as the Revive China Society or the Society for Regenerating China—in Honolulu, Hawaii, in 1894. Those admitted to the society swore the following oath: "Expel the northern barbarians [Manchurians], revive Zhonghua [Han China], and establish a unified government." It was later merged into the Tongmenghui in 1905, which in turn became the Kuomintang (abbreviated KMT in the Wade-Giles Romanization or GMD in the pinyin Romanization), the first modern political party in the history of China. The KMT launched the Xinhai Revolution of 1911, and the Republic of China was founded on January 1, 1912.

The first surge of Chinese student nationalism was seen in 1919, in what is now widely referred to as the May 4th Movement, when thousands of students demonstrated against the Treaty of Versailles's transfer of Chinese territory to Japan. Marxist ideas started to spread widely in China after this. The 1917 Russian October Revolution had attracted the attention of Chinese intellectuals, and many gained inspiration from Marx's class struggle and Lenin's anti-imperialist theories. With the help of the Comintern (the Communist International, also known as the Third International), some May 4th Movement leaders went on to form the Chinese Communist Party (CCP) in 1921.[29]

In their early phase of development, both the KMT and the CCP, the two political parties that dominated Chinese politics in the twentieth century, placed "mass awakening" as their priority. They needed to awaken and to mobilize as many people as possible to participate in their revolution. Even though they were enemies most of the time, the KMT and CCP united briefly during the Northern Expedition in 1926 to fight against their common enemies: warlords and imperialists. From 1937 to 1945, they reconciled again to fight together against the full-scale Japanese invasion. With the establishment of the two political parties, the awakening movement and the discourse of nationalism had entered a new phase of development.

"OVERTHROW THE FOREIGN POWERS"

The Chinese song "*Dadao lie qiang*" ("Overthrow the Foreign Powers" or "Let's Beat Together the Great Powers") is also known as the "Revolution of the Citizens Song" ("*Guomin geming ge*"). It was written by officers of the Huangpu (Whampoa) Military Academy and was released on July 1, 1926. Sung to the tune of "Frère Jacques," the song was the provisional anthem of the Republic of China.

> Overthrow the foreign Powers,
> Eliminate the warlords;
> The citizens strive hard for the Revolution,
> Joint affair to fight.
>
> Laborers, farmers, students, and soldiers,
> Make a great union!
> Overthrow the imperialism,
> Joint affair to fight.

Overthrow the foreign Powers,
Eliminate the warlords;
The Revolution is successful;
Joyfully sing in unison.

It was also the official army song during the KMT and CCP's joint Northern Expedition, which was launched in July 1926 to eliminate the warlords and abolish the unequal treaties with the foreign powers.

At the turn of the twentieth century, China was a land in ferment, politically and culturally. The old imperial order as well as its ideologies such as the *tianxia* concept was collapsing. China's traditional culture and Confucian orthodoxy were also in crisis, no longer able to provide a direction for moving the country forward or even to hold it together. There existed a big cultural and spiritual vacuum. For the KMT and CCP, or any other modern political parties established at this juncture of history, their success depended on whether they could introduce a new ideology and new culture to fill that vacuum. They needed to tell their people what the problems of China were and their solutions—to provide a road map and vision for this lost country. Otherwise, they would not be able to mobilize the Chinese people.

Both the KMT and CCP chose nationalism as a way to fill this vacuum. And both connected imperialism and unequal treaties with China's problems. In public pronouncements, both parties claimed a patriotic role to "save the country" (*jiuguo*). Both the KMT and the CCP saw the abolition of the unequal treaties as the key to saving China and gaining national independence. And they were both vocal in airing opposition to imperialism and warlordism, the two targets of their polemic on the unequal treaties.[30] They demanded the unconditional termination of all unequal treaties. As Wang notes, popular outrage against the whole idea of the unequal treaties was channeled to produce a "controlled awakening," a means to produce a "party-inspired consciousness" among the masses.[31]

For a period of time, the propagandists of the two parties actually worked together in the same building. In his book *Awakening China*, John Fitzgerald uncovers the previously untold story of Mao Zedong's role in the Nationalist Propaganda Bureau: Mao was the head of this bureau in 1925 and 1926. Fitzgerald's book highlights the role of Sun Yatsen as "director of awakenings" in the Nationalist Revolution and Mao's place as his successor in the politics of mass awakening. According to this book, Mao was a "master of propaganda and discipline," rather than just a peasant movement activist.[32] However, the two parties also had major differences in their approach to ideology and mobilization.

Kuomintang was translated as the Nationalist Party, and it was indeed a party of nationalism. Sun and his colleagues later adjusted the party's original racialist approach ("Expel the northern barbarians") to focus on an anti-imperialist nationalism. The cancellation of all unequal treaties was emphasized as a top issue of the party. In the declaration of the KMT's First National Congress on January 31, 1924, Sun clearly stated:

> All Unequal Treaties, including foreign concessions, consular jurisdiction, foreign management of customs services, and all foreign political rights exercised on China's soil, are detrimental to China's sovereignty. They all ought to be abolished so as to leave the way open for new treaties based on the spirit of bilateral equality and mutual respect for sovereignty.[33]

In a 1924 speech, Sun referred to all the unequal treaties as China's "self-selling indenture" (*maishen qi*).[34] In December 1926, after conquering the warlord-occupied Wuhan, the Nationalist Expedition forces built an iron tower on Mount Turtle engraved with the seven characters *Feichu bupingdeng tiaoyue*, "Abolish the Unequal Treaties," each character measuring 15 meters wide and more than 13 meters high.[35]

Chiang Kai-shek, Sun's successor, was also very keen on abolishing the treaties. Interestingly, every day for two decades Chiang wrote "*Xuechi*" (雪耻, "avenge humiliation" or "wipe clean humiliation") and a method to avenge the humiliation in the top right corner of his dairy as a daily reminder.[36] He started this practice shortly after the Jinan Incident.

The Jinan Incident (also known as the May 3rd Tragedy) was an armed conflict between the Japanese Army allied with northern Chinese warlords against the KMT's southern army in Jinan, the capital of Shandong, in 1928 during the Northern Expedition. On May 3, 1928, during cease-fire negotiations, the Japanese resumed fire on Chinese civilians. Approximately five thousand Chinese civilians were killed in this conflict. Chiang's chief negotiator Tsai Kung-shih was later tortured to death by having his face disfigured. Grace Huang records how Chiang started his daily "*Xuechi*" entry:

> A week after the start of the incident, he stated, "From this day on, I will rise out of bed at six o'clock. I will remind myself of this humiliation and continue to do so until the national humiliation is wiped away

completely." Four days later, he added to his reminder by creating a "method to avenge humiliation" (*xuechi tiaoyue*) column in his diary: "Every day, [I] will record a method on how to destroy the 'dwarf pirates' [*wokou*, Japanese] to avenge national humiliation." With few exceptions, Chiang contributed to this column faithfully until Japan's defeat in World War II.[37]

According to Huang, on March 27, 1934, Chiang wrote in his diary of his decision to issue a textbook focusing on the people's obligation and responsibility to the country. He also sent a telegram to his chief of staff listing thirty-eight items to be included in the textbook. Several items explicitly attempted to inculcate Chiang's idea of the Chinese nation through a description of humiliations:

> Item Three aimed to educate the people on the size of China. Though Chiang left the size unspecified, he mentioned four days earlier in his avenging humiliation column: "Recover Taiwan and Korea. Recover the land that was originally part of the Han and Tang dynasty. Then, as descendants of the Yellow Emperor, we will have no shame." Item Four aimed to give a brief history, including the year and month, of the territory China lost.[38]

Chiang used *xuechi* as a main political platform and mission of his party. He even wrote a book, *China's Destiny*, systematically reviewing the causes of the unequal treaties and their political, economic, social, moral, and psychological effects on China. In this 1943 book, Chiang concluded, "The weakening of China's international position and the deterioration of the people's morale during the last hundred years have been due chiefly to the unequal treaties." Describing the "most important lesson that history taught China," Chiang wrote:

> The Chinese people cannot hope to make their country strong and wipe out their national humiliation unless they struggle to the utmost for the attainment of their goal, and the goal can only be attained thorough a national revolution which will unify the people's will and fulfill the people's aspirations. The history of the last ninety-three years from the Taiping Revolution onward has fully proved that national revolution and the Three Principles of the People sponsored by Dr. Sun Yat-sen constituted the only right path along which the Chinese people can march to national rebirth.[39]

A close review of the CCP's statements and reports from its party congresses in the 1920s and 1930s indicates that they mentioned national humiliation and unequal treaties much less than the KMT did. The CCP documents, including articles by Mao Zedong and Chen Duxiu, focused more on class struggle and class oppression. The CCP ideologies insisted strongly on the importance of class consciousness rather than national consciousness.

I do not agree with Dong Wang's assertion that the KMT and CCP "tapped into the same vocabularies and specifics of the unequal treaties for their own political ends."[40] Even though the KMT also wanted to seize the patriotic high ground, its national-humiliation narratives during this period of time had their own styles and vocabularies. As Wang herself has suggested, in CCP documents China's experience was often portrayed as part of a global humiliation shared by other nations in a similar situation.[41] According to Fitzgerald, the CCP theorists placed the domain of class struggle in the field of international relations. The unit of class analysis was the nation itself: nations suffering imperialist oppression were labeled members of the international "proletariat," and the oppressor nations were thought to make up a transnational "bourgeoisie."[42]

To a certain extent, the differences between the two parties' narratives were due to differing target population of supporters. The Communist Party focused its mobilization work on the rural areas rather than among the intellectuals and the city dwellers. People on the bottom of the Chinese society—farmers in the interior provinces and factory workers—often felt victimized less by foreign imperialism than by their own government's policies.[43] Compared with the CCP, the Kuomintang was more an elite party than a mass party; it relied more on intellectuals and urban educated people—the groups of people who felt more strongly about the national humiliation and were able to place China in the global context.

While Chiang Kai-shek was writing his daily entry of *xuechi*, national humiliation was not common in Mao Zedong's speeches and articles. The Communist leader took a more pragmatic approach in the Anti-Japanese War. Mao once cautioned his generals: "To fight with Japanese is not real patriotism. By doing so, you are just patriotic to KMT's China. Our enemy is the KMT." It was reported that Mao also issued this order to the senior members of his party in 1937:

> Our aim is to develop the military power of the CCP, in order to stage a coup d'état. Therefore this main directive is to be strictly followed:

> 70% of our efforts for expansion, 20% for dealing with the Kuomintang, and 10% for resisting Japan. All party members and groups are hereby ordered not to oppose this paramount directive.[44]

During the eight years of the Anti-Japanese War, the CCP built up its sphere of influence wherever opportunities were presented. Through land and tax reforms, it gained increasing support from the poor peasants.[45]

The two parties had also different attitude towards China's traditional culture. The CCP was much more critical of Confucian orthodoxy. The Communists saw it as a cause of China's weakness and humiliation. The party's mission was to overthrow "the Three Big Mountains" (*sanzuo dashan*)—imperialism, feudalism, and bureaucratic capitalism. Chinese traditional culture was viewed as "feudal culture" and therefore became the target of the Communist revolution. The CCP embraced Communism and Marxism; it wanted to use Communism to replace Confucian orthodoxy and to create a brand-new ideology based on Communist orthodoxy and Maoism. On the contrary, the KMT viewed China's elite cultural tradition as a foundation for the regulation and maintenance of the social life of the Chinese society. It assumed that the deterioration of national culture and morality were caused by imperialism and the unequal treaties. For example, Chiang believed that China's good habits "were swept clean by the prevalence in the Concessions of the vices of opium-smoking, gambling, prostitution, and robbery."[46]

These differences between the two parties had far-reaching influence on China's politics, culture, and society in the twentieth century. For example, one of the key factors contributing to the CCP's final victory over the KMT was Mao's effective use of grassroots mobilization. The Cultural Revolution from 1966 to 1976 epitomized Mao's efforts to eliminate feudal culture from his "new" China.

Due to the efforts of both political parties and the early awakened intellectuals (such as Lu Xun), the Republican era saw much stronger popular nationalism. William Callahan finds that national humiliation was part of the construction of citizenship and national identity in the Republic of China.[47] The phrase "Never Forget National Humiliation" (*Wuwang guochi*) had been popularized in newspapers since 1915; it was "a slogan painted on walls, coined into trademarks, and imprinted on stationery."[48] Paul Cohen's research indicates that throughout the 1920s and into the 1930s the newspaper *Shenbao* ran ads linking the May 9th anniversary of the Twenty-One Demands with everything from cigarettes and wine to towels, machinery, parasols, watches, straw hats, silk stockings, cotton cloth, tooth powder, and banking service.[49] According to Dong Wang, in 1924, initiated by more than fifty intellectual organizations in Beijing, the Unequal Treaties Cancellation Movement and the Grand Anti-imperialists Alliance were formed.[50]

The late-Qing, intellectual-led, middle-out nationalism transformed in the Republican era into a much stronger movement of nationalism that included both state-led, top-down nationalism and bottom-up, popular nationalism. According to Xu Jilin, Chinese nationalism developed as an unbridled "wild horse" during this period of time:

> The May Fourth came to an end, replaced by a new age of nationalism. Like a wild horse, jingoism, once unbridled, could no longer be restrained, thus laying the foundations for the eventual outcomes of the history of China during the first half of the twentieth century.[51]

Nationalism supported China's fight with Japanese during the eight years for national survival. However, soon after the end of the war, the whole of China fell into a civil war between the Kuomintang and the Chinese Communist Party. It was one of the most brutal civil wars in human history. National humiliation provided the context for the founding moment of the People's Republic of China (PRC). On October 1, 1949, Mao Zedong declared the victory of the CCP and the founding of the PRC in Beijing. "Ours will no longer be a nation subject to insult and humiliation," he said. "We have stood up."[52] With Mao at the helm, the Communist Party would soon draw legitimacy not from the humiliating past, but from the victories of the Revolution.

THE EAST IS RED

For most Chinese over thirty years old, "The East Is Red" ("*Dong fang hong*") is a song that they can still sing when asked:

> The east is red, the sun is rising.
> China has brought forth Mao Zedong.
> He amasses fortune for the people,
> Hurrah, he is the people's great savior.
> Chairman Mao loves the people,

He is our guide,
To build a new China,
Hurrah, he leads us forward!
The Communist Party is like the sun,
Wherever it shines, it is bright.
Wherever there is a Communist Party,
Hurrah, there the people are liberated!

In the 1960s and 1970s, radio and television programs usually began with this song and ended with "The Internationale." It was the de facto anthem of the People's Republic of China during the Cultural Revolution.

Max Weber identified the three sources of political legitimacy as traditional, charismatic, and legal-rational. *Traditional legitimacy* is based on long-held norms, customs, and divine power. *Charismatic legitimacy* rests on the charisma of the leader, often partly based on the perception that this leader has certain extra- or supernatural attributes. *Legal-rational legitimacy* is rooted in the perception that a government's powers are derived from rationally created set principles, rules, and procedures.[53] In the *tianxia* system, as Xu Guoqi notes, state legitimacy was determined by divine right (son of heaven), by bloodline, and by the so-called mandate of heaven, which was not specific to any one national identity.[54]

Through my own experience, it is apparent that "The East Is Red" was the Chinese Communist Party's statement of legitimacy during Mao's era (1949–1976). Many people today view Mao's government as one of the most brutal, totalitarian regimes in human history. However, during Mao's era, very few Chinese Communists were concerned about their party's legitimacy. The charisma of Chairman Mao was no doubt an important source of this confidence. During the Chinese Civil War (1945–1949), Mao led the People's Liberation Army to defeat Generalissimo Chiang Kai-shek and expel the Kuomintang government from the mainland to Taiwan. As Mao alleged, "Political power grows out of the barrel of a gun."[55] This sentiment guided the legitimacy of his party. In the CCP's propaganda, the victory in this civil war has been glorified as the Chinese people's great liberation, and Mao therefore became the people's "great savior."

For Mao, his "mandate of heaven" was derived not just from the battlefield but also from his books, which presented his theories and ideology. In his books, including his famous Little Red Book (*Quotations from Chairman Mao Zedong*), which is possibly the most printed book in human history, Mao painted a wonderful picture of China's future—a communist paradise where everybody enjoys justice and equality, a place where there is no exploitation or suffering. This official communist ideology was crucial to the institutionalization of the CCP's legitimacy. The theories of historical materialism, class struggle, and scientific socialism provided a comprehensive conceptual framework of moral justification for the new party-state. Mao skillfully localized Marxism and contextualized it in terms of China's tradition. After Mao and his colleagues dressed it up, the communist ideology bore a great resemblance to the ideal Confucian *datong* society.[56] In Confucian thought, *datong* is harmony and unity in human society and harmonious relations between heaven, man, and earth.

Mao was a genius writer; his political articles, including his poems and calligraphies, were endlessly appealing to the Chinese people. At the peak of the Cultural Revolution, Mao had achieved god-emperor status in China. If there had been popular elections in China in the 1950s or 1960s, Mao would surely have been elected. In a sense, we can say that the CCP had successfully attained all three types of legitimacy that Weber identified. The party's Constitution of 1969 proudly stated: "The Communist Party of China with Comrade Mao Zedong as its leader is a great, glorious, and correct party and is the core of leadership of the Chinese people."

During Mao's time, however, China's national history and especially the national-humiliation narrative were not used by the CCP leaders as a major ideological tool or source of legitimacy. As Parks Coble notes, in Mao's era, the memory of the Anti-Japanese War had virtually disappeared from public space in China.[57] The orthodox Communist Party approach to the memory of the war was not the "dominant narrative" in China—it was the *only* narrative. Beijing maintained tight control over publishing, which prevented other voices from being heard.[58] For example, according to Callahan's research, the records of the National Library of China indicated that there were no books on the subject of "national humiliation" published in China between 1947 and 1990.[59]

Kirk Denton finds that historiography of the Nanjing Massacre was consciously suppressed during the Maoist period. In 1962, for example, scholars at Nanjing University's Department of History wrote the book *Japanese Imperialism and the Massacre in Nanjing* (*Riben diguozhuyi zai Nanjing de datusha*), based on extensive materials they uncovered during a two-year investigation into the massacre. After it was written, the book was labeled a classified internal document and could not be published openly.[60] Ian Buruma believes that it was only after 1982 that the Communist government paid any attention to the Nanjing Massacre at all.[61]

There are several reasons for the CCP putting aside national humiliation during this period of time. First, much like what the Bolsheviks did after the Communist takeover of Russia in 1917, the CCP made class distinction rather than ethnicity the foundation of political identity.[62] It claimed not to be a national or ethnic party but rather a revolutionary party. Moreover, it did not seek support or representation from all Chinese people, but only from the proletariat—the workers and peasants. The CCP relied on a system of majority tyranny as a basis for its legitimacy. During the Cultural Revolution, nationalism and even patriotism were rejected as "bourgeois ideology."[63]

Second, in the eyes of the Communist Party, any nationalist claims would contradict Mao's "internationalism." Inspired by the victory of Chinese revolution, Mao saw himself as a leader of an international communist revolution and thus became an active champion of the communist movement of internationalism. This was one of the reasons for his decision to be involved in the Korean and Vietnam wars. Mao called for his party to oppose "narrow" nationalism and patriotism:

> We must unite with the proletariat of all the capitalist countries, with the proletariat of Japan, Britain, the United States, Germany, Italy and all other capitalist countries, before it is possible to overthrow imperialism, to liberate our nation and people, and to liberate the other nations and peoples of the world. This is our internationalism, the internationalism with which we oppose both narrow nationalism and narrow patriotism.[64]

During the Cultural Revolution, China became the center of world revolution and publicly deemed itself the most "progressive" force on the international scene.[65] From Mao's perspective, historical grievance based on ethnicity was typical narrow nationalism.

Third, Mao and the CCP used class struggle theory to explain the Chinese revolution, foreign imperialism, and the Chinese civil wars. According to this theory, China's decline and suffering in modern history were caused mainly by internal corruption and incompetence of the feudal or capitalist rulers—the Qing Court and the nationalist KMT. Therefore, foreign invasions became only a secondary factor in explaining China's traumatic national experience.

Fourth, "victory" was the key word of the CCP's legitimacy claims. Mao was a master when it came to "hero" or "victor" narratives intended to mobilize popular support. The CCP's propaganda machine taught people again and again that it was under Mao's brilliant leadership that the party achieved one victory after another. But any Chinese nationalist narrative would inevitably have to involve the discourse of China's modern history, which was centered on national humiliation. This victim narrative would not be in tune with Mao's main theme of victor narratives. The Chinese suffering during the one hundred years of national humiliation was therefore deemphasized.

Besides the above mentioned reasons related with the CCP's ideology, there was also a very special but important reason behind the CCP's silence about Japanese atrocities during Mao's era. Compared with the KMT, the Communists had actually made little contribution to the war against Japan. During the war, the Chinese Communist forces fought as a nominal part of the KMT National Revolution Army, but kept up their guerrilla status all the time. As Buruma comments:

> Little was made in the People's Republic of the Nanking [Nanjing] Massacre because there were no Communist heroes in the Nationalist capital in 1937. Indeed there had been no Communists there at all. Many of those who died in Nanking [Nanjing], or Shanghai, or anywhere in southern China, were soldiers in Chiang Kai-shek's army. Survivors with the wrong class or political backgrounds had enough difficulty surviving Maoist purges to worry too much about what had happened under the Japanese.[66]

In all the official speeches and publications during this period, the CCP claimed all the credit of the victory of the war and the redemption of a century of national humiliation. The role of the KMT forces was virtually invisible in any open publications. Of course, the CCP did not want the discussion surrounding the Anti-Japanese War to go into detail, because any detailed research about the war would unavoidably involve the historical facts such as the major military engagements, the involved troops, and the processes of the battles. They did not want their people to find out that "there had been no Communists there at all."

Mao and his colleagues even felt some gratitude toward the Japanese. Without the Japanese full-scale invasion from 1937 to 1945, the Communist troops could have already been eliminated by Chiang Kai-shek.

During the eight years while the KMT troops battled with the Japanese and suffered huge numbers of casualties, the Communists, hiding in the mountain areas of Shanxi Province, developed from a weak power of about 30,000 people to a strong army of more than 1 million. The secret for this unthinkably quick expansion was Mao's strategy of avoiding direct military engagement with the Japanese main force.

As Barmé notes, Mao Zedong saw the relationship between the Japanese invasion and his party's rise to power in a very particular way. When he met with Japanese prime minister Tanaka Kakue on September 27, 1972, Mao expressed his views with "characteristic irony." "We must express our gratitude to Japan," Mao said to Tanaka. "If Japan didn't invade China, we could have never achieved the cooperation between the KMT and the Communist Party. We could have never developed and eventually taken political power for ourselves. It is due to Japan's help that we are able to meet here in Beijing." Tanaka observed, "By invading China Japan created a lot of trouble for China," to which Mao repeated, "If Japan hadn't invaded China, the Chinese Communist Party would not have been victorious, moreover we would never be meeting today. This is the dialectic of history."[67]

Not surprisingly, this "great, glorious, and correct" Party began to encounter a profound legitimacy crisis after the death of Mao on September 9, 1976. Beginning to learn the truth about the Cultural Revolution, many Chinese people, especially intellectuals, began to see Mao as China's tyrant leader. Chairman Mao could no longer be the people's "great savior." Suddenly, the entire foundation of the party's legitimacy collapsed.

"MARCH OF THE VOLUNTEERS"

A national anthem is normally a song of praise. Ideally, it should be characteristic of pride, joy, and celebration. However, much to the contrary, the theme of the PRC's national anthem is rebellion, salvation, and national survival:

> Arise,
> Ye who refuse to be slaves!
> With our very flesh and blood,
> Let us build our new Great Wall!
> The Chinese nation faces its greatest peril,

Everybody must roar his defiance.
Arise!
Arise!
Arise!
Millions of hearts with one mind,
Brave the enemy's gunfire, March on!
Brave the enemy's gunfire, March on!
March on!
March on!
On!

This song, "March of the Volunteers," was written by Tian Han, a famous modern writer, and was set to music composed by Nie Er. In 1932, one year after the Japanese invasion of Manchuria, "March of the Volunteers" was written as a patriotic tune dedicated to the Chinese who rose to defend the nation before Japan formally declared war on China. The song urged people to join the resistance movement against the Japanese invasion, and as a result, it immediately swept the nation.

It was reported that when the Chinese leaders discussed the selection of a national anthem in 1949, there was considerable controversy over the line "The Chinese nation faces its greatest peril." Some people suggested that the lyrics should be revised. Historian Guo Moruo, for example, recommended changing the line to "The Chinese people have come to their moment of emancipation." However, Premier Zhou Enlai supported the use of the original lyrics. He said that the soul-stirring tune and its lyrics were just what China needed to fight foreign menaces. The idea was that China would need this kind of spirit and that this song could inspire people forever.[68]

During the Cultural Revolution, however, the "March of the Volunteers" was banned and "The East Is Red" became the unofficial national anthem. At a time when the cult of Mao Zedong was at its peak, how could China's national anthem not mention either Mao or the Communist Party of China?

After the death of Mao in 1976, the new leader Hua Guofeng restored "March of the Volunteers" as the national anthem in 1978, but with changed lyrics:

March on! People of all heroic nationalities!
The great Communist Party leads us in continuing the Long March,
Millions with but one heart toward a communist tomorrow,

Develop and protect the country in a brave struggle.
March on, march on, march on!
We will for generations,
Raise high Mao Zedong's banner, march on!
Raise high Mao Zedong's banner, march on!
March on! March on! On!

The new lyrics, however, never caught on. On December 4, 1982, after the downfall of Hua and the reemergence of Deng Xiaoping as China's leader, the National People's Congress resolved to restore Tian's original 1935 lyrics as the official national anthem.

The change of national anthems in China is meaningful. From "Overthrow Foreign Powers" to "March of the Volunteers" to "The East Is Red," the different lyrics highlighted the different state narratives as well as the ruling parties' statements of legitimacy under the different domestic and international contexts.

From the founding of the Chinese Communist Party in 1921 to the establishment of the People's Republic in 1949, the CCP claimed its legitimacy and mobilized people by focusing on two of the Revolution's fundamental missions: that the Revolution would create a new communist society in China characterized by universal justice and equality, and that it would change China's "weak" country status and revive its central position on the world scene.[69] The rhetorical banners that the CCP raised as ideological tools for mobilization during this period read communism and nationalism.

It was in the period between the founding of the PRC and the end of the Cultural Revolution in 1976 that Chairman Mao's personal charisma and vision of a communist future provided the CCP with the strongest foundation for its legitimacy. As analyzed earlier, however, the party put aside the banner of nationalism during these years. National history and the memory of humiliation were not used by the CCP leaders as major ideological tools or sources of legitimacy.

The next fifteen years, from 1976 to 1991, marked a period of transition. The party was facing a legitimacy crisis, but it needed some time to make the necessary adjustments away from the long-held communist and Maoist narratives and practices. In 1982, for example, the party launched a "Three Loves" movement: "Love the party, love socialism, and love the motherland." Most notably, the party had begun to reintroduce national patriotism as an ideological tool.

For the government in Beijing, these fifteen years were crisis ridden. After several years of reform, Deng Xiaoping's policies had liberalized the economic system considerably and opened China up to substantial external influences, especially from the West, thereby creating an increasingly pluralistic society. This, of course, marked the creation of competing interests. Chinese society was undergoing a profound transformation. This process of transformation unavoidably led to conflicts and crises, especially when forceful social transition was coupled with political succession. Indeed, the major political issue in mainland China during the 1980s was leadership succession.

As Deng and his Long March–generation colleagues had become octogenarians by the late 1980s, such a leadership succession was clearly inevitable. But the problem was that, within the leadership, there was intense debate surrounding the succession issue. The debate was about not only the actual successors themselves but also basic policies, especially about the party's ideology and identity in the new situation. The party was basically devoid of internal consensus and its identity and ideology policies—to use the CCP terminology, the party's "propaganda, thoughts, and cultural fronts" (*xuanchuan sixiang he wenhua zhangxian*)—were full of ambiguities. Hua Guofeng's new anthem is a case in point. On the one hand, he restored "March of the Volunteers" as the national anthem, but on the other hand, he changed the original patriotic lyrics to "raise high Mao Zedong's banner," glorifying the party and not the nation. Put simply, the party was going through a serious identity crisis.

Following the Cultural Revolution, the most serious challenge facing the CCP in the 1980s was the "Three Belief Crises" (*san xin weiji*): crisis of faith in socialism (*xinxin weiji*), crisis of belief in Marxism (*xinyang weiji*), and crisis of trust in the party (*xinren weiji*).[70] When the official communist ideology lost credibility, the Communist regime became incapable of enlisting mass support behind a socialist vision of the future. A spiritual vacuum resulted from decades of Communist repression of both the traditional and Western belief systems. Under these circumstances, some intellectuals adopted liberal ideas and called for Western-style democratic reform.

The belief crises thus evolved into a prodemocracy movement and eventually led to the large-scale Tiananmen Square demonstration in the spring of 1989. Some scholars believe that there is a direct link between the Tiananmen Incident and the belief crises: "The Tiananmen Incident could be seen as a result of the bankruptcy of the official ideology. Indeed, when the old official ideology was shattered, the CCP was not able to advance a new one."[71] China's Communist rulers feared that, in the mind of ordinary Chinese citizens, they had already lost the mandate of heaven to rule. These crises became even more evident following the international collapse of communist ideology itself.

Shortly after the Tiananmen protests, the international situation changed dramatically. The Soviet Union disintegrated, and the Communist regimes in Eastern Europe were toppled and replaced by pro-Western governments. This revolution came as a gigantic shock to China. As a result of these changes, China became the largest remaining Communist country in the world and, unavoidably, a focal point for Western criticism. Dominant themes of Western countries' China policy became: exerting pressure on China, promoting Eastern Europe–style liberalization in China, and preventing the emergence of a threatening China.

China's international strategic value was also going down. The West no longer needed China as an ally against the Soviet Union. This attitude was expressed by the title of Roger Sullivan's 1992 *Foreign Policy* article "Discarding the China Card." In this article, Sullivan noted that "it was not so much that China had changed, but that the world had changed."[72] The international community's perception of China also experienced a dramatic change. As American scholars Scott Kennedy and Michael O'Hanlon observed:

> Since the Spring of 1989 China has gone from being perceived as reformist, poor, and weak to being seen as totalitarian, prosperous, and strong. The primary causes for this change in attitude are: in politics, the crushing of the protest movement in 1989 and the continuation of Chinese Communist Party role; in economics, China's most recent boom and our growing bilateral trade deficit; and in security, China's increasingly assertive defense posture. This has led some Americans to regard China as a political pariah, an economic competitor and a potential strategic rival.[73]

Sino-American relations, the most important bilateral relationship for China, experienced a general downturn after 1989. The United States began pressuring China in the fields of human rights, arms control and proliferation, trade, and the Taiwan question. Many Chinese see the U.S.

policy of "comprehensive engagement"—the Clinton administration's China strategy—as a euphemism for comprehensive containment. The U.S. Congress's resolution against China's Olympic bid in 1993, the search of the *Yinhe* vessel for chemical weapons precursors that same summer, the high price of China's admission to the World Trade Organization, and the United States' improvement of relations with Taiwan, India, and Vietnam all fit with a strategy of containment in Beijing's eyes.

After the military crackdown on the student protests—once again, political power grew out of the barrel of a gun—the CCP desperately needed to rebuild its legitimacy as China's ruling party.

4

FROM VICTOR TO VICTIM: THE PATRIOTIC EDUCATION CAMPAIGN

THE POWERFUL link between collective memory and history is particularly salient within the educational system. Forging a country's collective memory is an integral part of nation building.[1] Schools are the primary social institutions that transmit national narratives about the past. All nation-states, whether Western democracies or nondemocratic societies, have placed great emphasis on teaching their national history with the aim of consolidating the bond between the individual citizen and the homeland.[2] This is particularly evident in the case of political transitions. As Richard J. Evans suggests, "Seldom does history seem so urgently relevant or important as in moments of sudden political transition from one state form to another."[3]

History textbooks have been regarded as major components in the construction and reproduction of national narratives. The Chinese Communist Party (CCP) is not the only ruling party that "uses the past to serve the present." Vladimir Putin's Russian government, for example, has been restoring Soviet-style patriotic education in order to nurture Russia's wounded self-esteem after dramatic political change.[4] From post-Communist Eastern Europe to East Asia to South Africa, political transitions have often necessitated, among other things, the rewriting of school history textbooks.[5] What is the relationship between history education, historical memory, and the formation of national identity? What are the implications of the uses and abuses of national history for political purposes?

What role do history and history education play in political transition and foreign relations? An exploration of these questions would provide a unique and important approach in the study of politics.

In his study of the CCP's historiography on the frequent peasant rebellions in ancient China, historian James Harrison calls the party's rewriting of Chinese history "the most massive attempt at ideological reeducation in human history."[6] The patriotic education campaign, which began in 1991, was another wide-scale attempt at ideological reeducation. However, when compared with the former ideological education campaigns that the party launched in the 1970s and 1980s, its scope and implications are considerable. This chapter contains an exploration of why and how patriotism and the discourse of national humiliation rose to political prominence in China after the Tiananmen Square Incident and the collapse of Communism in Eastern Europe. I then examine how the content of history and memory has become institutionalized in China's education system, popular culture, and the public media.

THE REFORM OF HISTORY EDUCATION

The outbreak of the Tiananmen Square protests and the shift in the international environment shocked the CCP leadership. Shortly after the suppression of the rebellion, the party began to reflect on the past to find the incident's root cause. The Chinese leader, Deng Xiaoping, concluded that the biggest mistake for the CCP in the 1980s was that the party did not focus enough attention on ideological education.

> I have told foreign guests that during the last ten years our biggest mistake was made in the field of education, primarily in ideological and political education—not just of students but of the people in general. We didn't tell them enough about the need for hard struggle, *about what China was like in the old days* and what kind of a country it was to become. That was a serious error on our part.[7] [emphasis added]

The patriotic education campaign launched shortly after the Tiananmen Incident was exactly a history education campaign "about what China was like in the old days"— the old days of the party, the Anti-Japanese War, and foreign aggression. The major goals of this campaign were to educate Chinese people, especially the young people, about China's humiliating experience in the face of Western and Japanese incursions and how the CCP-led revolution had changed China's fate and won national independence.

The campaign was made official by two documents issued in August 1991: "Notice about Conducting Education of Patriotism and Revolutionary Tradition by Exploiting Extensively Cultural Relics" and "General Outline on Strengthening Education on Chinese Modern and Contemporary History and National Conditions."[8] It should be noted that both documents were inspired by a letter from the CCP leader, Jiang Zemin.

In the past, any written instruction from a Chinese emperor was called an "imperial edict," *shengzhi*. Officials who received a *shengzhi* had to implement the emperor's instruction immediately and thoroughly. Under the autocratic leadership of the CCP, instructions from the top are still received by lower officials as imperial edicts. As a normal procedure of political operation in this system, the top leaders give their policy instructions through well-drafted internal or public speeches or by letters to the related officials. After receiving the leaders' instructions, the concerned departments of the CCP Central Committee, or the ministries of the State Council, work diligently to draft an official document. Though these documents use titles such as "notice" (*tongzhi*), "outline" (*gangyao*), or "proposal" (*yijian*), they carry the same, if not greater, weight than laws and regulations. After receiving these official documents from higher authorities, the local governmental agencies and institutions are responsible for implementing the instructions. The CCP tries to ensure that all employees study these documents and understand the Central Committee's ideas.

In China, most schools, from primary schools to universities, are run by the state. This ensures that nearly all school officials are appointed by education agencies of local governments. As a result, most schools have established CCP committees or branches, and therefore school employees are required to study official documents.

Jiang's letter was addressed to the education minister and his deputy and was also published in the *People's Daily*. In this letter, dated March 9, 1991, Jiang wrote:

> We should conduct education on Chinese modern and contemporary history and national conditions to pupils (even to the children in kindergarten), middle school students and to the university students. The education should go from the easy to the difficult, and should be persistent.[9]

An education comprised of modern and contemporary Chinese history—"about what China was like in the old days," as Deng Xiaoping had remarked five days after the massacre in Beijing in 1989—became the common strategy that the CCP leadership implemented nearly two years later to deal with the challenge of the belief and legitimacy crises.

In his letter, Jiang also provided an illustrative summary of modern Chinese history. Since its publication, this portrayal has been used in many versions of government documents, and it became a sort of "master narrative" of China's version of modern history. Jiang wrote:

> To conduct the education [of China's citizens], we should at least make clear the following main points:
>
> 1. Because of the corruption of feudal rulers, in more than 100 years after the Opium War, Chinese people were subjected to bullying and humiliation under foreign powers. This can be further illustrated by listing some main historical facts.
> 2. During this period of time, many people, including those with high ideals, shed their blood and lay down their life. Each one would step into the breach as another fell, to resist foreign aggression. They were resolved to defend the Chinese nation.
> 3. After the "May Fourth Movement," the CCP was created. Under its leadership, Chinese people of different ethnic groups went through the Agrarian Revolution, the War of Resistance against the Japanese, the Liberation War, and finally, the new China. Chinese people have stood up for themselves since the implementation of this movement. After the liberation, China also experienced several anti-aggression wars. These demonstrated that the Chinese people cannot be bullied.
> 4. Chinese citizens have, of course, always been opposed to foreign invasions. They wish to uphold justice, and have never feared brutal exogenous forces.[10]

In his narrative, Jiang emphasized the "bullying and humiliation" of Chinese people under foreign powers. In essence, he repeated the CCP's usual interpretation of Chinese history: If not for the CCP's successful revolution and sacrifices, China would still be a weak and divided country. In other ways, however, his interpretation was different. Instead of emphasizing a class-struggle narrative as the leadership had done in the past, Jiang focused on the struggles with outside forces.

In August 1991, the National Education Council issued the "General Outline on Strengthening Education on Chinese Modern and Contemporary History and National Conditions," which instructed the education administrations of different levels to require all their officials and teachers to study the document. President Jiang's letter and the general outline served as the guide for administering a proper history education. The framework of the outline also demanded that all schools take no longer than three years to incorporate the requirements of the document into the school curriculum. This outline also stressed that "history education reform" is China's fundamental strategy to "defend against the 'peaceful evolution' plot of international hostile powers . . . [and is] the most important mission for all schools."[11] After the Tiananmen Incident, the CCP believed that Western countries had a master plan to peacefully change China by influencing the thoughts and beliefs of the younger Chinese generation. Accordingly, the general outline states that "strengthening education on Chinese modern and contemporary history and national conditions is of strategic significance."

Although the campaign officially started in 1991, it was not carried out full-scale until August 1994, when the CCP's Central Committee issued the "Outline on Implementing Patriotic Education." According to Suisheng Zhao, a period of relative political stability and intellectual stagnation, along with an economic upswing after Deng Xiaoping's southern tour in 1992, created the possibility for a confluence of different interests under the umbrella of patriotism.[12] After three years' preparation, Beijing was able to implement the massive patriotic education campaign throughout China.

The CCP did not hesitate to tell people why it had launched this education campaign. The 1994 outline explicitly laid out a series of major objectives:

> The objectives of conducting the patriotic education campaign are to boost the nation's spirit, enhance cohesion, foster national self-esteem and pride, consolidate and develop a patriotic united front to the broadest extent possible, and direct and rally the masses' patriotic passions to the great cause of building socialism with Chinese characteristics.[13]

"This says it all," comments Kenneth Pyle.[14] Since the CCP was no longer supported by communist ideology, the Beijing leadership needed to find a new source of legitimacy. Patriotic education stressed the role of the communist state as the bearer of China's historic struggle for national independence and therefore reinforced CCP authority.

Paul Cohen believes the campaign was "the logical choice" of the regime:

> Many factors contributed to this revival of nationalistic sentiment. In the aftermath of 1989, there was a felt, if unstated, need on the part of the Chinese government to come up with a new legitimating ideology to burnish the rapidly dimming luster of the original Marxist-Leninist-Maoist vision, and in the eyes of Deng Xiaoping, Jiang Zemin, and other key leaders nationalism, to be inculcated via multifaceted program of patriotic education, was the logical choice.[15]

The leaders also wanted to use this campaign to shift the focus of students' youthful energies away from domestic issues and back to foreign problems. As William Callahan suggests, the campaign was not so much one of reeducation as of redirection; it was an effort to redirect young people's anger away from the party.[16] And also, as Cohen argues, a sizable majority of the Chinese population in the 1990s had been born after 1949 and had never directly experienced the onslaught of imperialism and national humiliation. Since the victory over imperialism and the closure this brought to the "century of humiliation" were crucial parts of the justification of Communist rule in China, these individuals "had to be reintroduced to the imperialist past, to re-experience its bitterness and shame."[17] In this way, the history education campaign was used to relegitimize the Communist government.

This campaign is a nationwide mobilization effort targeted mainly at Chinese youths. As a central part of the campaign, Beijing called upon the entire nation to study China's humiliating modern history and how much the country has been changed by the Communist revolution. The CCP has set the entire propaganda machine in motion for this initiative, the content of which has become institutionalized in China—embedded in political institutions and inaugurated as the CCP's new ideological tool.

NEW NARRATIVE, NEW CURRICULUM

The Chinese Communist Party has a long history of "using the past to serve the present." In his 1993 book, Jonathan Unger describes how the party has used history and memory to enhance its political legitimacy and rally domestic support:

> Even more so than the emperors, the party leaders who entered the former imperial capital in 1949 were determined to control the messages imparted in works of history—to bend those messages in ways favorable to official lines and to extirpate any manifestation of dissent or opposition that might be hidden within historical allegory.[18]

As Anne Thurston puts it: "Memory has become politicized since 1949. The Party has served as the official mediator of both collective and individual memory."[19]

After the foundation of the People's Republic of China (PRC) in 1949, the Marxist historiography gained orthodox status in the writing of Chinese history. For Karl Marx and Frederick Engels, class struggle was the motor force of historical progress, and therefore the concept of class struggle was particularly emphasized in communist historiography. Specifically, communist historians use the class struggle theory to explain such events as peasant rebellions, foreign imperialism, and the Chinese civil wars between the CCP and the nationalist Kuomintang (KMT). Under the class struggle narrative, many peasant rebellions in Chinese history, including the brutal Taiping Rebellion (1851–1864), were revered as heroic class struggles against oppression. The CCP also depicted the Anti-Japanese War in Marxist terms, portraying Japanese workers and peasants as fellow victims of militant imperialists.

As Geremie Barmé observes, "Every policy shift in recent Chinese history has involved the rehabilitation, re-evaluation, and revision of history and historical figures."[20] In the 1990s, the CCP once again used the past to serve the present, but this time the class struggle theory no longer served its interests. The ruling regime found it necessary to conduct a major revision of history education. In prompt response, the official People's Education Press published new history textbooks for both middle and high schools in 1992.[21] In fact, there were no Chinese history courses in high school before the 1992 reform because students had already learned the history of China in middle school and were supposed to study world history only in high school. The focus of the new books was on the foreign powers' invasions and oppressions. Thus, the previous class struggle narrative was replaced by the patriotic narrative, and the Taiping Rebellion and the capitalist KMT were no longer important.

Because of the official change in historical perspectives, the descriptions and commentary of past events and well-known historical figures were also changed. An example of this is the depiction of General Zuo

Zongtang of the Qing dynasty. Zuo played a critical role in the defense of the Qing dynasty, both stifling the Taiping Rebellion and overpowering the Russians during the invasion of Xinjiang. In the new textbooks, General Zuo is no longer a peasant-suppressing devil but a foreign-defeating national hero.

The narrative of the Anti-Japanese War has also been revised. The emphasis is placed on the international and ethnic conflict between China and Japan, rather than the internal and class conflict between the CCP and KMT. In the early 1980s, history textbooks provided detailed descriptions about KMT corruption and impotence along with its nonresistance policy. Also, the textbooks purported that the Anti-Japanese War was fought solely by Communist troops. However, in the new textbooks, the narrative gives considerable credit to the KMT's military resistance.

Another major narrative change during the patriotic education campaign was from a victor to a victim narrative. As discussed in chapter 3, the educational emphasis during the Mao era was on China as a victor, glorifying Communist victories over the nationalist KMT and foreign invaders.[22] Mao Zedong was a master of using "heroic" or "victor" narratives to mobilize popular support. Because success in gaining national independence gave legitimacy to the Communist Party, victory in the War of Resistance (against Japan) and the civil war (against the KMT) were central to official postwar histories.[23]

However, in the post-Tiananmen era, the CCP leaders realized the very survival of the party depended largely on whether (and how soon) they could change the younger generation's attitude toward both the Western powers and the party itself. The victor narrative had not been helpful in cultivating the young generation's hateful attitude toward China's old enemies, and this made them less appreciative of the Communist revolution. Essentially, the patriotic education campaign was designed to present Chinese youths with detailed information about China's traumatic and humiliating experience in the face of Western and Japanese incursions. The CCP-led revolution changed China's fate and won national independence, thus ending national humiliation.

In the new textbooks approved after 1992, the official Maoist victor narrative was superseded by a new victimization narrative that blamed the West for China's suffering. "China as victor" was slowly replaced by "China as victim" in nationalist discourse. This change of narrative is found in the official documents, history textbooks, and popular culture. The new emphasis on foreign powers' brutality and Chinese misery during the past has forced many Chinese, especially the younger generation, to confront the foreign atrocities and Chinese suffering that occurred during the century of humiliation. They were exposed to many details that had previously been suppressed by the Maoist victor narrative. This transition from China as victor to victim reveals a great deal about recent changes to Chinese national identity.[24]

In implementing the "General Outline on Strengthening Education," modern and contemporary Chinese history has become a required core course in high school since 1992. According to the official *Teaching Guideline for History Education*, a required course meets three class-hours per week for a total of ninety-nine hours in two semesters.[25] Other history courses, such as Chinese ancient history or world modern and contemporary history, are elective courses, with two class-hours per week or sixty hours over two semesters. The "teaching guidelines" are detailed curricular standards the Ministry of Education formulates for each course. They exercise direct authority over educational content and teaching methods. In the beginning of the teaching guidelines for the new high school history course, an official narrative of modern Chinese history was provided:

> Chinese modern history is a history of humiliation in which China gradually degenerated into a semi-colonial and semi-feudal society; at the same time, it is also a history that Chinese people strived for national independence and social progress and persisted in their struggle of anti-imperialism and anti-feudalism. It is also the history of the success of the New-Democratic Revolution under the leadership of the Chinese Communist Party.[26]

In China, the national entrance examinations required prior to attending a university have been called the "conductor" of high school education. Because of the limited resources of higher education, many high school graduates do not have the opportunity to attend universities. Admission decisions are heavily based on the candidate's scores in these very competitive examinations. Therefore, students study the required subjects diligently. In China's education system, a candidate can take the nationwide examination in one of two categories: humanities or science/engineering. History is a testing subject only for humanities majors; however, all students are tested on politics, which mainly focuses on Marxism, Mao's thoughts, and the CCP's current policies. The 1991 outline stipulates that knowledge of modern and contemporary Chinese history should be included in the politics section for those students concentrating in the science/engineering major. After these reforms, modern and contemporary Chinese history—"education on national humiliation" (*guochi jiaoyu*)—has become one of the most important subjects in the national education system.

PATRIOTIC EDUCATION BASES: CHINA'S MEMORY SITES

Museums and public monuments have played very important roles in the formation of a national memory and identity in different societies. Today, the Chinese people are living in a forest of monuments, all of which are used to represent the past to its citizens through museums, historic sites, and public sculptures. Although people all over the world cherish their own memorials, the special effort made by the Chinese government since 1991 to construct memory sites and use them for ideological reeducation is unparalleled.

In 1991, the CCP Central Propaganda Department issued the "Notice about Conducting Education of Patriotism and Revolutionary Tradition by Exploiting Extensively Historical Relics." This document explains the rationale for using historical sites for patriotic education:

> Using the rich historic relic resources to conduct education of the masses about loving our motherland, loving the party, and loving socialism has the characteristic of visualization, real and convincing. In some aspects, this approach has better educational effectiveness compared with that of normal oral lessons and written propaganda materials. It provides a very important method and vivid textbook for younger generations to know about national history, to understand the country's current situation, and to learn from our tradition.[27]

The CCP Central Committee's 1994 "Outline on Implementing Patriotic Education" set off an upsurge of patriotic education throughout the country. It further required local governments of all levels to establish "patriotic education bases" as one of the most important elements of the campaign:

> Different sorts of museums, memorial halls, buildings in memory of martyrs, sites of important battles in revolutionary wars, protected historic

> relics, and scenic sites are important places for conducting patriotic education. The propaganda departments of different levels' party organizations should work with the local education and relic and civil affairs agencies to select and determine the local education bases. Work units of different levels in both the urban and rural areas should actively use these bases to conduct educational activities. Schools should incorporate this kind of educational activities into the curriculum of moral education.[28]

Setting up typical examples or models is a customary way for the CCP to launch a new political agenda or campaign. In March 1995, the Ministry of Civil Affairs announced that, after a careful nomination and selection process, 100 sites had been selected as the national-level "demonstration bases" for patriotic education (see table 4.1). In the history of CCP political campaigns, the selection of typical examples has always represented the party's interests, values, and strategies in a specific period of time. Among the 100 bases, forty are memory sites of China's past conflicts or wars with foreign countries—including battlefields, museums,

TABLE 4.1 THE HUNDRED NATIONAL-LEVEL PATRIOTIC EDUCATION BASES

Category	Subject
External conflicts (40 sites)	Anti-Japanese War, 1931–1945 (20 sites) Opium Wars, 1839–1842 and 1856–1860 (7 sites) Korean War, 1950–1953 (4 sites) Russian invasion, 1858 (1 site) China-India War, 1962 (1 site) War with the Dutch over Taiwan, 1662 (1 site) Invasion of the Eight Nation Alliance, 1900 (1 site) Other general anti-imperialism museums/sites (5 sites)
Civil wars (24 sites)	Civil wars between the CCP and KMT, 1927–1949 (24 sites)
Myths (21 sites)	Wonders of ancient architecture and civilizations (15 sites) Relics for prehistoric civilization (4 sites) Great achievements after 1949 (2 sites)
Heroes (15 sites)	Chinese Communist Party leaders (7 sites) Model workers (4 sites) Patriots (4 sites)

memorial halls, and monuments in memory of fallen soldiers—half of them in remembrance of the Anti-Japanese War (1931–1945). Twenty-four other sites represent a memory of the civil wars between the CCP and the KMT (1927–1949). Thus, altogether nearly two-thirds of the demonstration bases were actually memory sites of past wars and conflicts.

The remaining sites can be categorized into two groups: myths and heroes. Twenty-one are wonders of Chinese civilization, including ancient architecture such as the Great Wall, museums of ancient civilizations, and great achievements or relics of prehistoric civilizations. The rest are in memory of Chinese heroes, including memorial halls for CCP leaders such as Chairman Mao and Premier Zhou, for the party's "model workers" or soldiers, and for patriots—people who were not members of the CCP but made a special contribution to the Chinese revolution.

The Korean War was not fought on China's territory, and therefore two of the Korean War memory sites are actually commemorations of Chinese soldiers built in the soldiers' hometowns. Both of the soldiers are well known in China because of CCP propaganda since the 1950s. The Memory Hall of Huang Jiguang was built in Sichuan Province. Huang was fatally wounded during the Sangkumryung Campaign in Korea in October 1952. After throwing out his last hand grenade, he threw himself against the machine-gun slit of a dugout manned by American troops. The machine gun was silenced and the height was taken by his comrades, but Huang died. The website of this memory hall calls Huang "a good solider of Chairman Mao" and asks people to learn from his "spirit of patriotism and internationalism."[29]

After they had been selected as demonstration bases, most memory sites received government financial support for construction or renovation and enlargement. Their status means that they will receive a large number of organized visits from schools, army groups, and government agencies. For example, the Chinese People's Memorial Hall of the Anti-Japanese War was built in 1987 and enlarged in 1995. It has received more than 9 million visitors since 1987. Chinese leader Jiang Zemin wrote an inscription for its reopening in 1997 that reads: "Hold high the patriotic banner, use history to educate people, promote and develop Chinese national spirit, and rejuvenate the Chinese nation."[30] Jiang also wrote an inscription for the reopening of the September 18 Historical Museum in Shenyang in 1999. Renovation work on the museum, originally built in 1991, took two years and cost 130 million yuan (about $16 million). Jiang's dedication, "Never forget September 18" (*Wuwang 9-18*), was inscribed on a huge marble stone.

The Memorial Hall for the Victims in Nanjing Massacre by Japanese Invaders is another large-scale demonstration base. It was built in 1988 and was enlarged and renovated in 1995. The memorial hall has received more than 10 million visitors since 1985. More than 80 schools and other organizations have established affiliation partnerships with the memorial hall for regular visits and ceremonies, such as the ceremony for people joining the Communist Party and the Youth League.

Beijing's impetus for sustaining the 100 national-level demonstration bases was to set an example for local governments. Shortly after the 1994 "Outline" was issued, each of the PRC provinces, autonomous regions, and centrally administered municipalities (CAMs) established their own provincial-level patriotic education bases. Further, a large number of local-level bases have also been created. Many local governments support "leading groups" to coordinate the work. According to an interview with the deputy minister of the Propaganda Department, a dozen provinces put more than 10 million Chinese yuan into the development of the patriotic bases annually.[31] Available information indicates that five provinces or CAMs—Beijing,[32] Hebei,[33] Jiangsu,[34] Jiangxi,[35] and Anhui[36]—have established more than 434 provincial-level bases and 1,938 county-level patriotic education bases (see table 4.2). Given the fact that the PRC has thirty-one provinces, autonomous regions, and CAMs, the number of memory sites for the whole of China could be over ten thousand. Visiting these memory sites has become a regular part of the school curriculum.

TABLE 4.2 PATRIOTIC EDUCATION BASES IN FIVE PROVINCES

	Patriotic education bases			
Province	National level	Provincial level	County level	Visitors
Beijing	9	88	500	250 million since 1994
Hebei	6	38	113	100 million since 1995
Jiangsu	11	154	800+	N/A
Jiangxi	9	45	268	Over 4 million in 2004
Anhui	6	71	257	N/A

In February 2004, Beijing issued "Proposals of the CCP Central Committee and the State Council on Further Strengthening and Improving Ideological and Moral Education of Minors."[37] This document again emphasized the importance of conducting education on Chinese history, especially modern and contemporary history. It asks the educational institutions to "guide the minors to know about the history and tradition of the Chinese nation, to know especially about the grave calamity that Chinese nation has suffered and the brave struggle Chinese people have conducted since the modern times." In particular, it calls for all the patriotic education bases to be free of charge for all group visits by elementary and middle school students and for individual student visits to be half the normal price. In a marketized China, this is a very practical and important move for improving the campaign.

"MAKE ENTERTAINMENT A MEDIUM OF EDUCATION"

Compared with previous propaganda campaigns launched by the CCP (especially those in the Maoist years), the patriotic education campaign was carried out in a much more practical and sophisticated way of selling the CCP's ideas and agenda.[38] In the past, traditional propaganda campaigns were dominated by empty political slogans and preaching. Knowing the Maoist approach to propaganda no longer appealed to ordinary people, especially the younger generation, the patriotic education campaign was "dressed up."

The CCP set the entire propaganda machine in motion for this campaign. State-run newspapers, magazines, radio, and television had special columns or programs on the theme of patriotic education. Artists were summoned to propagate historical myths and trauma through literature, theater, and films. The state-controlled popular culture producers have produced a large number of films, songs, and books on the theme of patriotism, drawing in materials from China's modern and contemporary history. The campaign, therefore, does not merely focus on the educational system but actually permeates all Chinese pop culture and media.

In October 2004, ten government ministries and CCP departments issued a new document, entitled "Opinions on Strengthening and Improving the Work of Patriotic Education Bases." This publication directs government agencies and educational institutions to "liberate thoughts" and improve teaching methods, especially those that involve communication with the younger generation. It also notes that officials should try to "make entertainment a medium of education."[39]

That same month, Beijing put forward a new patriotic education project, the Three One Hundred for Patriotic Education. The "three one hundred" are a hundred each of films, songs, and books with a common theme of patriotism. Seven PRC ministries and CCP departments, including the Ministry of Education and the Propaganda Department, jointly recommended 100 films, 100 songs, and 100 books to the whole society. Many of these works were about modern and contemporary Chinese history—and one selected book is entitled *Never Forget Our National Humiliation*.[40]

Since the 1950s, Chinese filmmakers have made many films on such historical events as the Anti-Japanese War, the Opium War, and the Korean War. For example, *Sangkumryung Campaign*, a recommended film, tells the story of the brutal battles between the Chinese and Americans in Sangkumryung during the Korean War. The government often provides the financial support to produce these films, which normally generate lucrative profits. One reason for these high profits is that government agencies and schools frequently organize their employees and students to screen the recommended films.

To attract more people to selected patriotic education bases, the CCP Central Committee and State Council launched a new program called "Red Tourism." The purpose of Red Tourism is to encourage people to visit the former revolutionary bases and landmarks. In 2005, China's National Bureau of Tourism (NBT) published a list of 100 Red Tourism scenic spots and recommended them to tourists. The NBT also named 2005 the "Year of Red Tourism."[41] Many of the 100 scenic spots are also patriotic education bases established in 1994. Essentially, the CCP skillfully replaced the term "education" with "tourism." According to a report from the Xinhua News Agency, more than 150 major Red Tourism sites in thirteen provinces and municipalities received 20 million visitors in 2004.[42] From 2004 to 2007, more than 400 million people participated in Red Tourism in different provinces in China. Popular destinations include Shaoshan, Chairman Mao Zedong's hometown in the southern province of Hunan, and Yanan, the CCP's "holy place of revolution" (a small town in Shaanxi Province that was the site of the CCP headquarters during the Anti-Japanese War).[43]

In addition, the CCP Central Committee asked local governments to make use of important legal holidays and national traditional holidays to carry out patriotic education. According to the 1994 "Outline," "The patriotic content should be especially stressed during the important celebrations such as the New Year, Spring Festival, Women's Day, Labor Day, Youth Day, Children's Day, the Party's Birthday, Army Day, and National Day." The government organized a series of activities to celebrate several important anniversaries of historical events. According to the research of Suisheng Zhao, in 1995 there were more than ten thousand official events and various celebrations commemorating the fiftieth anniversary of the victory in the Anti-Japanese War.[44] In 1997 and 1999, a series of large-scale activities were organized all over the country to celebrate the return of Hong Kong and Macao to the homeland. The celebration activities for both events lasted more than six months. The resumption of Chinese sovereignty over the two cities was widely heralded in the Chinese press as *xuechi* or the "wiping away of a humiliation."[45] In 2005, the CCP launched a special propaganda campaign to memorialize the sixtieth anniversary of the Anti-Fascist and Anti-Japanese War.

Clearly, the CCP did not limit education policy to the sphere of the classroom. Throughout Chinese society, evidence of the political education campaign can be seen. From recommended literature and films to patriotic songs and holidays, the campaign has been a success in penetrating the citizens' everyday life. With the use of this pervasive tactic, the campaign has raised awareness of national humiliation and spurred national pride.

INSTITUTIONALIZATION

In 2006, the Chinese government proudly announced that its "One Child per Couple" campaign, which started in 1976, "helped China prevent 400 million births by the end of 2005."[46] But how do we evaluate the effectiveness and implications of the patriotic education campaign, which is inherently an ideological education campaign? Actually, as Andrei Markovits and Simon Reich suggest, the politics of collective memory are impossible to quantify and hard to measure with the methods of survey research.[47] Elizabeth Cole and Judy Barsalou have also advised that evaluating the impact of history education on individual students and the larger society is extremely difficult.[48]

According to Robert Keohane and Judith Goldstein, once ideas or beliefs become institutionalized, they constrain public policy.[49] In chapter

1, institutionalization was introduced as one of the three causal pathways through which beliefs or ideas can serve to influence political actions. The term *institutionalization* is used here to denote the process of embedding particular values and norms within an organization, social system, or society. Once these ideas are institutionalized, they can have lasting impact for generations to come. Furthermore, once a policy choice leads to the creation of reinforcing organizational and normative structures, the policy idea can affect the incentives of political entrepreneurs long after the interests of its initial proponents have changed.[50]

Tyrene White writes that one of the defining characteristics of the Maoist era in Chinese politics (1949–1976) was the continual use of "mass mobilization campaigns" (*qunzhong yundong*) to achieve socialist goals.[51] Deng Xiaoping officially announced that the CCP would abandon bottom-up mobilization, in which the elite party membership is beholden to the nonelite masses (as in the Cultural Revolution). The top-down model of party-controlled mobilization, on the other hand, has remained an integral, active part of the political process. To this day, the top-down model is still an important leadership device for the CCP.

The party's official definition of a "mass mobilization campaign" is "organized mobilization of collective action aimed at transforming thought patterns, class/power relationships, and/or economic institutions and productivity."[52] White lists three specific indicators of campaign activity: informational, organizational, and mass participation indicators.[53] *Informational indicators* are those that are apparent in the media: newspaper articles, slogans, mobilization meetings, targets for criticism, stories for emulation, pamphlets, signs, banners, and exhibits. *Organizational indicators* occur when the fundamental organization of a society is altered, which might include sending in outside cadres, creating work teams, reallocation of resources, disruption of work routines, or reorganization of the unit. Finally, large-scale involvement of the citizenry constitutes *mass participation indicators*. Examples of this are participation after regular work hours; mobilization of minority, youth, or other special groups and organizations; study groups; and local, regional, or national rallies.[54] Virtually all of the above tools were utilized in the patriotic education campaign.

The campaign started in the early 1990s as an education campaign targeting young people and school students. Over time, it has gradually become a nationwide mobilization. Patriotism, along with history and memory, has become the most important subject for ideological education of the party-state system. The CCP set the entire propaganda machine in motion for this campaign. School teachers and administrators, military officers and soldiers, and all the employees of state agencies and state-run organizations have been required to take regular political classes on patriotic education and to participate in various activities and events on the theme of patriotic education.

In comparison with previous propaganda campaigns launched by the CCP, the patriotic education campaign was carried out in a new social context. During the twenty years since the campaign's launch, the political, social, and economic context of Chinese society has been undergoing a great transformation. The changes experienced by China's 1.3 billion people are increasingly pluralistic; a new middle class is growing, and civil society is emerging. China is also now engaging more closely with the international system. According to a report from *China Daily*, China now has more than 150 million private enterprise owners, technicians, managers, independent professionals, doctors, lawyers, and employees of private and foreign companies who contribute one-third of the country's total tax revenues.[55] At the same time, between 100 million and 150 million Chinese peasants have quit working in their villages and headed to the cities.[56] These people are no longer contained within the system, meaning that they no longer have to attend the CCP's political studies or other organized events. They are not only outside the system but also outside the CCP's grasp. Consequently, at least in terms of the proportion of the population participating, the party's mobilization campaigns are no longer as powerful as those of the past.

Having realized the changes in the situation, the CCP regime has correspondingly changed its approach to mobilization and propaganda. In comparison with previous propaganda campaigns, the patriotic education campaign has been dressed up and carried out in a much more practical and sophisticated way, as discussed in the previous section. In particular, the party has made special efforts to make entertainment a medium of education and to penetrate every facet of people's lives with the educational content.

Even the employees of private and foreign companies and migrant workers are not totally outside the campaign of patriotic education. While the average citizen who does not want to be influenced can easily turn off a TV program on humiliation history or skip a newspaper story on that topic, it is much more difficult for them to deal with these kinds of programs when they are everywhere in the state-controlled media. From the Olympic Games opening ceremony to a new monument erected on a street corner, it is difficult to ignore the message of this campaign when the government has so meticulously themed patriotic education in all the important activities of the people's lives.

The CCP leaders also replaced the Maoist approaches of mass campaign with the creation of routine; radicalism gave way to "systems engineering." The implementation process has gradually evolved into a pattern of institutionalized mobilization. This has become the biggest difference between the patriotic education campaign and other political campaigns the CCP has launched. The party has set up some permanent "leading groups" or offices at the different levels of government and party agencies to coordinate the work of patriotic education. Routine procedures have also been developed to administer work and coordinate with other relevant departments. In addition, funding and personnel have been increased and regularized.

One of the important roles that these leading groups play is to keep a watchful eye on the emergence of any different ideas that may challenge the institutionalized beliefs. They will also act quickly to suppress the possible proliferation of the new ideas. In January 2006, Yuan Weishi, a professor of philosophy at Zhongshan (Sun Yat-sen) University in Guangzhou, published a long article in a magazine strongly criticizing one of the required middle school history textbooks.[57] This essay, entitled "Modernization and History Textbooks," was published in *Bingdian* (*Freezing Point*), a weekly supplement of the popular national newspaper *China Youth Daily*.[58] In this article, Yuan accused the government's history text of feeding the students "fake pills" and fostering blind nationalism and closed-minded antiforeign sentiment.[59] Citing two case studies, Yuan argued that this official history textbook published by People's Education Press provides a one-sided account of two historical events—the burning of the Yuanming Yuan and the Boxer Rebellion.[60]

Two weeks after the publication of Yuan Weishi's article, party officials ordered *Bingdian* closed and the chief editors of both *China Youth Daily* and *Bingdian* replaced. Propaganda authorities even issued an order barring all media from reporting the suspension, all reporters from participating in any news conference about it, and all websites from carrying any discussion about it.[61] This case demonstrated that the system has a very quick response capability to heretical beliefs. Even a single scholarly article published in a weekly supplement could activate the institution's response system, and a series of actions was conducted to "correct" the wrongdoing. However, one might also note that the same government has been strongly criticized in recent years for its failure to deal quickly and responsibly with such public health crises as AIDS and tainted baby milk.

Most CCP political campaigns are short-term mobilizations that temporarily intensify coercion and vary from region to region in timing, intensity, and scope. However, in the "Outline on the Implementation of Education in Patriotism," the CCP leadership emphasized that the patriotic education campaign is a long-term project and should be carried out "unwaveringly" and "tirelessly."

> Patriotic education must persist in stressing construction. Particularly, we should focus on theoretical construction, curriculum construction, and base construction of the patriotic education. We must do this in accordance with the series of important speeches by comrade Deng Xiaoping on patriotic education. We should penetrate patriotic education in all forms of ideological and political education, and make it the foundation project of the construction of socialist civilization. We should make patriotism the main melody of our society, and we must make unremitting efforts and work tirelessly on this project for the long-term.[62]

Since 1991, the Communist government has turned words into action. As discussed in previous sections, history and memory have become embedded in Chinese education systems, party-state systems, popular culture, and public media.

In the past, many of the CCP's political campaigns started with great momentum but lost steam early on. A change of leadership often contributed to these failures. Very often, new leaders launched their own political campaigns to demonstrate differences between themselves and their predecessors. But the patriotic education campaign is an exception. Started in 1991, the campaign is still well under way without any signs of decline. Initiated by Jiang Zemin, the patriotic education campaign continues to be promoted by the current CCP leader, Hu Jintao. For example, a 2007 initiative of education reform in higher education has made Chinese modern and contemporary history a required core course for all college students in China.[63] Interestingly, this new core course on post-1840 Chinese history replaced the traditional courses on Marxism-Leninism and Maoism that had been compulsory across undergraduate curriculum for decades. As one observes, for lack of a better alternative, the reliance on patriotism as unifying ideology is most likely to continue in the future.[64]

THE POLITICS OF HISTORY EDUCATION

In the 1994 "Outline on the Implementation of Education in Patriotism," the CCP Central Committee set a goal for the campaign:

> If we want to make the patriotic thoughts the core theme of our society, a very strong patriotic atmosphere must be created so that the people can be influenced and nurtured by the patriotic thoughts and spirit at *all* times and *everywhere* in their daily life. It is the sacred duty for the press and publishing, radio, film and television departments of all levels to use advanced media technology to conduct patriotic education to the masses.[65] [emphasis added]

Many indicators suggest that this top-down propaganda campaign has realized its objectives. During this process, the ruling party tried its best to use the education campaign to penetrate every facet of people's daily lives so that the masses can be "influenced and nurtured." As Julia Lovell notes, "With its regimen of flag-raising, anthem-singing, film-watching, textbook-reading, museum-visiting and so on, post-1989 Patriotic Education has offered a full-body workout for China's growing generations of potential nationalists."[66]

The patriotic education campaign represents a major shift in Beijing's identity politics. When the CCP launched the campaign of patriotic education in 1991, shortly after the Tiananmen Incident, the party faced a serious crisis—the official Marxist and Maoist ideologies were bankrupt. The campaign has proven to be one of the most important maneuvers the party has conducted for its survival in the post-Tiananmen and post–Cold War eras. As Suisheng Zhao observes, the Communist government launched this campaign to redefine and reinvigorate the legitimacy of the post-Tiananmen leadership in a way that would "permit the Communist Party's rule to continue on the basis of a non-Communist ideology."[67] Through this nationwide educational campaign, Beijing has creatively used history education as an instrument for the glorification of the party, the consolidation of the PRC's national identity, and the justification of the political system of one-party rule by the CCP. During the course of the campaign, the party skillfully utilized China's humiliating past to arouse its citizens' historical consciousness and to promote social cohesion.

The 1990s and 2000s have witnessed a surge of nationalism in China, and some scholars believe that the campaign for patriotic education has greatly contributed to this rise in nationalism. For example, Zhao attributes the nationalistic sentiments of the mid-1990s to the dependence on patriotism and the patriotic education campaign, both designed by the Communists to build support for the government.[68] Geoffrey Crothall finds that while Chinese students usually hate to take political science classes and study Marxist doctrine with Communist Party propaganda, they nevertheless find the new patriotic education appealing.

> All the indications are that patriotic education has worked where political science failed. Today's students are far less willing to criticize the party because to do so would be seen, somehow, as being unpatriotic. Furthermore, the students have seen living standards rise and China's position in the world improve markedly over the past five years.[69]

Some foreign leaders and international media have also viewed China's history education as the foundation of the rising grassroots nationalism in China. Japanese foreign minister Nobutaka Machimura, for instance, connected China's anti-Japan sentiments with China's history education, suggesting that China should "modify" its education on history.[70] According to a survey released by Japan's *Asahi* newspaper in April 2005, more than eighty percent of Japanese believe that China's nationalistic education system encouraged the recent protest.[71]

I have no intention of measuring to what extent the campaign for patriotic education has promoted the rise of nationalism in China. However, full comprehension of this campaign is a precondition to understanding the rapid conversion of China's popular social movements from the internal-oriented, anticorruption, antidictatorship democratic movements of the 1980s to the external-oriented, anti-Western nationalism of the 1990s. Most participants in China's nationalism protests in the 1990s and 2000s were college students and young people in their twenties. Given that the patriotic education campaign started in 1991, this means that most of those students began to receive patriotic education as soon as they entered primary school or middle school. They are the "generation of patriotic education."

:::

In this chapter, I have explored how historical memory of national humiliation has been reinforced by the current regime's educational socialization through the national patriotic education campaign after 1991. The next chapter further investigates how the content of history and memory has become embedded in patterns of political discourse in China. There, I focus on how the Communist government, especially its top leaders, uses history and memory to construct the rules and norms of the CCP, and how the discourse of national humiliation has played an integral role in the construction of Chinese nationalism.

5

FROM VANGUARD TO PATRIOT: RECONSTRUCTING THE CHINESE COMMUNIST PARTY

JIANG ZEMIN'S "PATRIOTIC TURN"

After 1991, the Chinese Communist Party (CCP) had no choice but to put aside the banner of communism and wholeheartedly embrace nationalism. As Thomas Christensen has observed, nationalism became the sole ideological glue that holds the People's Republic together and keeps the CCP government in power in the post–Cold War era.[1] Lacking the procedural legitimacy of democratically elected governments and, at the same time, facing the collapse of communist ideology, the CCP has frequently fallen back on using nationalism as its societal glue. "Since the CCP is no longer communist, it must be even more Chinese."[2]

Developments in China have not occurred in isolation. The end of the Cold War has seen the revival throughout the world of national aspirations and interests.[3] As Geremie Barmé suggests, the new revival of nationalism in China should be understood in the broader context of Chinese society and the international situation. Beyond the bounds of official culture, nationalism or patriotism has actually functioned as a form of consensus for the post-Tiananmen and post–Cold War Chinese society.

> The rapid decay of Maoist ideological beliefs and the need for continued stability in the Chinese Communist Party have led to an increased reliance on nationalism as a unifying ideology. . . . Both economic realities

and national priorities call for a strong central state and thus tend to give an ideologically weakened Communist Party a renewed role in the broader contest for the nation.[4]

Beijing was indeed using patriotism as a unifying ideology. In a 1990 speech titled "Patriotism and the Mission of the Chinese Intellectuals," Chinese leader Jiang Zemin openly asked all Chinese, especially the young intellectuals—those "troublemakers" during the 1989 democracy movement—"to unite under the banner of patriotism." In this speech, Jiang stated that his party would embrace patriotism as new tool of mobilization: "In the history of China, patriotism has always been the banner to mobilize and inspire people to unite together; it is the common spiritual pillar of the Chinese people of all nationalities."[5]

At the international level, the government's crackdown on the demonstrations of the spring of 1989 caused global protests. Many countries, especially in the West, took a hostile attitude toward Beijing. However, the hostility toward the regime was perceived by many Chinese, including many intellectuals, as Western discrimination and aggression toward the whole of China. In a collectivist society, social identity theory tells us that individuals often see themselves more as group members than individuals; they also closely connect their self-identity and -esteem with group membership.[6] The negative response of the world to China therefore encouraged a "us-against-the-world mentality" among elements of the Chinese leadership and populace.[7] Western unfriendliness activated Chinese patriotic sensibilities and provided Beijing with opportunities to use external pressure to strengthen internal solidarity.

On the other hand, the troublesome transformation in Eastern Europe and the Soviet Union in the 1990s has also been used by the CCP to deliver a message to the Chinese people: China would fall right into the same disorder and chaos if the Communist Party were toppled down. For many people who supported the 1989 student movement, there is the added realization that if China had then successfully undergone a major political upheaval, the nation could well have been faced with the disorder that now grips Russia's rulers.[8] The CCP leaders gained an unusual breathing spell after the military crackdown, and they seized the opportunity to start their own reforms.

In its efforts to promote a new surge of nationalism, the Communist government has a habit of digging up history. As discussed in the previous chapter, China's national humiliation in its modern history has been used as the principal tool to conduct national ideological reeducation. The Beijing government—more specifically, its top leaders—also used historical memory to construct the rules and norms of the ruling party. In fact, history and memory have provided a complete set of theories to redefine the identity of the Chinese Communist Party. The chief engineer of this redefinition project was Jiang Zemin.

When Deng Xiaoping chose Jiang as his third successor twenty days after the Tiananmen crackdown, many people considered him merely a transitional figure. Jiang had been a relative outsider to Beijing's elite politics. He lacked his own power base and had little experience in the central government. Furthermore, he had virtually no authority or prestige within the military. However, Jiang proved politically astute and appeared to learn from the failures of his predecessors.

Jiang knew that his opponents were eagerly awaiting any mistake he might make and reasoned that the only way to avoid making mistakes was to shadow Deng's policies instead of putting forward his own. Casting himself as a devout disciple and defender of Deng, Jiang avoided putting his own stamp on official policies in the first several years in his post. Between 1989 and 1992, Chinese politics were stagnant, and few new policies and reforms were put into effect. At this, even Deng could not hold himself back and, in 1992, he made his famous "inspection tour of southern China," after which he urged Jiang and the rest of the party to speed up economic reform. Deng told them "to stop being afraid, to make bigger and faster movement forward."[9]

However, after securing his power, Jiang became an entirely different leader. During the eight years from 1994 to 2002, Jiang carried out a series of bold reform policies. Under his leadership, China experienced substantial developmental growth and made important breakthroughs in the market-oriented economic reform. It was during his leadership that China joined the World Trade Organization. His term also saw the peaceful return of Hong Kong and Macao. Jiang improved China's relations with the Western world and other major powers, especially the United States and Russia.

Today when people talk about Jiang's legacy, they primarily focus on his economic reforms and foreign policies. However, very little attention (by either the media or scholars) has been paid to another major reform that Jiang launched: a quiet revolution that transformed the CCP from a revolutionary party to a nationalist party. In this reform, Jiang used nationalism and patriotism to replace communism and socialism as China's new ideology.

In the previous chapter, I looked at how Jiang used history education to promote the patriotic education campaign. The following sections present a detailed account of how Jiang Zemin used history and memory to reconstruct the ruling party's narrative in terms of its membership, its legitimacy, and its objectives.

As part of the institutional culture of the Communist Party, any major political reform always begins with the formation of new narratives, which are transcribed in party documents. Normally, the contents of these documents are presented in political reports to the CCP's National Congress. In the three political reports Jiang made at the party congresses of 1992, 1997, and 2002, he provided a comprehensive narrative of the CCP's new legitimacy and objectives and redefined the meaning of its membership.

The Party Congress has been the most authoritative public event in the politics of China since 1949. It convenes every five years and fulfills three basic functions. First, the members assess party work in major policy arenas from the previous five years. Second, they work to define the party's overarching general task as well as the priorities and approaches—the party line—for all significant policy realms in the coming five-year period. Last, they appoint (or reappoint) the party's top leadership.[10]

The first two tasks are addressed in the long "political report" delivered to the congress by the party general secretary in the name of the last congress's Central Committee. Because these functions are fundamental, preparations for convening party congresses are intensely political. Once endorsed by the full party congress, the ideological themes and policy lines contained in the congress's political report become the most authoritative expression of the party's policy in the areas they address. In principle, at least, all party leaders must justify policy actions in terms of the party line adopted at the congress or as modified at subsequent Central Committee plenums.

As Neil Renwick and Cao Qing suggest, Chinese political discourse is characterized by three features: building a consensus (*gongshi*), a drive for unity (*tuanjie*), and the need for the propagation of this "consensus" through education (*jiaoyu*).[11] Although the CCP's top leader—today's general secretary, or the chairman during Mao's era—delivers the main political report to a party congress, the political report is a consensus document. The top leader often plays a dominant role in drafting the report, and it may, therefore, bear this person's heavy influence. But most often the political report finally delivered to the congress is the product of a long process of drafting and review, so that it reflects much more than just the top leader's singular view.

For example, the drafting of the political report of the Fifteenth Congress in 1997 took ten months and ten successive drafts, drawing on more than eight hundred revisions. One draft saw broad review by more than 4,000 senior party members, government and military officials, and nonparty people.[12] For both the Fourteenth Congress five years earlier in 1992 and the Sixteenth Congress five years later in 2002, over 3,000 senior party members reviewed the drafts of the final report.[13] It took the CCP headquarters over a year to draft the political report of the Sixteenth Congress.[14] This elaborate process produces what is intended to be a highly authoritative consensus document.[15] Table 5.1 provides a summary of the drafting processes of three political reports.

The political reports were major sources of information for earlier generations of China watchers, for whom the ability to interpret CCP scriptures was a basic skill. In recent years, however, attention to these texts has decreased. In recent decades, Chinese society has evolved inexorably

TABLE 5.1 POLITICAL REPORTS OF THE CCP NATIONAL CONGRESS

Political report	Time	Length (words)	Reporter	Drafting processes
14th Party Congress	Oct. 12, 1992	26,348	Jiang Zemin	The drafting took 7 months and 10 successive drafts, drawing on more than 620 revisions. One draft saw broad review by more than 3,000 party, state, military, and nonparty people.
15th Party Congress	Sept. 12, 1997	28,400	Jiang Zemin	The drafting took 10 months and 10 successive drafts, drawing on more than 800 revisions. One draft saw broad review by more than 4,000 party, state, military, and nonparty people.
16th Party Congress	Nov. 8, 2002	28,184	Jiang Zemin	The drafting took 13 months. Eight research groups went to 16 provinces and held 80 focus group meetings, attended by 914 people. One draft was reviewed by more than 3,100 people.

from a simple to a complex system. More importantly, market economy and political relaxation have coalesced to create a popular culture market comparable to those in Western countries. Consequently, many China scholars have turned their attention from party documents to these new texts and "voices" (e.g., mass-circulation books, magazines, movies, posters, cartoons, television shows, and Internet chats), which are much more intriguing and colorful in comparison. These novel "texts" have no doubt enriched and expanded studies on Chinese society; however, this approach is insufficient, even misleading, when it comes to policy making. The leaders of the ruling party make decisions on foreign policy without parliamentary hearings or public canvassing. Despite increased attention to public opinion, Beijing has not made any fundamental change in its decision-making process in the last two or three decades.

THE CCP'S NEW MEMBERSHIP

The classic definition of the membership of the CCP is the "vanguard of the Chinese working class." According to the party's 1969 constitution, "The Communist Party of China is composed of the advanced elements of the proletariat; it is a vigorous vanguard organization leading the proletariat and the revolutionary masses in the fight against the class enemy."[16] In his 1996 speech, Jiang Zemin used several superlatives to describe his party's "new" membership:

> Our Party has inherited and carried forward the Chinese nation's outstanding tradition, and has made the *biggest* sacrifice and the *biggest* contribution in the struggle of national independence and safeguarding of national sovereignty. We have therefore won the heartfelt love and support from people of all nationalities in China. The Chinese Communist is the *firmest*, the *most* thoroughgoing patriot. The Chinese Communist Party's patriotism is the *highest* model of conduct for the Chinese nation and the Chinese people.[17]

In this statement, Jiang emphasized that the party had made "the biggest sacrifice and the biggest contribution" in the struggle of national independence and safeguarding national sovereignty. As such, he sought to introduce the new identification of the party—the Chinese Communist as the "firmest and most thoroughgoing patriot."

Jiang's campaign of "Three Represents" is an attempt to transform the Communist Party from a vanguard revolutionary party driven by the proletariat to a ruling party representing the majority of the people. According to Jiang's speech at the Sixteenth Congress in 2002, the Communist Party should represent "advanced productive forces, advanced Chinese culture and the fundamental interests of the majority."[18] That is, the party can be all things to all people, promoting the interests not just of workers and farmers but of wealthy entrepreneurs and university professors as well. In actuality, this is a farewell statement to the old Communist Party, and some political analysts believe that, sooner or later, the Chinese Communist Party will transform itself into a socialist democratic party.

If we apply social identity theory, we see that people identify with groups in which they feel they belong. Because of this, we sometimes think of ourselves in terms of "us" versus "them" or, alternatively, the in-group versus the out-group. The more we identify with our group, the more we will differentiate our group from other groups. In his speech at the sixth plenary session of the Fourteenth CCP National Congress in October 1996, Jiang Zemin divided Chinese people into two categories: the "ardent patriots" and the "scum of a nation."

> The Chinese people have never lowered their head in front of the invaders. They have the glorious tradition of loving freedom, pursuing advancement and preserving national dignity and sovereignty. They hate the foreign invaders furiously. They particularly despise the scum of a nation who turns traitor for their personal gain. They incomparably respect ardent patriots. These have already become our valuable national personality.[19]

He also emphasized the qualifications of being a "right" Chinese citizen. One should hate the foreign invaders, despise traitors, and respect patriots.

Social identity theory also indicates that when social identity is unsatisfactory, individuals will strive either to leave their existing group and join some more positively distinct group (social mobility) or to make their existing group more positively distinct (social change). The CCP Central Committee stated clearly in the "Outline on the Implementation of Patriotic Education":

> The purpose of conducting patriotic education is to inspire the national spirit, to strengthen the national cohesion, to set up people's sense of self-respect and sense of pride, and to consolidate and develop the most

> widely united front. Our purpose is also to lead the people's patriotic enthusiasm to the great cause of building socialism with Chinese characteristics, and to unite our people striving for the realization of the four modernizations and the rejuvenation of Chinese nation.[20]

In other words, the party hoped the education campaign could promote positive social change and also make China a better place in order to prevent the spread of "social mobility"—people leaving the party or, worse yet, the country.

Historical memory has also been used to explain China's foreign policy and especially the different relationships with countries of varied forms of government. As a common foreign policy statement, Chinese leaders always say that China and the Third World have a better mutual understanding and share good relationships due to the fact that they went through similar experiences throughout history and were similarly subjected to colonial aggression and Western oppression. While reading Hu Jintao's political report of the Seventeenth Party Congress in November 2007, we need to pay attention to the different wording and the tone that he chose to describe China's relationship with two categories of countries:

> For developed countries, we will continue to strengthen strategic dialogue, enhance mutual trust, deepen cooperation and properly manage differences to promote long-term, stable and sound development of bilateral relations. For developing countries, we will continue to increase solidarity and cooperation with them, cement traditional friendship, expand practical cooperation, provide assistance to them within our ability, and uphold the legitimate demands and common interests of developing countries.[21]

For many Chinese, the countries of the world can be divided into two groups: those who have bullied China in the past—all of them are the developed countries—and those who have the similar experiences with China—the other Third World countries.

"WE ENDED THE HISTORY OF HUMILIATING DIPLOMACY"

Jiang Zemin's speech at the Meeting Celebrating the Eightieth Anniversary of the Founding of the Communist Party of China in July 2001 is another valuable source because it reviews the eighty-year history of the

CCP. This lengthy speech—over 20,000 words—provides a comprehensive new narrative of the CCP's legitimacy.

> We have thoroughly put an end to the loose-sand state of the old China and realized a high degree of unification of the country and unparalleled unity of all ethnic groups. We have abrogated the unequal treaties imposed upon China by Western powers and all the privileges of imperialism in the country. The feudalistic segmentation of the country has gone forever on this land of China. . . . We have forged a people's army under the absolute leadership of the party and built a strong national defense. . . . We have thoroughly ended the history of humiliating diplomacy in modern China and effectively safeguarded State sovereignty, security and national dignity. . . . The international standing and influence of socialist China are growing with each passing day.[22]

Each of these accomplishments—from a high degree of unification to the abrogation of the unequal treaties—is closely connected with the hundred years of national humiliation. By emphasizing these achievements, Jiang introduced the central myth of the Communist narrative of modern Chinese history: Were it not for the CCP's successful revolution, China would have remained a weak, corrupt, and divided country. This is perhaps the most important justification for the CCP's one-party reign.

The relationship between collective memory and society's legitimization is best evidenced by the typical attempt of nationalist movements to create a master commemorative narrative that legitimizes their aspirations for a shared destiny by emphasizing a common past for its members.[23] Such narratives have a tremendous power to build legitimacy based on common experiences. To explain this concept more clearly, we can look to this statement in Jiang's 2001 speech:

> From the Opium War (1840–42) to the founding of the Communist Party of China, and from the founding of the party to the present, China has experienced two completely different periods of 80 years. The comparison of the two periods of 80 years has made the Chinese people and all the patriotic forces of the Chinese nation fully aware that it is precisely the leadership of the Communist Party of China that has enabled the country to materialize the great historical transformation from the most miserable circumstances to a situation that promises a bright future. Without the Communist Party, there would have been no New China.

> With the Communist Party, China has put on an entirely new look. This is the fundamental and most important conclusion drawn by the Chinese people from their long years of struggle.[24]

In this lengthy statement, Jiang presented the CCP's "master narrative" of Chinese history—that the leadership role of the CCP has been entrusted to it by the history of the past century through the party's sacrifice and its contribution to the struggle for national independence and the safeguarding of national sovereignty. The essence of this narrative is the notion that "without the Communist Party, there would have been no New China."

The cognitive content of history and memory often describes how group membership is maintained and even explains how the world works for this group of people through a series of cause-and-effect relationships. In China's case, the CCP has been very effective in using historical memories to propagate the party's world perspective. The party's propaganda machine has tried every means to impose such ideas on the Chinese people, as Jiang said in his political report at the Fifteenth Congress:

> Our conclusion drawn from the great changes over the past century is as follows: Only the Communist Party of China can lead the Chinese people in achieving victories of national independence, the people's liberation and socialism, pioneering the road of building socialism with Chinese characteristics, rejuvenating the nation, making the country prosperous and strong and improving the people's well-being.[25]

According to this statement, the "theory" that has been used to explain how the world works for the Chinese people is fairly clear: Only the Communist Party of China can save China; only the party can develop and rejuvenate China. As Anne Thurston points out, the legitimacy of the CCP depends on fostering a perception that the "country" so loved by Chinese patriots must be governed by the Communist Party.[26]

The CCP is certainly not the first political party that has used national historical memory to boost its legitimacy, nor will it be the last. What is important to recognize, however, is the significant link between Chinese historical memory and political legitimacy. The politics of memory has proven central to the transition to democracy throughout the world. Perceptions of the past are essential to both delegitimating previous regimes and, at the same time, grounding new claims to political legitimacy.[27]

This is even more true in China's case; the CCP has used history and memory to generate a whole set of theories to explain the role of the party in China's history. The view is that the CCP has made the largest sacrifices and contributions in the struggle to "put an end to the past humiliation." Under this set of theories, it was history—the record of the past century and the need to put an end to the national humiliation in particular—that entrusted the CCP with the leadership role of governing China. As Renwick and Qing suggest, the CCP has claimed legitimacy on portraying itself as the historic agency that restored national unity and practical independence.[28]

REJUVENATION: THE KEY WORD

"Invigorating China" (*zhenxing zhonghua*) was probably the most popular political slogan in China in the 1980s. The four Chinese characters associated with this motto were painted on walls all over China at that time. This phrase was actually first used by Sun Yat-sen in 1894 when he created the Hsingchung Hui—the Society for Invigorating China—which would later become the Nationalist Party of China (Kuomintang).

For any political party, it is vital to have a vision for the future that serves to provide compelling ethical or moral motivations to inspire people's participation in the party's cause. Therefore, it is necessary for a party to make clear its mission and to elucidate its vision for the future—these are prerequisites to the party's construction of its political legitimacy. After the end of the Cultural Revolution in 1976, the CCP's traditional objective of the realization of a communist society was no longer attractive to the Chinese people. The party badly needed a new vision for the future that could retain the support of its people. "Invigorating China" thus became Deng Xiaoping's favorite slogan and the mission statement for the CCP in this period of redefining its identity.

After Jiang Zemin came into power, he used the word "rejuvenation" (*fuxing*) to replace "invigoration" (*zhenxing*). The new catch phrase was "the great rejuvenation of the Chinese nation" (*zhonghua minzu de weida fuxing*). This change of words was indeed meaningful. The word *rejuvenation* is deeply related to China's history and historical memory. By using this word (as opposed to *invigoration*), Jiang rekindled in people the memory of China as a central power in the world and emphasized that his party's work was to restore China to that former position and glory.

According to Yan Xuetong, an international relations scholar at Tsinghua University, the term *rejuvenation* refers to the psychological power contained in the concept of China's rise to its former superior world status. Yan also believes that the Chinese see this rise as regaining China's lost international status rather than obtaining something entirely new; at the same time, they also consider the rise of China as a restoration of fairness rather than gaining advantage over others.[29]

In his 2001 speech, Jiang put forth his party's new mission statement:

> Every struggle that the Chinese people fought during the 100 years from the mid-19th to the mid-20th century was for the sake of achieving independence of our country and liberation of our nation and putting an end to the history of national humiliation once and for all. This great historic cause has already been accomplished. All endeavors by the Chinese people for the 100 years from the mid-20th to the mid-21st century are for the purpose of making our motherland strong, the people prosperous, and the nation immensely rejuvenated. Our Party has led the entire Chinese people in carrying forward this historic cause for 50 years and has made tremendous progress, and it will successfully attain the objective through hard work in the coming 50 years.[30]

This statement presents the two major roles of the CCP—what Jiang calls two great "historic causes"—that the CCP has performed and will accomplish: putting an end to the history of national humiliation and making the nation immensely rejuvenated. Both of these goals originate from China's history and memory.

This history and collective memory have provided the ruling party with socially appropriate roles to perform. The identification of its roles can best be understood through the theory of chosen traumas and chosen glories. Again I reiterate that the assumed fundamental role of the ruling party is to put an end to past humiliation and to restore the past glory of the nation. The mission of the party is no longer the realization of communism but has veered toward a very nationalistic objective.

Hu Jintao became the CCP's new leader in 2002. Even though he made many changes to Jiang's policies, he continues Jiang's narrative of rejuvenation. Compared with Jiang, Hu is even more of an enthusiastic proponent of the "great rejuvenation." In fact, many of his public speeches have ended with a call for people to "strive harder for the great rejuvenation of the Chinese nation."

Hu's political report presented at the Seventeenth Party Congress in October 2007 was described as the "general guidelines for the great rejuvenation of the Chinese nation" by Beijing's ideological scholars. In this report, Hu called the "great rejuvenation of the Chinese nation" the "historical mission" of his party:

> Ever since its founding in July 1921, the CCP has bravely dedicated itself to the historical mission of leading the Chinese people in striving for a happy life and for the great rejuvenation of the Chinese nation. Chinese Communists have been fighting one generation after another to fulfill this mission, and countless revolutionaries have sacrificed their lives in the course. Party members in contemporary China must continue on this mission.[31]

The report also discussed the process by which this great rejuvenation can come to fruition. For example, Hu said that "reform and opening up are the only way of rejuvenating the Chinese nation" and that "education is the cornerstone of national rejuvenation." Hu also believed that "the great rejuvenation of the Chinese nation will definitely be accompanied by the thriving of Chinese culture." In particular, he emphasized the relationship between national rejuvenation and the reunification of China and Taiwan: "The two sides of the Straits are bound to be reunified in the course of the great rejuvenation of the Chinese nation."[32]

If the central myth and legitimacy of the government are highly dependent upon ending China's history of humiliation and safeguarding state sovereignty, it becomes quite natural and understandable why national reunification is an important mission for the CCP. The Taiwan question is directly related to the CCP's legitimacy. As Jiang Zemin said in his 2001 speech:

> The status of Taiwan as a part of China shall in no way be allowed to change. The Chinese Communists are rock firm in their resolve to safeguard State sovereignty and territorial integrity. . . . It is the bounden duty of the Chinese Communists to end the state of separation between Taiwan and China's mainland and achieve the complete reunification of China.[33]

One has to know this historical context to understand why Jiang and the Beijing government have repeatedly emphasized that it is the "bounden duty" of the CCP to achieve the complete reunification of China and that the Taiwan question is in China's core interests.

"Backwardness incurs beatings by others" (*luohou jiuyao aida*) is another popular political slogan in China. It has been used as a political theory to explain China's national experience during the century of humiliation. President Hu also used this to explain why the great rejuvenation of the Chinese nation has become the "unswerving" goal of the Chinese people:

> History and reality tell us that backwardness incurs beatings by others. Only through development can rejuvenation be realized. China was bullied by foreign powers in modern times. A major reason for that was that China was chronically poor and weak during that period. Since then, the great rejuvenation of the Chinese nation has become the unswerving goal that each Chinese generation has striven to realize.[34]

The CCP has been drawing upon this theory to justify its arms development, nuclear program, and manned space program.

Table 5.2 (see next page) provides a summary of the change of narrative of the CCP's membership, legitimacy, and mission during two periods of time: from 1949 to 1976 and from 1991 to present. As discussed before, the fifteen years from 1976 to 1991 is basically a transitional period when the CCP was searching for its identity after the end of Cultural Revolution. As we can see, the content of history and memory has provided a whole set of theories to define the CCP's new membership, legitimacy, and objectives in the post-Mao and post–Cold War era.

DISCOURSE OF NATIONAL INTEREST

Anyone familiar with Chinese official foreign policy statements in the 1980s and 1990s would undoubtedly recognize the moralizing tone that pervades such pronouncements. Although most nations provide moral justification for their foreign policies, the pervasive and patronizing nature of Beijing's ethical rationalizations was striking.[35] Many visiting foreign leaders and negotiators found that prior to dealing with the issues at hand, their Chinese hosts would talk about ethics, principles, and Chinese philosophy. They got down to business very slowly and very often were unpredictable players. It was hard to know whether the Chinese

TABLE 5.2 CCP'S NARRATIVE CHANGE ON MEMBERSHIP, LEGITIMACY, AND MISSION

	1949–1976	After 1991
Membership	• The political party of the proletariat. • The vanguard of the Chinese working class.	• The firmest, most thoroughgoing patriot.
Legitimacy	• Victory of the Chinese revolution. • Chairman Mao Zedong is the people's great savior. • Wherever there is a Communist Party, there the people are liberated. • Only the Communist Party of China can save China.	• We have abrogated the unequal treaties imposed upon China by Western powers and all the privileges of imperialism in the country. • We have thoroughly ended the history of humiliating diplomacy in modern China and effectively safeguarded state sovereignty, security, and national dignity. • Only the Communist Party of China can develop and rejuvenate China.
Mission/ objectives	• The complete overthrow of the bourgeoisie and all other exploiting classes. • The establishment of the dictatorship of the proletariat. • The triumph of socialism over capitalism. • The ultimate aim is the realization of communism.	• Making our motherland strong, the people prosperous, and the nation immensely rejuvenated. • To end the state of separation between Taiwan and China's mainland and achieve the complete reunification of China.

were rational and "normal" negotiators, since it seemed that they believe that ethics and principles were more important than their own interests. Whether citing the principles of world revolution or the "Five Principles of Peaceful Coexistence" or quoting Chairman Mao's anti-imperialist thoughts or Deng Xiaoping's anti-hegemonist theories, Chinese hosts often subjected their foreign visitors to ethical diatribes—what Kenneth Lieberthal calls "moralism." "We have been bullied and humiliated by industrial powers for the last 150 years. You owe us a lot. We are right, and you need to recognize the moral correctness of our stance—and then we can talk about specifics."[36] Few Westerners, if any, were spared this special "treat."

The Chinese intelligentsia have long been dissatisfied with this "morality diplomacy." Their criticisms first publicly surfaced in 1996 with the publication of two influential books. *China Can Say No* (*Zhongguo keyi shuo bu*), by Song Qiang, Zhang Zangzang, and Qiao Bian, created an unusual cultural phenomenon, drawing unexpectedly wide attention from both inside and outside China and becoming the best seller ever on foreign affairs.[37] Although the book has been routinely interpreted as a manifesto of "anti-Americanism," at the level of foreign-policy decision-making, the book touched off heated discussion about Chinese national interests. *Analysis of China's National Interests* (*Zhongguo guojia liyi fenxi*), was written by Dr. Yan Xuetong, a Berkeley-educated international relations professor, and became a national book prize winner.[38] The book makes it clear that specific national interests, not abstract principles, should determine China's foreign policy and that China should not shy away from talking about its own national interests.

The Chinese government's different responses to the crises during the Kosovo War in 1999 and the Iraq War in 2003 demonstrated a major shift in the way that Beijing pursues its foreign policy. For example, comparing Chinese foreign minister Tang Jiaxuan's speeches during the two wars, people may come to the conclusion that Tang has mutated from a moralist into a realist (some might say pragmatist). At a press conference in March 2003, when the minister was asked whether China would use its veto at the UN Security Council, Tang answered as a realist diplomat, pure and simple: "You asked how China will vote. China's practice is always to make an independent judgment and judge the matter on its own merits, follow China's foreign policy and proceed from the fundamental interests of the Chinese people."[39] Tang did not mention one word about principles such as mutual nonaggression and noninterference in states' internal affairs that he had emphasized during the Kosovo War four years earlier.[40] This time, throughout the Iraq conflict, Beijing maintained a low profile. Publicly, China stood with France and Germany in urging that UN arms inspectors in Iraq be given more time to complete their jobs. But China's tone was much milder than France's or Germany's vitriolic condemnation of invaders and hegemonists (as during the Kosovo War) was replaced with smooth talk. Chinese officials have also found that national interest statements can help them gain domestic understanding and support, including from the nationalists. Some officials see that realism is often more effective than moralistic principles in justifying the regime's legitimacy.

Recent visitors to China have noticed that China's new leaders can quickly get down to business and focus on the issues at hand.[41] Instead of talking about principles and morals first, Chinese officials now openly tell the world that their foreign policy serves their interests. Slowly and quietly, China has in effect discarded the old principles, such as the famous Five Principles of Peaceful Coexistence, that used to be the cornerstone of its foreign policy. It is true that even during Mao's time, Chinese national interests were clearly operating in some of its foreign affairs behaviors, such as the Sino-Soviet "alliance" in the 1950s and the Sino-American rapprochement in the 1970s. However, Chinese officials today no longer mask national interests in moralistic statements. Beijing has moved significantly from its previous moral high ground to a much more normal or typical foreign-policy position that recognizes explicitly that it has national interests.

Beijing's new national interest discourse should be understood in the context of Jiang Zemin's "patriotic turn" and the subsequent narrative changes regarding the ruling party's membership, legitimacy, and mission. Since the CCP is no longer the vanguard of the Chinese working class but the party of the firmest and most thoroughgoing patriots, it is natural that the party now needs to dress itself as the guardian of Chinese national interests. Also, the central myth and the legitimacy of the ruling party come from its historical "sacrifices and contribution"—putting an end to the history of humiliating diplomacy in modern China. Therefore, as Peter Gries points out, the legitimacy of China's current rulers is also highly dependent upon successful performance on the international stage. The ruling party is responsible for maintaining China's "national *mianzi*" (face) in its dealings with other nations.[42]

By the end of 1990s, in the years following the patriotic turn and the patriotic education campaign, domestic changes were influencing China's foreign policy. Beijing gradually placed greater emphasis on nonmaterial interests. For this ruling party, some nonmaterial interests that have been defined by historical memory, such as national dignity, face, and respect from other countries, have become equally important or even more important than China's material interests such as trade, security, and territory. Given the fact that the mission of the party is no longer the realization of communism but a nationalistic objective of the "great rejuvenation of the Chinese nation," the important indicators of China's national rejuvenation, such as the reunification with Taiwan and international respect and recognition, have become top objectives in Beijing's foreign policy.

A QUIET REVOLUTION

Jiang Zemin's patriotic turn was a quiet revolution in the history of the Chinese Communist Party. As a major activity of this ideological project, the leadership of the CCP used the content of history and memory to reconstruct the rules and norms of the ruling party. History and memory have provided new resources for the ruling party to redefine its membership, mission, and role.

As discussed in chapter 1, definition and measurement are two problems that hamper the more systematic incorporation of identity as a variable in explaining political action. According to the analytical framework introduced in chapter 1, when collective identity serves as constitutive norms, this identity should:

- Specify rules for group membership (categorization) and accepted attributes (identification).
- Consist of an element of group self-esteem and myth.
- Provide actors with socially appropriate roles to perform.
- Organize actions in ways that help to define the interests of groups.

In this framework, when examining the role of historical memory in the CCP's identity reconstruction, we should first find out what role historical memory plays in the process of this group's categorization, identification, self-esteem, and role identity. Table 5.3 provides a summary of history and memory as constitutive norms in constructing the Chinese Communist Party's new identity.

As discussed in this chapter, the CCP is no longer the vanguard of the Chinese working class and therefore must create a new identity. This new categorization of the party has been developed through the legitimizing affects of historical memory. The CCP is now the "firmest and most thoroughgoing" patriot. The responsibilities and leadership associated with this new role have been based in large part on the history of the past century—that is, in its struggle to put an end to the past humiliation, the

TABLE 5.3 HISTORY AND MEMORY AS CONSTITUTIVE NORMS

Categorization	*Does the content of history and memory specify rules that determine group membership and attributes?* • "The Chinese Communist is the firmest, the most thoroughgoing patriot." • "The responsibility and leadership role of the CCP have been entrusted to it by the history of the past century. The Party has made the biggest sacrifices and the biggest contribution in the struggle of national independence and safeguarding national sovereignty. Only the party can develop and rejuvenate China."
Identification	*Does the content of history and memory help to define the interests of groups?* • The CCP is the guardian of Chinese national interests. • Some nonmaterial interests that are defined by the content of history and memory, such as national dignity, face, and respect from other countries, are equally important or even more important than China's material interests such as trade, security, and territory.
Pride and self-esteem	*Is the content of history and memory an element of group self-esteem and myth?* • "We have abrogated the unequal treaties imposed upon China by Western powers and all the privileges of imperialism in the country. We have thoroughly ended the history of humiliating diplomacy in modern China and effectively safeguarded State sovereignty, security and national dignity. The international standing and influence of socialist China are growing with each passing day."
Role identity	*Does the content of history and memory provide the ruling party socially appropriate roles to perform?* • The two major roles for the ruling party to perform are to "put an end to the past humiliation" and to restore the past glory of the nation, "making the nation immensely rejuvenated."

party portrays itself as having made the greatest sacrifices. This identification also constitutes the basis of the group's self-esteem, myths, and, more importantly, legitimacy for ruling China.

As Jiang Zemin proudly stated, the CCP has "thoroughly ended the history of humiliating diplomacy in modern China and effectively safeguarded state sovereignty, security, and national dignity." By keeping the humiliation of the past embedded in the Chinese mind, the CCP has created an opportunity to become the redeemer of national pride. The central myth of the party is exemplified in the following mantra: "Only the Communist Party of China can save China; only the party can develop and rejuvenate China."

The content of history and memory has also provided two major roles for the ruling party to perform—putting an end to past humiliation (chosen trauma) and making the nation immensely rejuvenated (chosen glory). Without the context of history and memory, it would be difficult to understand Beijing's new narratives on national interests. Achieving some nonmaterial interests that are closely connected with Chinese historical consciousness, such as protecting and advancing China's image and face (*Guoji xingxiang*) in the international theater, has thus become an important priority in Beijing's diplomacy. To maintain its chosen glory of rejuvenating Chinese nationalism, the CCP must achieve these nonmaterial interests.

PREMIER WEN JIABAO'S CHILDHOOD WAR MEMORY

After reading this chapter on the current CCP leaders' use of history and memory as ideological instruments to construct the rules and norms of the ruling party, one might wonder whether the leaders themselves actually *believe* in the message they pass on to their people. When considering the function of culture and identity in the decision-making process, an explanation by an instrumentalist might be no different than an explanation set forth by a realist. In realist theory, actors often deploy culture and identity strategically, like any other resource at their disposal, for the purpose of furthering their own interests. Are the current Chinese leaders simply cool-headed and cold-hearted rationalists who use historical memory instrumentally? Although a few examples may not be sufficient for arriving at conclusive answers to the above questions, the story of Chinese premier Wen Jiabao's childhood war memories can provide us with another perspective in understanding these questions.

Premier Wen paid an official visit to the United States in December 2003. Prior to his visit, the premier participated in a one-on-one interview with the *Washington Post*, and while in the United States, he gave a speech at Harvard University and spoke at a reception dinner given by Secretary of State Colin Powell. On each of these occasions, Wen brought up his childhood war memories and explained why they are important to him. In his opening remarks at Harvard University, for example, Wen said:

> As the speaker today, of course I think I need to introduce myself a little bit to my audience, and I owe you this because in this way we can have a heart-to-heart discussion. As you probably know, I'm the son of a schoolteacher. I spent my childhood mostly in the smoke and fire of war. I was not as fortunate as you as a child. When Japanese aggressors drove all the people in my place to the Central Plaza, I had to huddle closely against my mother. Later on, my whole family and house were all burned up, and even the primary school that my grandpa built himself all went up in flames. In my work life, most of the time I worked in areas under the most harsh conditions in China. Therefore I know my country and my people quite well and I love them so deeply.[43]

Speaking at the dinner Secretary Powell held for him, Wen further elaborated on the reasons he talked about his childhood war memories and used this as his personal introduction.

> It is very difficult to understand someone's thinking and to know this person without knowing his growth experience. I was born during China's Anti-Japanese War. I can never forget the scene when I huddled against my mother stood in front of the bayonets of Japanese soldiers. My hometown was all burned up, including the primary school that my grandpa ran. If my American friends would ask me about my political beliefs, I can tell you clearly and definitely, I myself and my people will use our own hands to build my country well.[44]

At his first press conference shortly after being formally appointed China's premier in March 2003, Wen also talked about his family experiences during the war. "The untold suffering in the days of old China left an indelible imprint on my tender mind,"[45] Wen declared. He explained that knowing someone's early experiences is integral to "understand someone's thinking" and to "having a heart-to-heart discussion" with someone. By saying this, he also emphasized that his childhood memories are an important part of his life and help define who he is. These childhood experiences were instrumental in formulating his political beliefs, and he uses them, he says, "to build my country well."[46]

One of the questions the *Washington Post* reporter asked Wen was, "Is there anything that has made a particular impression on you in your reading about the United States?" The premier answered that he was most impressed by a speech given by President Abraham Lincoln in 1861: "The mystic cords of memory, stretching from every battlefield and patriot grave, to every living heart and hearthstone, all over this broad land, will yet swell the chorus of the Union, when touched again, as surely they will be, by the better angels of our nature."[47] Wen said he had used a red pencil to underline these words when he first read them, and in fact, he was even able to recite the Chinese translation of the whole paragraph. It is very interesting to note that these lines of Lincoln's about memory resonated with Wen over a century after they were uttered. We do not know what exactly in these lines touched him, but it seems apparent that the cords of memory stretching from his burned-out hometown and his grandfather's school still touch him today, and the bayonets of Japanese soldiers were his most unforgettable childhood memory.

The focus in this chapter has been on uncovering how the Chinese Communist Party leaders have utilized historical memory as a tool to regain legitimacy and to mobilize the population. The patriotic education campaign is no doubt an elite-led, top-down political movement. In this campaign, the CCP is the primary educator, setting the entire state machine in motion for this purpose. Likewise, Beijing is the manipulator that controls the content of such education. However, we need to also note that, for the Chinese people, the state patriotic education campaign is not the only source of their knowledge of national history. The foreign invasions, the military defeats, the unequal treaties, and all the details of invaders' atrocities during the "century of humiliation" are not merely a recounting of national history—these stories have become intergenerational narratives, passed down from parents and grandparents. The Anti-Japanese War was fought in most provinces of China and took as long as fourteen years to resolve, beginning from the time Japan invaded Manchuria. Many Chinese families had experiences similar to those of Wen's family, as their houses were burned and they were forced to migrate.

The current CCP leaders utilize China's past history of humiliation to awaken people's historical consciousness and build cohesion. As a

Communist leader, Wen Jiabao is one of the organizers of the party's patriotic education campaign; however, as an individual, his family experiences and childhood war memories have helped shape his own identity and beliefs. Numerous times, I have quoted Beijing's other leaders, such as Jiang Zemin and Hu Jintao, whose actions, both spoken and written, illustrate that each considers himself as one of the people. Each leader has expressed a very strong historical consciousness about China's traumatic national experiences and a determination to make the country a better place. It seems that these leaders are not only educators and manipulators but also believers in their new ideology. While this may not provide them with sufficient justification for that ideology, it does illustrate the importance that this discourse has in Chinese culture and society.

From the official history textbooks to Premier Wen's memories of war, China's national humiliation discourse is not a one-way street of top-down propaganda. The different stories of this chapter have indicated that primordialism (family stories), constructivism (school textbooks), and instrumentalism (elite-led ideological education) are not mutually exclusive, but that they can in fact work together to provide a more comprehensive interpretation of the humiliation discourse in China.

:::

The next chapter explores how historical memory can explain China's behavior during the 2008 Summer Olympic Games and during the relief efforts following the tragic Sichuan earthquake on May 12, 2008.

6

FROM EARTHQUAKE TO OLYMPICS: NEW TRAUMA, NEW GLORY

SAME BED, DIFFERENT DREAMS

For China, 2008 was the year of Olympics. The Olympic torch relay was one of the many unusually elaborate projects that the Chinese leadership prepared for the 2008 Summer Games. After an ornate lighting ceremony in Greece, the torch began its attenuated "journey of harmony" along 85,000 miles, making stops in 135 cities on five continents. It was the longest Olympic torch relay in history, but the tranquillity of the ironically christened relay was short lived. Throughout the torch's journey, protesters heckled, jeered, and even attempted to douse the emblematic flame, all in an effort to bring attention to various problems in China, from human rights abuses in Tibet to environmental issues to Beijing's foreign policy. Amid the chaos as protesters attempted to grab the flame, security officials were often forced to transport the torch past demonstrators via bus.

Protests against China's hosting of the Olympic Games were not unexpected. Controversy had surrounded Beijing since it began bidding for the right to be the host city of the 2000 Olympic Games. The unsuccessful 2000 bid generated very strong anti-Western fury in China. Many Chinese even believed it had been a Western conspiracy, but it wasn't until after Beijing won the 2008 bid that controversy really began brewing. In the months leading up to the Beijing Games, newspapers and nightly news abounded with criticisms about China. A *Foreign Affairs* article even suggested that the upcoming games would be Beijing's "nightmare."

> Demands for political liberalization, greater autonomy for Tibet, increased pressure on Sudan, better environmental protection, and an improved product-safety record now threaten to put a damper on the country's coming-out party. As the Olympic torch circled the globe with legions of protesters in tow, Beijing's Olympic dream quickly turned into a public-relations nightmare.[1]

The Games began to be compared to the xenophobic sentiments of the Boxer Rebellion of 1900 and the Nazi Olympics of 1936. As China built the famed Cube swimming pool and the Bird's Nest National Stadium, turmoil grew around the world and within China.

Yet, what apparently took the world by surprise was that demonstrators targeting the Olympic torch relay to protest the Chinese government were met with equally or more emotional counterdemonstrations by Chinese living and studying overseas. A new tide of nationalism began encompassing not only the younger generation inside China but also the well-educated nationals overseas. In London, Paris, San Francisco, and Canberra, China's national flag was everywhere on the Olympic torch route. For every pro-Tibetan protest, there were considerable pro-Chinese demonstrations. It was reported that more than 20,000 overseas Chinese gathered together in Canberra to "protect" the Olympic torch, many of them students from China studying in various universities in Australia.[2] On the campuses of Duke, Berkeley, Chicago, and many other American universities, Chinese international students staged pro-China demonstrations.[3]

Inside China, anti-French sentiment has grown ever since the disruption of the Olympic torch relay in Paris and French president Nicolas Sarkozy's threat to shun the Olympic Games' opening ceremony. The supermarket chain Carrefour, perhaps the most visible sign of France in China with 112 outlets across the country, became the target of Chinese aggression. In April 2008, demonstrations against branches of Carrefour erupted in more than twenty cities across China.[4] On April 19, for example, hundreds of Chinese demonstrated their frustration with the foreign presence by protesting in front of an outlet of Carrefour in Qingdao, a coastal city of eastern China's Shandong Province. One large placard that protesters brandished gave a comprehensive list of issues, including one that dated back to 1860.

> Say no to Carrefour!!! Say no to French Imperialists!!!
> Strongly protest the Anglo-French invasion of China in 1860;
> Strongly protest the slander of Beijing Olympics in 2008;
> Strongly protest France's interference of China's internal affairs;
> Strongly protest the French media's distortion of the facts;
> Strongly protest France's connivance with criminals to grab our holy flame;
> Strongly protest Carrefour's financial support to Dalai Lama.
> Chinese? Stand up!!![5]

The century of humiliation has indeed provided the Chinese with plenty of historical analogies to use, and they often draw parallels between current and historical events.

"One World, One Dream" was the slogan chosen for the 2008 Summer Olympic Games by the Beijing Olympic Committee after conducting a worldwide search, which included 210,000 possible entries.[6] But is it truly possible for a world full of divergent cultures, national experiences, beliefs, and levels of development to share the same dream? Although this slogan is meant to be one of unity, it is reminiscent of an old Chinese idiom: *tong chuang yi meng*, "Same Bed, Different Dreams." This idiom is used to describe two people whose lives are intimately intertwined yet have very different agendas. Although "One World, One Dream" is a beautiful slogan, "Same Bed, Different Dreams" is often a more accurate expression of the current world situation.

2008 was an eventful year for China. With the New Year came the harshest winter in half a decade, leaving hundreds of thousands stranded over the Spring Festival holiday. No sooner than the snow had melted in March, riots broke out in Lhasa, Tibet, with participants hoping to use the lead-up to the Beijing Olympics to garner international attention for the cause of Tibetan independence. With all eyes on Beijing and the race for Olympic preparation under way, western China suffered yet another natural disaster. On May 12, 2008, an earthquake measuring 8.0 on the Richter scale rocked Sichuan Province, leaving tens of thousands dead or missing and millions homeless. It was this tragedy and the frenzy of Olympic preparations that sparked a zealous nationalism. A casual observer during the spring and summer of 2008 might have been in awe of the sight of thousands upon thousands of Chinese youths, both at home and abroad, shouting "*Zhongguo jia you!*" "Come on, China!" Through the lens of historical memory and national humiliation, let us examine China's behavior during these major events more closely.

GOLD MEDAL

In the summer of 2008, the U.S. Olympic men's gymnastics team won the bronze medal at the National Indoor Stadium in Beijing, while China took the gold and Japan came in second. The U.S. team members hugged one another in excitement after the medal ceremony. With smiles on their faces, they posed for photographs with their bronze medals held high. During an interview, teammate Jonathan Horton told reporters, "I think the most important thing for us was to be on that podium, which we knew that we could do. Bronze, silver, gold, it doesn't matter." While the American team was pleased with their win, a hot topic with Chinese online chat rooms that evening was: "Why were the Americans so happy with a bronze medal?"

In China, bronze medals mean failure, because for many Chinese, only gold medals count. If you visited China during the 2008 Olympics, you would have found a gold medal list on the front page of almost all the newspapers. The table was always ranked by the number of gold medals that each country had won, as people were counting their country's gold medals every day. However, for those Chinese athletes who did not win gold medals, even if they did win silver or bronze medals, the treatment they received from the media, the government, and the general public was totally different from that of the gold medalists.

CCTV's seven o'clock evening news, which serves as a fugleman in reporting on national politics, is the most popular news program in China. If you had watched this program during the Olympic Games, you would have found that nothing else was more important than China's gold medals. Instead of providing coverage of each day's games, it gave detailed reviews of each medal ceremony for Chinese gold medalists. As an integral part of this program, China's national anthem "March of the Volunteers" was played daily (as Chinese athletes took gold medals every day during the games) and took up much of each half hour. In each of these medal ceremonies, the medalists approached and faced the podium steps of different heights. The gold medal podium step was higher than the others and located in the center. Then, as the national anthem for the champion's country was played, the flags of the medalists' countries were raised high in the air. For the thirty-minute CCTV broadcast, time allotment was a challenge because there were so many events each day, and CCTV was required to report on all appearances by senior members of the Politburo.

It is worth noting that CCTV's special coverage of medal ceremonies was not just party propaganda; Chinese people loved watching the medals being awarded. Many people wrote to CCTV and the newspapers saying that what they enjoyed most during the Games was watching the medal ceremonies with Chinese athletes standing on the highest podium as the Chinese national anthem played. Some overseas Chinese wrote to *People's Daily* complaining that they missed the medal ceremonies because the local television stations did not broadcast any of them. Indeed, it is not an exaggeration to say that the medal ceremonies have become a celebration and rite of passage for the whole nation.

To accumulate as many gold medals as possible in the Summer Olympics has been China's national strategy since returning to Olympic competition in 1984. China even has a ministry-level sports authority, the General Administration of Sport of China. The major task of this administration is to prepare for China's participation in the Olympic Games and other major international sporting events. The administration's most important program is the gold medal strategy (*jinpai zhanlue*). The efficient implementation of this program was the secret to passing the United States in the gold medal count in Beijing in 2008. The core of this program is to conduct comprehensive research on Olympic events and then carefully select China's target sports—those disciplines in which the Chinese would have better opportunities to make breakthroughs.

The gold medal strategy has become a national project. The General Administration of Sport of China drew up a comprehensive strategic plan called "The General Outline for Winning Honor at the Olympics, 2001–2010" (*Aoyun zhengguang jihua*).[7] This Cabinet-approved document urged the different governmental ministries and all of the provincial governments to cooperate with each other for the common objective of "winning honor" at the 2004 and 2008 Olympic Games.

Swimming and track and field are historically the two largest and most competitive sports in the Olympic Games. Given the fact that the United States and a few other countries, such as Russia and Germany, have traditionally held supremacy in these disciplines, it would be very difficult for China to make a breakthrough. With this in mind, these competitions were not selected as target sports for Chinese athletes. Most of the target sports are the medal-rich Olympic disciplines that offer more gold medals because of different weight classes, race lengths, and athlete combinations. Shooting and weight lifting, for instance, each have fifteen golds, while canoeing/kayaking has sixteen. China also tends to choose sports that rely on athletes' individual skillfulness and long-term training, such as diving and weight lifting, rather than the disciplines that need more teamwork and physical contact, such as soccer. To the General Administration of Sport of China, it does not matter whether those sports are popular among Chinese people; what matters is the potential for gold medal achievement.

This gold medal strategy proved to be successful in 2008. With home court advantage, China successfully topped the gold medal count with fifty-one, while the United States received thirty-six gold medals, the Russian Federation got twenty-three, and the United Kingdom took home nineteen. However, only one of China's gold medals in Beijing came from swimming or track and field, and China did not get any golds at all from popular sports such as soccer, basketball, volleyball, or tennis. The Chinese won seven of the eight available gold medals in diving, though, and all four of the available golds in table tennis, as well as nine for gymnastics, eight for weight lifting, and five for shooting.

For Chinese athletes, gold medals mean far more than just the usual fame and endorsements; cash bonuses and many other unimaginable perks make Olympic gold medalists very rich people and change their lives forever. As an incentive, the different levels of government, from national to provincial to county, all present cash awards to the medalists. But there is a clear delineation between gold medals and other medals; the government's most lucrative incentive policies are for gold medalists only.[8] Gold medalists also receive many other benefits that silver or bronze medalists do not get, such as apartments or houses, awards from entrepreneurs, preferential admission to prestigious universities, and even another "gold medal" that is made of one kilogram of pure gold—a special gift from the Hong Kong–based Henry Fok Education Foundation.

In his Olympic debut at the 2008 Summer Games in Beijing, Zou Kai, a gymnast from Sichuan Province, won three gold medals—the team gold and individual gold medals for floor exercise and the horizontal bar. According to Chinese media, the handsome rewards he has received since the end of the Games include: 1.05 million yuan (equivalent to $150,000) from the General Administration of Sport of China, 1.5 million yuan from the Sichuang provincial government, 3 million yuan from the government of his hometown of Luzhou, 1.5 million yuan from Hong Kong businessman Tsang Hinchi, 720,000 yuan from the Hong Kong–based Emperor Group, and three pure gold medals and $240,000 from the Henry Fok Education Foundation.[9] Zou also received a 2,000-square-foot apartment and a Volkswagen. Altogether, Zou has received more than 10 million yuan ($1.43 million) in cash bonuses, not including his real estate awards and other income from advertisements and images.[10]

However, what if Zou had earned three silver medals instead of three golds? Then the total award he would have received would have been no more than 2 million yuan ($280,000), and he would not have had many opportunities for advertising endorsements. For those athletes who win only one silver or bronze medal, what they receive is far less.

For example, Zhang Lin, a twenty-one-year-old swimmer from Beijing, won a silver medal in the men's 400-meter-freestyle at the 2008 Summer Olympics—the first-ever Olympic medal in China's men's swimming history. Even though some sports experts praised Zhang's silver medal as a landmark victory with historic significance, he did not receive much media attention. All the media at that time were busily reporting China's growing stash of gold medals. What if Zhang had won a gold medal? If that were the case, he would have soon become the brightest star in China. Unfortunately for him, Zhang was 0.58 seconds behind South Korean gold medalist Park Taehwan, and so Zhang was pushed from the spotlight in favor of gold medal winners in other events.

Why are gold medals so important to the Chinese? To answer this question, we need to first understand the politics of sports in China. China's leaders have a long tradition of using sports as a political tool to strengthen the CCP's legitimacy and the country's social coherence. In 1959, table tennis player Rong Guotuan made history as China's first world champion in any sport. Mao deemed the victory a "spiritual nuclear weapon." In the early 1980s, the whole nation was obsessed with the five consecutive world title victories that the Chinese women's national volleyball team achieved, including the gold medal in the 1984 Summer Olympics. Deng Xiaoping and other Chinese leaders skillfully used this volleyball team and their heroic victories to spur national pride, which had suffered during the Cultural Revolution. At the same time, they also used this team as a kind of symbol of China's reform and rejuvenation. The Chinese government has long viewed winning international games, especially in Western sports, as a rite of passage into the top tier of world power.[11]

Nor is it is only the government—many ordinary citizens also care very much about the color of the medals. It is obvious that the titles of world champion or gold medalist are not just used for the sole purpose of political mobilization. What is behind the Chinese people's "gold medal mentality"? What do the Olympic gold medals mean to the Chinese people?

We would not be able to fully understand these questions without understanding China's history and historical memory of national humiliation. Nowhere is this more evident than in the discourse of the so-called Sick Man of East Asia (*dongya bingfu*).

SICK MAN OF EAST ASIA

In a survey of more than a million Chinese respondents at the end of 2007, the Chinese public's No. 1 Olympics wish was to witness China's 110-meter hurdler, Liu Xiang, win the gold medal in the Bird's Nest Stadium; staging a successful Olympics was ranked only fourth by the Chinese public.[12] Four years prior in Athens, even though Liu was his country's first male Olympic gold medalist in track and field, he was just one of China's thirty-two gold medal winners. The 110-meter hurdles event is not particularly popular in China, especially compared with table tennis and diving, so why was the public so excited about Liu and the 110-meter hurdles?

It's hard to overestimate this young man's popularity in China. Liu's face is everywhere in the country, advertising for Nike, Coca-Cola, and Cadillac as well as many domestic brands. *Forbes*, which ranked Liu second on its list of richest Chinese entertainers, estimated his income at $23.8 million in 2007, behind only the NBA Houston Rockets' center Yao Ming.[13] In China, however, Liu is more popular than Yao. He is the darling of the whole country, known as China's "national treasure," as evidenced by the fact that his legs are insured for $13.3 million.[14] He is also the only athlete to be handed the Olympic torch by President Hu Jintao in Tiananmen Square.

A *China Daily* report explains the special treatment he receives: "Nobody asks him out for a meal in case the food has something bad in it. There is a group of men following him 24 hours a day. He can't even drink a bottle of water if he doesn't know exactly where it comes from." Unfortunately, Liu never got to the first hurdle in Beijing due to a heel injury. His withdrawal was called China's "national mourning,"[15] and Vice President Xi Jinping even called for the entire nation to give Liu their understanding.

To fully understand the Liu Xiang phenomenon in China, we have to know the special national discourse of the Sick Man of East Asia in China. The "Sick Man of East Asia" has long been regarded by many Chinese as a humiliating epithet used by Western imperialists to refer both to the poor physical health of the Chinese people and to China itself.[16] More than a hundred years ago, Chen Tianhua, a late-Qing writer and revolutionary, wrote in a famous 1903 article "Jingshizhong": "Shame! Shame! Shame! This great China, which for many centuries was hailed as the Celestial Empire by neighbors, is now reduced to a fourth-rate nation! The foreigners call us the sick man of East Asia, call us a barbaric, inferior race."[17]

The Sick Man of East Asia discourse must be understood in the context of late Qing Chinese society, when the country was weakened by foreign invasion, natural disasters, domestic unrest, and widespread opium addiction. As more Chinese became addicted to opium during this time period, it became common for well-to-do Chinese to frequent opium dens, neglecting family and community responsibilities. This recreational drug use deteriorated people's health and caused many social problems.

This situation worried many Chinese intellectuals, as they came to feel extremely anxious about the decline of physical prowess of the Chinese people. Liang Qichao, one of the most influential scholars and reformists in the late Qing, was the first person to use *dongfang binfu*—a term he translated from an October 1896 article written by a British man in a China-published English newspaper, the *North China Daily News* (*Tzu lin hsi pao*).[18] Liang frequently used the phrase to emphasize the importance of improving people's physique and called for a national "body reform movement" as part of his package of political reform.[19]

As Susan Brownell notes, for a century this phrase has loomed in the Chinese imagination as an insulting label applied to China by Japan and the West.[20] However, Jui-Sung Yang, a professor at Taiwan's National Chengchi University, argues that the "Sick Man of East Asia" is actually the Chinese people's "imaged humiliation."[21] According to his research, this phrase was initially utilized by the West to describe the weak and corrupt condition of the Qing Empire in the late 19th century, corresponding to the Sick Man of Europe, which referred to the weakening Ottoman Empire during the same period. Yang believes it was not a reference to the Chinese people's health or physique, but that the meaning of the phrase was "reinvented" by some Chinese thinkers, such as Liang Qichao and Yan Fu. These reform-minded intellectuals used this phrase to amplify the sense of national crisis in order to stimulate people's will to reform. Ironically, as time went on, the Chinese people came to regard the term as purely a contemptuous criticism of the Chinese body.

The Sick Man of East Asia discourse is also closely related to sports and the Olympics in China. At the official website of the Beijing Organizing

Committee for the Olympic Games, an article appeared entitled "From 'Sick Man of East Asia' to 'Sports Big Power.'" The website introduction tells us that this is actually a part of Beijing's education campaign to help youths learn more about the history of the Olympics.

> Before 1949, Chinese athletes attended three Olympic Games altogether, but every time came back with failure. They did not get even one medal. A foreign newspaper once put out a cartoon: Under the Olympic five-ringed flag, a group of thin and emaciated Chinese people, wearing mandarin robes and jackets, carry a huge duck egg—zero. The title of this cartoon is "Sick Man of East Asia." This is a humiliation and satire of the Chinese athletes but also indicates that the disaster-ridden old China has no status in the world.[22]

According to Chinese author Zhai Hua, however, this cartoon about Chinese athletes carrying a duck egg was not published in a foreign newspaper, but was actually in a Chinese-language newspaper published in Singapore for the local Chinese community.[23]

A name that has been frequently mentioned in the Sick Man discourse is Liu Changchun, China's first Olympic athlete. As the sole representative from a nation of 400 million, Liu attended the 1932 Los Angeles Summer Olympics. He almost could not make the trip to Los Angeles, as he did not get any financial support from the Nationalist Government, and his trip was made possible only after warlord general Zhang Xue-liang (Chang Hsüeh-liang) provided a personal gift to him. The Chinese government has often used this story to tell people how bad the "old China" was. Liu's story has been adopted by various history textbooks and documentaries in China, and in May 2008, shortly before the Beijing Olympics, a movie based on this story, *The One-Man Olympics*, premiered in Beijing.[24]

Without knowing this background, it would be hard to understand why Chinese officials and media have said that the Beijing Olympics is the fulfillment of China's hundred-year-old dream. As author Xu Guoqi commented in *Olympic Dreams: China and Sports, 1895–2008*, sports in modern China have never been simply for personal fun or physical competition; it is about national honor or shame, about political legitimacy, and even about the Chinese position in the world. Many Chinese enthusiastically believe that victory in international sports games, especially in the Olympics, is the best way to "wipe away" the national humiliation related to the being called the Sick Man of East Asia.

Let us now return to the first question: Why Liu Xiang, and why the 110-meter hurdles? For many Chinese, Liu's world-record-breaking sprints disprove the notion that Chinese bodies are somehow inferior to foreign ones, especially in sporting events. After his 2004 Olympic gold medal win, Liu became an instant symbol for China's ability to conquer the world in any new field that China wants to take on. As a London *Times* article commented: "He beat the West in one of their own events, a cross-cultural contest of speed and strength out of kilter with traditional métiers such as diving, shooting and table tennis."[25] Liu himself also made a famous but controversial statement in Athens in 2004: "My victory has proved that athletes with yellow skin can run as fast as those with black and white skin."[26]

So, why are gold medals so important to the Chinese? In truth, the Chinese championship mentality masks a lingering inferiority complex. As Chen Tianhua wrote in 1903, "Foreigners call us the sick man of East Asia, call us a barbaric, inferior race."[27] Being ridiculed by foreigners because of physical inferiority, even if the ridicule was only imagined, has been an integral part of the Chinese collective memory of national humiliation. Nothing could be better to heal these wounds than achieving gold medals in world-class sporting competitions. But only gold medals can make the Chinese more confident; silver and bronze medals still mean that the Chinese are inferior to the champions, and only gold medalists can enjoy the sound of their national anthem and the raising of their national flag during the medal ceremony. For many Chinese, the sound of "March of the Volunteers" immediately evokes historical sentiment about their country's traumatic national experience, but seeing a Chinese man or woman in the Olympic medal ceremony, standing on the highest podium with the gold medal hanging on his or her neck, erases that pain. Only in this moment can their historical sentiment be released, chosen trauma replaced by chosen glory.

It is because of the lingering memory of national humiliation that the Chinese government and Chinese Communist Party elite can legitimize their rule through sports. Gold medals in international sports have been effectively used as the currency of CCP legitimacy. Comparing today's achievements with that of old China, as in the article "From 'Sick Man of East Asia' to Sports Big Power," has been a common method of the CCP propaganda machine. It is a great achievement for China to go from just one participant and no medals in 1932 to 100 medals and 51 golds in 2008. The success of the CCP government and China's rejuvenation in power and wealth can be illustrated by the world-leading count of fifty-one gold medals, as well as by the splendid opening ceremony and the construction of expensive sports facilities.

Several days before the Beijing Olympics, Chinese president Hu Jintao held a press conference with overseas media who came to Beijing to report on the Games. During the meeting, a reporter from the *Australian* asked a question: The slogan of the Olympic Games is "One World, One Dream." What is your dream and what is the dream of China? Hu replied: "My dream is the same with that of the Chinese people. The dream of the Chinese people is to accelerate the modernization of China, realize the great rejuvenation of the Chinese nation."[28]

As mentioned in the previous chapters, Chinese national pride had been deeply wounded as a result of humiliating experiences in the wake of Western and Japanese incursions. The restoration of the nation's ancient central position on the world stage thus became the most profound factor in shaping China's modern and contemporary history. For many Chinese, including Hu, hosting the 2008 Summer Olympics was a symbol of China's rejuvenation. Through the extravagant opening ceremony, the Chinese government showcased China's historical glory and new achievements. Rejuvenation was indeed the key word and the central theme of the pageant.

The Chinese portray the Olympics as unassailable evidence that China has finally "made it." For many Chinese, fulfilling the hundred-year dream meant an end to the century of humiliation. However, they needed the approval and admiration of the rest of the world, particularly the Western world. As Paul Cohen notes, there was the polarity between "other-directedness" and "inner-directedness"; the former is dependent on the approval of others. If the approval is not granted or is granted only with qualifications, initial pride can suddenly morph into resentment, anger, and deepened insecurity.[29]

NATIONALISM AS A CULTURAL MISUNDERSTANDING

The politics of historical memory provides important explanations for China's motivations and attitude toward the Olympics. However, integral to understanding China's Olympic behavior as well as the politics of historical memory in China is recognizing the significance of China's national deep culture. The cultural value of collectivism and the unique disaster culture, variables uncommon in Western political analysis, have indeed played a crucial role in shaping Chinese politics and national identity. In fact, the recent controversies over the surge of nationalism in China—from emotional counterdemonstrations during the Olympic torch relays to reactions to the tragic Sichuan earthquake and to the Summer Olympic Games—were also generated by cultural misunderstandings.

The individualist-collectivist split is one of the most powerful differences between cultures. It also provides a key to understanding the norms and values that govern social relationships. In collectivist cultures such as East Asian and Latin American countries, a person's identity is deeply rooted in the group mentality. People often associate their individual self-esteem and reputation with that of their fellow social group members. Collectivists have a strong insider/outsider mentality. They tend to be harmonious and cooperative inside the group, and they pay great attention to the image of their own community and government and defend against any criticism from outsiders.

In stark contrast, most Western societies epitomize individualistic, do-your-own-thing cultures. Individualist cultures value independence and autonomy. In the eyes of most Westerners, the disruptions of the Olympic torch relay were conducted by a small group of individual activists. Whether they were citizens of France or the United States, their behavior represented only the limited few. However, for many Chinese people, the message from these demonstrations was understood as: You (the French, the Americans, the West as a whole) don't like us (all Chinese people and the nation of China).

The strong historical consciousness in China can be understood through China's collectivist cultural value. In a collectivist culture, people tend to view themselves as members of groups (families, work units, tribes, nations) and usually consider the needs of the group to be more important than the needs of individuals. As Jonathan Mercer asserts, the more collectivist a culture becomes, the stronger the intergroup discrimination. The more people identify with their own group, the more they will differentiate their group from other groups.[30] Social identity theory also explains the impact of collective identity and esteem on the individual. Individuals seek positive self-identity and esteem, and this is gained by group membership and the development of consensual, in-group identities. People see themselves more as group members than as individuals and act accordingly through "collective action." People who share the same collective identity think of themselves as having a common interest and a common fate.

Common history and collective memory of national experiences very often are important identity makers for a community. As mentioned in previous chapters, China's unique national experience—most significantly, pride in its ancient civilization as well as its collective memory of the century of humiliation—has played a crucial role in shaping the Chinese national identity. This historical consciousness has been reinforced by the current regime's educational socialization through history education and the national patriotic education campaign launched in 1991. A strong sense of victimization makes the Chinese very sensitive about slights to China's dignity, especially from Western countries.

Different political cultures also create communication barriers. Living in an authoritarian political culture, many Chinese people naturally think governmental intentions are at the root of everything. For example, many Chinese have interpreted the pro-Tibetan and anti-Chinese Olympic protests as a nefarious plot by Western governments seeking to prevent the rise of China. The media in China are used for education and propaganda, and most media outlets are the mouthpiece of the ruling party. With no freedom of speech, it is difficult for the Chinese to understand the culture of protest in Western societies. Therefore, Chinese people do not appreciate that internationally broadcast media outlets need to present a variety of opinions.

Another important cultural variable relates to face and face-saving, as showing respect is extremely important in communitarian societies. The Western style of communication, straightforward and direct, has often been interpreted in Eastern cultures as rude and lacking respect. Concern with face and face-saving is the reason politeness and avoiding confrontation are so highly valued. The protests against the Olympic torch relay, as viewed from the Chinese cultural perspective, were extremely rude and disrespectful. For Chinese people, hosting the Summer Olympics is much like a wedding ceremony for a family. This celebration is seen as being part of the "family's" new glory, with much hope and pride attached to it. What many in Western societies haven't realized is that the Chinese saw the attempts to grab the Olympic torch in Paris, London, and San Francisco as attacks on China's fundamental national dignity, face, and pride.

DISASTER CULTURE AND CHINESE POLITICS

In the history of China, the country has been wrought by frequent natural disasters. However, not many people know the striking facts about how China has suffered in this way. Records indicate that about 33 percent of the world's continental earthquakes and nearly 55 percent of all earthquake casualties occur in China.[31] Of the ten deadliest natural disasters in the world in the past two centuries, five happened in China.[32] The world's most damaging floods from 1980 to 2006 were in China.[33] During the course of just sixteen years, China suffered at least nine of them, including the 1998 Yangtze River flood that affected an estimated 200 million people.[34]

Since Chinese civilization originated in the Yellow River basin, it is appropriately termed the "cradle of Chinese civilization." This basin was the most prosperous region in early Chinese history. However, the river has been extremely prone to flooding. From 602 b.c. to the present, it has flooded more than 1,500 times, while its main course changed 18 times. Flooding of the Yellow River has caused some of the highest death tolls in world history, with the 1931 flood killing between 2 million and 4 million people, the deadliest natural disaster in recorded human history.[35]

Inevitably, natural disasters have become an important factor in shaping Chinese politics, economics, and social patterns, as well as the Chinese national character. To deal with the frequent natural disasters, especially the floods that have occurred almost every two years in the Yellow River basin, it was absolutely vital for people to work together and to collectivize power. The agricultural communities also needed strong leadership with the capability to effectively mobilize and organize relief efforts, because disease and famine often followed a major flood. Compared with the small city-states that formed in ancient Greece, a strong central government with a militaristic hierarchy had advantages to mobilize people and provide disaster relief. Scholars have used geography and natural disasters to explain why an autocratic, not democratic, political system was formed in early China.

People all over the world would like to have freedom of speech, self-determination, and popular government. However, living in a country where frequent natural disasters have become part of everyday life, it is understandable that Chinese people also care about whether their government is powerful and effective enough to cope with major calamities. For Western politicians, legitimacy comes from the popular vote, but for the Chinese governments—from the early dynasties to the present—legitimacy, or the "mandate of heaven," to a large extent has been derived from their responsiveness and performance during widespread catastrophes.

The current government's swift and effective response to the Sichuan earthquake of May 12, 2008, was a vivid demonstration of the Communist

Party's power to mobilize its resources. This earthquake measured 8.0 on the Richter scale and affected a large mountain area of about 100,000 square kilometers with a population of more than 15 million. Over 90,000 were killed or missing and at least 5 million people lost their homes.[36] Within the first 72 hours, Beijing dispatched more than 100,000 soldiers to the earthquake-ravaged areas.[37] Many people have contrasted the Chinese government's performance with the way the United States responded to Hurricane Katrina in 2005. Whereas President George W. Bush did not visit the area until a week after the hurricane struck, Premier Wen Jiabao was on the scene in Sichuan the night of the earthquake. International media, unusually, have acknowledged the enormous effort the Chinese government has put into this rescue mission.

In Chinese, the word for "crisis" is composed of two characters: *Wei Ji*. *Wei* means "danger," and *ji* is "opportunity." The current government clearly seized this opportunity. The work that it accomplished would seem to be a "mission impossible" type of situation for many other governments. And through its sincere humanitarian actions, the CCP brought the people closer to the government. Its leaders, especially Premier Wen, won a place in many Chinese people's hearts. The party did an admirable job during other recent large disasters, as well, such as the 1998 Yangtze River flood and the snowstorm in early 2008.

These disasters also exposed many serious problems of the government. For example, people were extremely angry to know that many of the lives lost in Sichuan (especially schoolchildren's) were not a result of the earthquake itself but of the shoddy construction of Chinese schools in Sichuan, which was linked to the corrupt dealings of local Chinese officials in the province. Still, many people believe that the current system has certain advantages in nationwide mobilization and organization during such dire situations. Because of this, the regime will most likely keep its mandate. The history of natural disasters in China is an important background for understanding Chinese politics and the people-state relationship.

The devastating Sichuan earthquake has indeed sparked a strong sense of unity and a surge of patriotism among the Chinese citizenry. On May 19, 2008, the first of three days of national mourning, hundreds of millions of people across China stopped what they were doing and observed three minutes of silence. Through such acts, the nation has demonstrated to the outside world its tremendous spirit and solidarity.

The natural disaster factor helps explain the formation of collectivism in China. In simple terms, collectivism is one effective way for human beings to deal with natural disasters. Cooperation, filial piety, interdependence, and self-sacrifice—values that are prized in collectivist settings—are crucial in fighting disasters.

The natural disaster variable could also help us to understand why many Chinese people share a very strong "One China" mentality. In a sense, the pursuit for national reunification has become a "holy task" for different Chinese governments. The reason is simple: a united central government is more effective in disaster relief. Most of the Yellow and Yangtze River floods affected vast areas across several provinces. Throughout China's history, whenever the central governments were weak and the country was divided into several parts, as in the late Qing dynasty and the warlord period in the late nineteenth and early twentieth centuries, the consequences of natural disasters became crueler and people suffered considerably more.

In fact, such disasters were directly related to the decline of the Qing Empire. The national economy was greatly weakened by the 1887 Yellow River flood, which had an estimated death toll of 2 million, and several other major catastrophes. The Taiping Rebellion further deteriorated the country. Not long after, the Qing dynasty was overthrown by the Nationalist Party (Kuomintang) led by Sun Yat-sen in 1911 and the Republic of China was established. But the young republic also suffered from a number of tragic natural disasters before the Japanese full-scale invasion in 1937: the 1924 Haiyuan earthquake (death toll, 240,000), the 1927 Gulang earthquake (40,000), the 1931 Central China flood (2 million to 4 million), and the 1933 Diexi earthquake (15,800).[38]

NEW GLORY, NEW TRAUMA

During the century following the Opium War, foreign powers carved out spheres of influence, forced the Chinese government to sign a series of unequal treaties, and frequently embarked on armed invasions of China to punish the Chinese for "acts of disobedience." Many Chinese believe that the Western powers took advantage of China's major catastrophes and the feeble leadership of the adolescent emperors in late Qing. Frequent natural disasters were a major contributor to the decline of the Chinese empire. Keeping in mind the collectivist culture, this hundred-year period remains absolutely vital to Chinese national identity.

For many Chinese people, hosting the 2008 Olympic Games is the country's new glory. This event is seen as part of the country's new achievement, with much hope and pride attached to it. However, the devastating Sichuan earthquake the same year is an unforgettable new trauma. As discussed in chapter 1, a country's glory/trauma complex is made up of key historical events that have been critical in defining a society's identity and worldview. Only time will tell how China's new history and new collective memories of the current events will influence the country's future.

While the Chinese believe that crisis creates both danger and opportunity, they also have a special understanding about disasters and traumas. In China, the traumas can sometimes also be used as validation of the idea of chosenness. The Chinese feel that since they have suffered so much, there must be a deeper meaning to that suffering, to be revealed in a positive, even glorious future. As Johan Galtung suggests, new traumas are then expected for the future, with a mixture of fear and lustful anticipation of self-fulfilling prophecies coming true.[39]

During the 2008 earthquake, the Beichuan Middle School lost over a thousand students, most of whom were in their classrooms when the earthquake struck. Two weeks after the earthquake, Premier Wen visited the school's temporary quarters and wrote four characters on a blackboard: *Duo nan xing bang*, "Distress rejuvenates a nation." After his departure, teachers and students could not bear to erase his chalk inscription, which was covered in plastic until the Sichuan Cultural Relics Bureau could devise a method for permanently preserving Wen's handwriting.[40] A *China Daily* article reports that Premier Wen's four characters inspired not only the surviving students but the whole nation.[41] *Duo nan xing bang* is a famous idiom in China. People also use this phrase to refer to the century of national humiliation. They believe that a nation can be successful only after experiencing some hardships and difficulties, as a disaster can also open new opportunities and bring new changes.

In fact, the earthquake and the Beijing Olympics have already brought about some visible changes in China. For example, in a country that has no tradition of volunteerism, both events have sparked widespread volunteerism among Chinese people. More than a million people applied to be volunteers for the Olympic Games, and hundreds of thousands of volunteers from different parts of China, many of them among China's new social class—entrepreneurs and self-employed individuals—went to the earthquake-ravaged areas to offer help. Many nongovernmental organizations and nonprofits, some of which were underground networks before the earthquake, have actively participated in various relief efforts, from fund raising to trauma healing. Some predict that the outpouring of civil spirit in response to the earthquake may reshape Chinese politics, and a civil society may emerge from the earthquake rubble.[42]

There is no doubt that the regime used the Olympics and the earthquake relief to mobilize support. However, even the top-down mobilization had its positive effects. For example, hundreds of thousands of Beijing's adult citizens studied English to prepare themselves to be good hosts in the summer of 2008. Susan Brownell suggested that the general command of English in the city would rise as everyone from volunteers to hotel employees to taxi drivers was expected to study it.[43] This is actually part of a larger process in which everyday people start to see themselves as members of a global community. The city also launched a campaign for "civilized behavior" with the purpose of encouraging its citizens to change some of their common behaviors such as spitting, littering, and jumping ahead in line. Cultural understanding can only be improved through more communication and cultural exchanges, and the Olympic Games are best suited for this. Top-down mobilization and bottom-up civil society, therefore, may not necessarily be mutually exclusive.

Finally, in a country with no free press, the Chinese media's response to the earthquake is intriguing. Newspapers, television, and online media reported events openly. National television provided round-the-clock live coverage. Even though the media are still not at liberty to provide critical commentary, it was already a "great leap forward" for Chinese media.

The series of major events in 2008—from the chaos during the Olympic torch relays to the devastating earthquake and to the Summer Olympic Games—has generated a new tide of nationalism in China. The earthquake indeed sparked a strong sense of unity and a surge of patriotism among the Chinese citizenry, although of course China is not unique in coming together after a national tragedy. Many other countries have endured major tragedies and catastrophes, which have had a similar effect of strengthening civil or nationalistic bonds.

Attempting to compare the situation with the xenophobic sentiments of the Boxer Rebellion of 1900 and the Nazi Olympics of 1936 is unfounded. As explained in the previous section, Chinese youths' emotional counterdemonstrations during the Olympic torch relays were also generated by cultural misunderstandings. Today's young patriots are no different than the young demonstrators in Tiananmen Square twenty years ago. The two generations share the same strong sense of historical consciousness and national pride, and both would like to make their country a better place.

China's long history of coping with great hardships—be they natural disasters or national humiliation—may shed light on the emergence of a new nationalism in China. Throughout such difficulties, China has always sought a strong centralized authority to address these problems effectively. So far, the CCP has been able to fill this role with little problem, thus gaining the support of the people. Unfortunately, the recent events have also exposed the fragility and inconsistencies of the current system.

In China, people apply the Confucian "Boat and Water" theory to describe the relationship between the state and the people: "Water can bear the boat, but it can also capsize it." The citizens uphold the state, but they can also overturn it. According to this theory, the CCP needs to be cautious about the "water," not overusing the people's support during the momentum of either disaster or victory. Furthermore, if the CCP is confident in its vision and capabilities, it does not need to be concerned about support. Why doesn't the CCP work with the people to build a new government, a government that truly represents the people? Special national conditions, such as natural disasters, should not be excuses for political reform.

This chapter has discussed questions such as what the Olympics meant to the Chinese government and its people and why the gold medals are so important to the Chinese. As suggested, it is impossible to fully understand China's Olympics behavior without a clear understanding of the Chinese people's historical memory. International sports provide a venue for symbolic competition between nations. In China, sports are often intertwined with historical memory, and it is this link with history that is explanatory. Generations of Chinese people have been enraged by the Sick Man of East Asia metaphor, which caused them to think Westerners somehow felt the Asian body was inferior. Gold medals in international sporting events have therefore become important measures by which Chinese people prove that they are strong and capable.

Sports nationalism can be seen everywhere in the world, but Chinese sports nationalism is given an especially sharp edge by the grievance over past humiliations. However, the Chinese elite should also listen to Xu Quoqi: "A nation that obsesses over gold medals to bolster nationalist sentiment and its domestic legitimacy is not a confident government. And a population that cannot gracefully accept losses in sports is not a composed and secure population."[44] The events of 2008, when understood in the context of historical memory, are telling not only of China's future but also of its past.

7

MEMORY, CRISES, AND FOREIGN RELATIONS

HISTORICAL CONSCIOUSNESS is rooted in deeply held, often unrecognized thinking patterns. As a part of national "deep culture," historical reminiscences often remain dormant and apparently forgotten. However, during periods of crisis and instability, memory can be activated, and people begin to recall the past more intensely than ever before. In other words, collective memories may become "hot" or "cold," depending on people's emotional temperature. We need to note this special characteristic of collective memory, for if we want to understand how historical memory works, we must examine what factors or circumstances activate historical reminiscences. In this chapter, I illustrate the circumstances under which historical memory can be activated to serve as a major motivating factor in China's conflict behavior.

In the previous chapters, I have discussed how the Chinese Communist Party (CCP) and the government have used history and memory to construct national identity, and particularly to construct the rules and norms of the party. After examining the CCP's new ideological policy in the 1990s, two further questions arise:

1. How did the patriotic education campaign and Jiang Zemin's "patriotic turn" influence Chinese people's worldview, especially their attitude toward and perception of Western countries?

2. How did this reconstruction of identity and the institutionalized historical consciousness influence China's foreign policy behavior during this time period?

If the historical memory explanation that I focus on in this book is a valid, and not just epiphenomenal, explanatory model for China's domestic politics and foreign relations, it should explain Chinese conflict behavior during the 1990s and 2000s. The focus here is on the three U.S.-China crises between 1995 and 2001 and several more recent examples of Chinese foreign affairs to illustrate the impact of the institutionalized historical consciousness on China's foreign affairs behavior.

While it is widely accepted that culture or other ideational factors impact China's foreign policy decision making, there is still uncertainty about to what extent ideational factors bring about conflict behaviors. For the purpose of conducting a systematic research of historical memory and how it helps to explain political outcomes, the analysis of this chapter is based on the analytic framework that I developed particularly for this research project (see table 1.3). According to this framework, there are three causal pathways in which ideas can influence policy behavior: as road maps, as focal points and glue, and as institutions. In other words, ideas influence policy when the principled or causal beliefs they embody provide road maps that increase actors' clarity about goals or ends-means relationships, when they affect outcomes of strategic situations in which there is no unique equilibrium, and when they become embedded in political institutions.

While the crises discussed here have been examined before, this study differs from previous examinations in that it uses historical memory as the main explanatory model. The three U.S.-China crises from 1995 to 2001 were actually China's only "hot" conflicts with foreign countries since the end of the Cold War. They therefore provide the perfect crucible in which to test the activation of historical memory at moments of crisis and conflict. It is for this reason that these events merit reexamination, to provide new perspectives and new interpretations of these crises.

This chapter is divided into three sections. The first section reviews China's conflict behavior during the three crises with the United States and particularly explores three phenomena during the crises: China's unusual escalation of the conflict, its conspiracy mentality toward U.S. foreign policy, and its constant demand for an apology. The second section examines the role of historical memory in perception, interpretation, and decision-making processes during these crises. Also included in this section is a discussion of how memories of past injustices functioned as filters, limiting choices by excluding other interpretations and options. The third section compares the three U.S.-China crises with several other conflicts and disputes that the Chinese government handled during the same time period. It examines how beliefs of history and memory can serve as focal points in influencing policy behavior by causing conflict and constituting difficulties to the settlement of the conflict.

CHINA'S CONFLICT BEHAVIOR

From 1995 to 2001, three major crises erupted between the United States and China: the 1995–1996 Taiwan Strait crisis, the 1999 crisis after the NATO bombing of the Chinese Embassy in Yugoslavia, and the 2001 crisis triggered by the collision of warplanes off the coast of China. Given that all three crises caused military confrontation between the two countries and that the latter two involved casualties, these crises can be considered China's only "hot" conflicts with foreign countries since the end of the Cold War.

The three events share a striking similarity. The escalation of an international incident or mishap in the resolution of a particular crisis was, in each case, caused by China's unusual and unexpectedly strong reaction to allegedly mischievous behavior on the part of the United States. Why did China react so strongly in these three cases? Why are there always conspiracy theories in China regarding U.S. intentions? And why are apologies so important to China? Answering these questions is an important step to understanding China's conflict behavior and foreign policy.

Scholars from different fields have provided various theories and studies on China's conflict behavior during this period of time.[1] Some theorists question whether conflict or even war is inevitable between an established superpower and a rising great power, reflecting the pattern in the two world wars, and whether recurrent conflict represents an inherent "clash of civilizations." Some maintain that the divergent domestic political systems make the United States and China unavoidable competitors.

The existing theories and explanations offer valuable insights into the causes of Sino-American frictions, but none of them fully addresses the questions above. Moreover, most of these studies focus on macroanalyses of institutions, policies, and decision making, without detailed discussion of perception and identity. Even though all three crises were political-military crises, such studies focusing only on political, socioeconomic, and security dimensions of bilateral relations have critical limitations in understanding the deep structure and dynamics of the conflict and cooperation between two countries. The first part of this section will examine the first phenomenon of China's conflict behavior in these crises: intentional escalation of conflict.

INTENTIONAL ESCALATION?

From July 1995 to March 1996, the Taiwan Strait experienced an unusual major crisis, which followed the U.S. decision to allow Taiwanese leader Lee Teng-hui to visit the United States in June 1995. Clearly angered by this decision, mainland China responded with large-scale military exercises and missile tests near Taiwan.

On the surface, Lee's trip to the United States seemed innocuous. He was invited by his alma mater, Cornell University, to pay a private visit to the United States to deliver the graduation address. However, the decision made by the Clinton administration to issue Lee a visa reversed a sixteen-year-old U.S. practice of barring Taiwanese leaders from visiting the country on the grounds that such a visit would antagonize Beijing and contradict Washington's "One China" position.

Beijing reacted quickly and furiously. Three days after Lee finished his six-day visit, on June 16, 1995, Beijing recalled its ambassador from Washington and rejected President Bill Clinton's appointment of a new U.S. ambassador to China. Diplomatic punishment, however, was not China's only strategy. It also responded with three large-scale military exercises and missile tests near Taiwan in March 1996. The three waves of maneuvers were designed to simulate an invasion of Taiwan and its outlying islands and marked a clear escalation of conflict.

In March, the United States deployed two aircraft carriers to the area to deter possible Chinese actions against Taiwan. This represented the largest U.S. deployment in Asia since the Vietnam era in 1975. For the first time since the 1950s, the armed forces of the United States and China confronted each other. Although armed conflict did not ensue, this incident marked the first of three major crises escalated by China. The other two would proceed differently from the Taiwan Strait Crisis. China's response to American action was marked by clouded interpretations of U.S. intentions and demands for an American apology.

The second major U.S.-China foreign relations crisis highlighted here is the NATO bombing of the Chinese Embassy in Belgrade, Yugoslavia, on May 8, 1999. The Chinese Embassy in Belgrade was struck by five 2,000-pound joint direct-attack munitions (JDAMs)—a satellite-guided, near-precision weapon—dropped by an American B-2 bomber flying from Missouri. Three Chinese were killed in the blast and 23 others were injured, leaving the embassy seriously damaged. A joint statement by Secretary of Defense William S. Cohen and Central Intelligence Agency (CIA) Director George J. Tenet issued the same day called the bombing an error. It would later be determined, according to the Department of Defense, that the Chinese Embassy was not correctly entered in databases listing objects that should be avoided. The embassy had moved from another location four years prior, but since it was still listed in the database at its old Belgrade location, the embassy did not appear in the electronic check and was mistakenly targeted.[2]

In the midst of chaos, an emergency meeting of the Politburo Standing Committee was held in Beijing on the night of the bombing, and the committee came to the following decisions:

1. To immediately issue a solemn declaration in the name of the government of the People's Republic of China (PRC) most strongly condemning NATO's bombing of the embassy in Yugoslavia
2. To have the Ministry of Foreign Affairs urgently summon the U.S. ambassador in China and charge him to deliver the strongest protest to the U.S.-led NATO command
3. To conduct organized demonstrations in the vicinity of diplomatic institutions of the United States in China, including those in Beijing, Shanghai, Guangzhou, and Shenyang, while increasing the police presence in surrounding areas to prevent any extremist acts.[3]

All these decisions were implemented in the days to follow.

Among these decisions, the most unusual was to conduct demonstrations in the vicinity of U.S. diplomatic missions. The Chinese government generally banned any large gatherings or demonstrations for fear of unrest, especially after the 1989 student movements. But this time, the government of China organized the demonstrations themselves.

Soon afterward, major cities in China saw their biggest and angriest demonstrations in decades. Thousands of students chanting anti-American and anti-NATO slogans marched in Shanghai, Chengdu, and

Guangzhou. In Beijing, about 100,000 protesters converged on the U.S. Embassy, pelting it with rocks and debris, wrestling with police, and attempting to set fire to embassy vehicles. Hundreds of police encircled the embassy to shield it from the protesters who surrounded the diplomatic mission. U.S. ambassador James Sasser and his staff became "essentially hostages" inside the embassy building. The residence of the U.S. consul general in the southwestern city of Chengdu was stormed and partially burned.[4]

The collision of warplanes off the Chinese coast in April 2001 was the third crisis embroiling the United States and China after the end of the Cold War. On April 1, a U.S. EP-3E Aries II airplane on a routine surveillance mission near the Chinese coast was intercepted by two Chinese F-8 fighter jets and subsequently collided with one of them. The damaged U.S. airplane and its twenty-four crew members made an emergency landing on China's Hainan Island at Lingshui, where Chinese officials detained the crew. The damaged Chinese fighter jet crashed into the water. Chinese efforts to find the pilot, Wang Wei, were unsuccessful, and it was later determined that he had died.[5]

After the April 1 incident, China immediately charged the United States with responsibility, stating that the U.S. airplane had turned suddenly into the Chinese jet and then landed at Lingshui without permission. The Chinese issued a statement on April 4 demanding a formal apology. The United States responded that the airplane had been operating outside Chinese territorial waters, that the EP-3 was a large, slow-moving airplane relative to the Chinese F-8, and that the airplane had issued a mayday alarm and landed in distress. Consequently, the United States determined that an apology was neither necessary nor appropriate and insisted that China allow the immediate return of the crew and the airplane to the United States. President George W. Bush said openly that he would communicate with China in a "tough, clear and open way." Following the United States' refusal to issue an apology and China's decision to detain the plane's crew while it investigated the collision, the incident escalated into a major crisis.

A review of the conflict processes indicates that China had intended to intensify the conflict during all the three crises. However, it was hard to understand why China wanted to take the lead in their escalation and reacted so strongly in these cases. If we look back at China's foreign policy during the course of these three crises in 1995–2001, we notice that China had actually desired simultaneously to develop a better bilateral relationship with Washington. Beijing has consistently tried to avoid direct conflict with the United States since the end of the Cold War, adopted moderate stances on numerous occasions, and at times even submitted to resolutions that it considered detrimental to China's national interests (e.g., the World Trade Organization [WTO] and arms control).

It should also be noted that China had also experienced high-level tensions and conflicts with other nations during this period of time, but did not choose to escalate those incidents. For example, there were territorial disputes between China and some Association of Southeast Asian Nations (ASEAN) countries. In the late 1990s, as a new strategy of strengthening their territorial claims, the Philippines and Vietnam took the lead to intensify the situation by seizing and attacking Chinese fishermen and fishing boats. However, the Chinese government demonstrated a very restrained response to these provocations. None of these disputes had been escalated into a major conflict or crisis. In 1996, large-scale anti-Chinese riots happened in Indonesia, but the Chinese government expressed only verbal concern and did not take any actions. It did not cause any diplomatic conflict between the two countries.

The question is why China was more aggressive in its approach to the United States, the only superpower of the world, yet more conciliatory toward smaller countries in managing conflicts. We need to know what factors generated these unusually vehement reactions. Moreover, why did China cooperate with the United States on some issues but turn aggressive in these instances?

Having raised these questions about China's unusual escalation of conflict, let us turn to the second phenomenon of China's conflict: a conspiracy mentality toward U.S. foreign policy. We will come back later to examine these questions in more detail.

AMERICAN CONSPIRACY

A conspiracy mentality toward U.S. foreign policy exists to a greater or lesser degree in all regions of the world and is alarmingly prevalent in China. Many U.S. diplomats and scholars have been surprised to find that every time there is an incident between the two countries, a horde of conspiracy theories in China is soon to follow. Such theories all carry the same assumption: that there is a larger, overarching U.S. scheme or hidden agenda behind current events.

There are various conspiracy theories regarding Washington's policies that have spread throughout the whole of China. David Shambaugh has concluded that, from the standpoint of many Chinese people, the United States has a master plan to "divide China territorially, subvert it politically, contain it strategically, and frustrate it economically."[6] Conspiracy theories have spawned their own discourse in China and captured the public imagination, exacerbating a heavy, pernicious political atmosphere between the two countries.

There are numerous examples of this conspiracy mentality in all aspects of China-U.S. relations. Many Chinese strategic analysts draw a parallel between Ronald Reagan's "Star Wars" plan and George W. Bush's Missile Defense and Space Weapons Program. The former contributed to the collapse of the Soviet Union, and they believe that the latter aims to do the same thing to China.[7] These theories are held not only among those within the government sphere but also by the common Chinese citizens, who have their own presumptions of America's intentions. Many Chinese interpreted the pro-Tibetan and anti-China Olympics protests in the spring of 2008 as a nefarious plot by Western countries seeking to prevent the rise of China. During the Severe Acute Respiratory Syndrome (SARS) outbreak in China in the spring of 2003, some Chinese believed the SARS virus to be a biological weapon manufactured by the United States.[8] The reason, many Chinese surmised, for the United States to administer this biological attack was perceived intimidation and the potential threat of China's rise to U.S. dominance in the world.

Information availability is no doubt a major concern for any research on contemporary Chinese foreign and security policy. In fact, it is often quite difficult to obtain information in any country on governmental decision making, particularly if such matters are relatively recent and remain classified. In this research, however, a special manuscript—*Zhu Rongji in 1999*—provides illuminating data on China's decision makers. This book contains an extraordinary collection of memos, speeches, notes, and other secret documents smuggled out of CCP archives. These documents reveal what top Chinese decision makers were thinking during the embassy crisis. One section of this book, "The Bombing of China's Embassy in Yugoslavia," provides detailed minutes of the emergency meeting of the Politburo Standing Committee held in the early morning of May 8, 1999.

Zhu Rongji in 1999 was first published in Chinese in the United States and then translated into English and published in the American academic journal *Chinese Law and Government*.[9] As a *New York Times* article comments, the book's appearance suggests there is a growing movement by a group of powerful Communist Party insiders to rewrite party history and influence China's future by leaking information to the West.[10] According to this article, many China scholars, including Andrew J. Nathan, the chair of the Department of Political Science at Columbia University who edited the English translation of the book, vouched for the book's authenticity and the integrity of the person or persons involved.

The Politburo's Standing Committee is China's supreme decision-making body, a group of seven to nine people who oversee the Communist Party of China. The power of the committee resides largely in the fact that its members generally hold simultaneous positions within the government of the PRC. In the early morning of May 8, 1999, several hours after the Belgrade bombing, an emergency meeting of the Politburo's Standing Committee was called to discuss the situation and decide countermeasures. Each committee members shared his view of the situation and the countermeasures proposed. The meeting minutes include a detailed record of all seven Standing Committee members' remarks. Below are those sections on the bombing incident.[11] I have added italics for emphasis and noted the speaker's party position at that time.

- Li Peng, chairman of the National People's Congress, ranked No. 2 in the Standing Committee of the Politburo: "Comrades! The blood-stained embassy incident is not an isolated matter and is not merely an *insult* and challenge to the Chinese people; it is *a carefully crafted plot* of subversion. The *anti-China forces* in the world are cunningly making use of various unfavorable factors both in and outside China to wantonly *provoke disturbances*. . . . The United States is typical of those who 'take a foot when given an inch' and who '*bully* the weak but fear the strong.' This incident, more than anything else, reminds us that the United States is an *enemy*. It is by no means a friend, as some say."
- Hu Jintao, vice president of the PRC, ranked No. 5, talked mainly about the countermeasures. He emphasized that the most important thing now is to "persist in normal work and studies and hit back at the *anti-China forces* with real actions to *reinvigorate China*."
- Li Lanqing, vice premier, ranked No. 7: "This is an open *provocation* to the people who have endured all the disasters of warfare and who love world peace. It is a serious challenge to the Chinese government! In the future, direct confrontation between China and the United

States will be unavoidable! The intention of the United States in doing this thing is quite obvious. It wants to *sound China out* and to *create chaos in China*. We must not play into their hands."

- Li Ruihuan, chairman of the Chinese People's Political Consultative Conference, ranked No. 4: "The possibility cannot be excluded that this was *a premeditated plot* of the United States *to create chaos in China*, to have China's young people vent their hatred of the United States on the Chinese government. . . . The Americans hope for nothing better than to *provoke contradictions* between the [Chinese] government and the broad masses of people, especially young students, and thereby shift the crisis. . . . In the face of the U.S. *provocations*, we must truly show the nation's strength and roar out that the Chinese people will not be *humiliated*."
- Zhu Rongji, premier, ranked No. 3: "Whatever the true reason for the bombing, there is no question that the United States feels absolutely *no respect* for China. Nor can the possibility be excluded that it is '*throwing a stone to probe the path*' and *sounding out China's strengths* with a view to dealing a strategic blow at China. The United States is claiming over and over again that the bombing was merely an accident and is making various inept statements in an attempt to cover up its true intentions—statements that do not sound plausible even to Americans' ears. This is 'advancing a foot when given an inch' and barefaced *bullying*! . . . The embassy bombing is no more than a *ploy* used by the United States."
- Wei Jianxing, chairman of the Communist Party's Central Commission for Discipline Inspection, ranked No. 6: "The bombing of our embassy was an out-and-out violation of and trampling on our sovereignty. It is an *insult* to the *dignity* of the Chinese people. . . . Chinese cannot remain silent any longer."
- Jiang Zemin, president of the PRC and chairman of the CCP, ranked No. 1: "If we analyze the world strategic setup and the situation in the Asia-Pacific and surrounding regions, we will easily see that, by wantonly using guided missiles to attack our embassy in Yugoslavia, *the United States is sounding out our support for the Yugoslav Federation and our reaction to, and stand on, international crises and conflicts*. The United States wants, by means of this incident, to ascertain the strength of China's reaction to international crises and conflicts and especially to sudden incidents; to ascertain the voice of the people, the stance of public opinion, and the government's opinion,

and the measures it will take. These things will serve the United States as important grounds for implementing the new NATO strategy, carrying out the U.S.-Japan security treaty, formulating its Asian-Pacific security strategy, and intervening in matters on China's periphery and even in China's internal affairs.

Hence the air attack on our embassy in Yugoslavia may be part of an even greater *plot*, such as forcing China to become involved in these crises and conflicts, distracting China's attention from the 'one center and two basic points'[12] and causing China to be bogged down in upheavals or saddled with the heavy burden of warfare. We must have a clear understanding of the situation and accurately forecast and grasp developments. If we analyze Sino-U.S. relations from the perspective of international strategy, we must, of course, reserve the right to react strongly to the bombing of our embassy in Yugoslavia."

A quick content analysis of those remarks indicates that, of the seven top leaders, five of them used the term *provocation* or *insult*, four of them regarded the bombing as bullying or used terms such as *dignity* or *humiliated*, four of them directly called the bombing a U.S. plot or ploy, and none of them accepted the U.S. explanation that the bombing was a technical error. For the majority of China's top leaders, their first response was to interpret the incident as an open provocation and insult to China and the Chinese people. It was "barefaced bullying" that hurt the dignity of the Chinese, and therefore China must "roar out that the Chinese people will not be humiliated."

Li Peng framed the incident as a "carefully crafted plot" of subversion. The majority of the Politburo members agreed that "the possibility cannot be excluded that it was a premeditated plot of the United States" or "may be part of an even greater plot." According to their interpretations, the American plot could include the following:

- Creating chaos in China—the United States hoping to use this incident to "provoke contradictions between the Chinese government and the broad masses of people."
- "Throwing a stone to probe the path"—using Jiang Zemin's words, the United States wanted "to ascertain the strength of China's reaction to international crises and conflicts; to ascertain the voice of the people, the stance of public opinion, and the government's opinion, and the measures it will take."

Jiang even presumed that the air attack could be part of an "even greater plot," such as forcing China to become involved in these crises and conflicts, distracting China's attention from economic development, or causing China to be bogged down in upheavals or saddled with the heavy burden of warfare. Whatever the proposed conspiratorial motive, Chinese leaders agreed that the American bombing was a plot to undermine China.

A *People's Daily* front-page editorial on May 19, 1999, echoed the leaders' interpretations: "We have maintained stability and development, and made achievements that the enemy forces in the West could no longer tolerate. That is why they attempt to disquiet us, so as to take action against us in a time of chaos and with menace."[13] In the CCP propaganda and information system, the *People's Daily*'s editorial can be read as the government's official statement. Many of China's international analysts also shared their leaders' view that the United States wanted to use the bombing "to create chaos in China."

At the time of the embassy bombing, I was working for a Beijing-based government think tank on international security. A report concerning the incident submitted to the top leadership by my institution determined that creating internal chaos in China was the No. 1 motivation for the United States to bomb the Chinese Embassy. During the internal discussions of the drafting of this report, several people doubted that the Clinton administration would be part of the conspiracy, as there was no evidence to support this assertion. However, the majority of researchers agreed that the bombing was an intentional action approved by top U.S. leaders.

The emergency meeting of the Politburo Standing Committee came to an unusual conclusion. The CCP headquarters in several major cities received this instruction on the morning of May 8, 1999:

> Conduct demonstrations, in an organized manner, in the vicinity of diplomatic institutions of the United States in such cities as Beijing, Shanghai, Guangzhou, and Shenyang, and at the same time have public security departments increase police presence in areas around American diplomatic institutions in China to prevent extremist actions.[14]

Again, it should be pointed out that the Chinese government generally prohibited large gatherings or demonstrations after the 1989 Tiananmen Square incidents. This time, though, it would go against its own fears of unrest in trying to make a statement to the world.

The student demonstrations and violent actions in several Chinese cities shocked the U.S. media, which quickly pointed blame at the Chinese government for inflaming the protests. It was also argued by some China watchers that the Chinese people's anger and placement of blame were genuine and understandable.[15] The key point of this debate is how the average Chinese, especially the student demonstrators, interpreted the bombing. Did *they* believe it was a technical mistake?

Dingxin Zhao conducted a research study focused on issues relating to the embassy bombing several months after the incident.[16] It included a survey of 1,211 students and interviews of sixty-two individuals in three elite universities in Beijing. According to Zhao's *China Quarterly* article, the majority of the respondents believed or strongly believed that the embassy bombing was premeditated by either the U.S. government (75.1 percent) or the U.S. military (77.8 percent). Only 3.8 percent of the respondents agreed that the bombing could be a technical error.[17] The survey also indicated that 70.7 percent of the respondents agreed or strongly agreed that the Chinese embassy was attacked because China was weak. According to the research, many students believed that if the United States took China seriously, the first thing it would do before planning an air strike would be to mark out the location of the Chinese Embassy on their maps so as to avoid any potential accidents. Thus, the students inferred that the United States did not take China seriously. This perception greatly hurt their sense of national pride. More than half of the respondents (54.2 percent) agreed or strongly agreed that the embassy bombing was intended to induce political instability in China.[18]

It could be argued that the students' views of the embassy bombing were influenced by government propaganda. However, the problem with this notion is that the Chinese students exposed to government propaganda were not the only ones with conspiracy theories. John Holden, the president of the National Committee on U.S.-China Relations, witnessed the anti-U.S. demonstrations in Beijing during the crisis. According to a *Duowei Times* interview with Holden, he was surprised that most Chinese people did not accept the U.S. explanation about the bombing; he was further surprised when Professor Ezra Vogel, who teaches Chinese politics at Harvard University, told him that most Chinese students at Harvard also believed that the embassy bombing was intentional.[19] Holden could not understand why the Chinese students at Harvard, who read American newspapers and watched American TV news programs every day, would share the same interpretation of this incident as the Chinese students living in China.

The events surrounding the bombing of the Belgrade embassy are still a mystery. Neither Chinese leaders nor the Chinese people seem to believe that the bombing of the embassy was a technical mistake. Instead, they perceive a vast conspiracy within the U.S. government to conduct the bombing. But why did Chinese leaders, the public, and even Chinese students in elite American universities all tend to reject U.S. insistence that the bombing was an accident? Why was it that the Chinese interpreted the incident as a conspiracy by the United States to humiliate, test, and bully China? The Belgrade bombing touched off the largest anti-American demonstrations in China since the height of the Cultural Revolution in the late 1960s. Although many scholars have conducted research on this incident, the above two questions have not been fully studied and answered.

For a military incident that occurred only a few years ago, there is still a lack of accessibility for academic researchers to determine the real reason behind the bombing on May 8, 1999. Was the bombing a pure technical mistake caused by the use of outdated maps, as the Department of Defense and the CIA assured the world? Or are there other untold motivations and secrets, as some have speculated? For example, according to an article in the *Observer*, NATO intentionally bombed the embassy because it was being used as a relay station for Yugoslav army radio signals.[20] There are two schools of thought: the accident school and the conspiracy school. Both in China and the United States, there continue to be different theories, including conspiracy theories, about the nature of the bombing.

The purpose of this chapter is not to investigate the secrets behind the incident. Rather, it is to focus on understanding the way in which the Chinese leaders conceptualized and interpreted this incident. Was the Chinese interpretation based on rational assessment of the evidence, intelligence, and knowledge of the American military and political leaders? What factor "tipped" their interpretation? Why did conspiracy theories regarding U.S. intentions constantly surround these crises? Before examining these questions, let us look at the third phenomenon of China's conflict behavior: the constant demand for apologies.

AMERICAN APOLOGIES

The demand for an apology has become commonplace in Chinese diplomacy. For many Chinese, the biggest hurdle to improving Sino-Japanese relations has been the Japanese reluctance to offer a formal apology to China for its World War II atrocities. Requesting apologies also became a sticking point in negotiations between China and the United States in 1999 following the NATO bombing of China's embassy in Belgrade and in April 2001 in the wake of the American EP-3 surveillance aircraft collision.

Following the incident in 1999, the Clinton administration offered an official apology almost immediately. On May 8, the same day the Belgrade tragedy occurred, Secretary of State Madeleine Albright sent an official letter to China's Ministry of Foreign Affairs, stating:

> I know Ambassador Sasser and other officials have already conveyed our deep regret about the tragic, accidental fall of bombs on your Embassy in Belgrade, but I wanted to express personally to you my sincere sorrow for the loss of life, injuries, and damage. On behalf of my government and as a member of NATO, I extend sincere apologies and condolences.[21]

On May 10, President Clinton spoke in front of the media: "Again I want to say to the Chinese people and to the leaders of China, I apologize, I regret this, but I think it is very important to draw a clear distinction between a tragic mistake and a deliberate act of ethnic cleansing, and the United States will continue to make that distinction."[22] Clinton also sent a letter to Chinese president Jiang Zemin making clear the U.S. government's deep regret. Clinton tried twice to talk with the Chinese president over the bilateral hotline, but Jiang refused to take his calls.[23]

On May 14, Jiang finally agreed to a phone conversation with President Clinton. Clinton expressed his sincere regrets for the tragedy in Belgrade and sent his personal condolences to the injured staff and family members of the victims. He promised that there would be an investigation of the incident and that he would let the Chinese people know the truth as soon as possible. On December 16, 1999, after lengthy negotiations, Beijing and Washington agreed on a compensation package.

The collision of warplanes in 2001, which set off the third major crisis between the United States and China, ended in lengthy negotiations focused on the issue of apology. Because the Chinese blamed the United States for the crash, Beijing demanded a formal apology:

> The US side should make a prompt explanation to the Chinese government and people about the US plane's ramming of the Chinese jet and its infringement upon China's sovereignty and airspace, *apologize* to the Chinese side and bear all the responsibilities arising from the incident.[24]

Although initially Beijing also called on the United States to stop reconnaissance flights over China's coastal waterways, eventually that demand was taken off the table. An official apology was Beijing's only request for the solution of this crisis.

The United States, however, was adamant that it would not apologize. Washington insisted that because the U.S. plane was outside China's territorial waters, it should not have been approached by the Chinese fighters. Furthermore, the EP-3 had issued a mayday distress call before making an emergency landing and therefore had acted in accordance with established international aviation procedures. Because of these circumstances, President George W. Bush would not apologize and demanded the Chinese government release the twenty-four crew members. "Every day that goes by increases the potential that our relations with China could be damaged," he declared.[25] Secretary of State Colin Powell flatly rejected China's demand for an apology. "I have heard some suggestion of an apology, but we have nothing to apologize for," Powell said on April 3. "We did not do anything wrong."[26]

The two governments found themselves in a dilemma. The Chinese made it clear they would not release the U.S. crew without an apology, but it seemed the United States was never going to offer a formal apology. The two positions seemed irreconcilable. As a Reuters article said: "The fate of 24 Americans, a state-of-the-art spy plane and perhaps the future of China-US relations, may in the end boil down to a single word."[27]

The standoff between the two governments lasted eleven days. On April 11, Ambassador Joseph W. Prueher sent a letter to Chinese foreign minister Tang Jiaxun reflecting the outcome of discussions between the two governments. It was the fifth version of the letter that was passed to the Chinese, containing the exact wording that was the object of days of struggle between U.S. and Chinese diplomats. The English-language version of the letter said President Bush was "very sorry" the EP-3 entered Chinese airspace and made an emergency landing on Hainan Island "without verbal clearance." It also asked Beijing to "please convey to the Chinese people and to the family of pilot Wang Wei that we are very sorry for their loss."[28]

The Beijing government did its own translation of the English text, in which the double "very sorry" became "*shenbiao qianyi*"—an expression of deep apology or regret, which was what Washington had gone to pains to avoid in its own Chinese version. The Chinese media were required to use this version in their reports.[29] On April 12, the Chinese government issued a statement: "Since the U.S. government has already said "*shenbiao qianyi*" (used "*very sorry*" in its English version) to the Chinese people, the Chinese government, out of humanitarian considerations, decided to allow the 24 people from the U.S. spy plane to leave."[30]

THE PUZZLES AND THE ARGUMENTS

The three conflicts discussed in the previous section create several foreign relations puzzles. Scholars from different fields have attempted to explain China's foreign policy decision making and conflict behavior during this period of time, but as we will see, each raises more questions than are addressed.

According to the realist model, the Sino-American conflict is a clash of national interests, caused by a struggle for power. For example, Abram Shulsky believes the confluence of two tendencies—China's search for a more active political-military role in the affairs of East Asia, and the U.S. policy of maintaining strong military forces in the region—inevitably raises the possibility of military conflict between the two countries.[31] Richard Bernstein and Ross H. Munro argue that Sino-U.S. competition will become the major global rivalry in the opening decades of the twenty-first century. This rivalry will occur due to Chinese desires to dominate Asia and the long-standing U.S. policy of preventing a single country from dominating that region.[32] The debate about China as a peer competitor revolves around simple realist notions of how international politics works: Power is what matters, and what matters in power is one's relative capabilities compared with those of others, especially other great powers.

Some scholars believe that the post–Cold War U.S.-China relationship represents a pattern of "superpower/great power competition."[33] When a nation that has become economically and militarily dominant on a global scale is confronted by a rapidly developing regional power with its own imperative needs for identity, dignity, and independence, history shows that the resulting conflict can easily escalate out of control. As Robert Gilpin explains, this scenario creates the risk of a "hegemonic war."[34]

For a realist critic, China's demand for an apology could be merely a "test-of-wills" power play. Apology or not is a contest over maintaining (for the United States) or (re)claiming (for China) relative power in the region. As Kevin Avruch and I have asked: "Why *apology*? The realist might say, in a clash of wills any issue will serve: why not apology?"[35]

The realist position is certainly plausible in some aspects. In both countries, there were nationalists who did take the apology as a test of wills. For example, President Clinton was strongly criticized by some U.S. media for "kowtowing" to China when he apologized five times for the embassy bombing. Even Henry Kissinger asked him to "stop apologizing."[36] In 2001, a *Weekly Standard* article called President Bush's offer of two apologies to China over the EP-3 incident the "profound national humiliation" of the United States.[37]

Scholars who have conducted research on the EP-3 crisis agree with each other on one point: As Peter Hays Gries and Peng Kaiping put it, "At the last stage of the EP-3 crisis, the two governments somehow were cooperating with each other to play-act."[38] Albert Yee explains the resolution of the incident as the outcome of two-level negotiations. Chinese and American leaders initially confronted a diplomatic impasse because their minimally acceptable positions did not overlap. Faced with strong domestic constraints, they reached a compromise in large part by jointly lowering their initial demands in ways that deflected the criticisms of their respective domestic hard-liners.[39] The two governments used their linguistic differences and the resulting resource of linguistic polysemy to write their respective "official" translations of final texts in ways that allowed both sides to please their domestic audiences.[40]

However, if it was merely a test-of-wills power play, why did the two governments cooperate with each other to play-act? Why did Clinton apologize five times for the embassy bombing in 1999? And why did Bush keep silent when China translated "very sorry" as a formal apology in 2001? In the case of the embassy bombing, any country that made such a tragic mistake should apologize, and Clinton did, for it was a normal international practice, not a test of wills. However, with regard to the EP-3 incident, initial Chinese demands included a demand that the United States halt all surveillance flights. In a national-interest calculation, this requirement should have been more important than an apology, but an American apology became the sole demand of the Chinese in the negotiations. Why were apologies from the U.S. government in particular so important to the Chinese government, and how do we understand China's "apology diplomacy"?

Critics of the realist model assert that realist approaches overlook the role of meaning and representation in explaining or accounting for state action. Some argue that mainstream international relations theory is ill suited to address the issue of intentions.[41] The realist model fails to explain why China often tried hard to avoid direct conflicts with the United States and other countries on issues that were vital to its national interests, such as trade (WTO membership), security (arms control), and territory (South China Sea), but took the lead in escalating conflicts on such occasions as the United States' failure to request permission for a private U.S. visit by Taiwan's president in 1995 and the EP-3 accident.

Differing with realists, Samuel Huntington provided a special model to explain conflicts in the post–Cold War era. According to him, the main lines of future world conflict will take the form of an impending "clash of civilizations." In terms of Sino-American relations, Huntington states: "With the Cold War over, the underlying differences between China and the United States have reasserted themselves. . . . A 'new Cold War' is under way between China and America."[42]

Culture is no doubt one of the most important divisions between the United States and China. However, there is very little consensus as to the role played by culture in Chinese foreign policy. Some scholars tend to use Chinese traditional cultural traits (especially Confucianism) to analyze Chinese conflict behavior. Others regard communist ideology and Maoism as the conceptual foundations of Chinese contemporary approaches to conflict. But how can we filter out communist behavior from Chinese behavior from Confucian behavior? The two groups of scholars would surely reach different conclusions regarding China's conflict style and approach to compromise.

In his book *Cultural Realism*, Alastair Iain Johnston suggests that there was no pacifist bias in traditional Chinese strategic culture; on the contrary, China's leaders have always regarded force as an important part of national prestige and survival.[43] On the other hand, some scholars suggest that even today, the nonviolent preaching of Confucian-Taoist philosophies manifests itself in the general desire of China's leaders for accommodation over violence.[44] However, culture is not timeless or changeless; even Confucianism is a dynamic and evolving doctrine. Nor is culture merely a set of customs.

Nobody would agree that the United States and China are doomed forever to misperceive and misunderstand each other. The 2001 crisis over the apology issue could not be ascribed simply to variant etiquette, moral law, or cultural semantics regarding the concept of "apology." Therefore, there must be more to the story of Chinese apology diplomacy than simply a cultural difference. The search for answers to these questions has led to the reexamination of history and memory—topics often neglected in foreign relations analysis. The following sections examine the three crises through the perspectives of historical memory.

HISTORICAL MEMORY AS A ROAD MAP

Collective identity affects the way actors understand and interpret the outside world and incoming information. Guided by the theoretical framework introduced in chapter 1, this section will examine several research questions to illustrate the relevance and importance of historical memory in explaining China's responses to the three crises. These questions examine the role of historical memory in perception, interpretation, and decision-making processes. A wide range of data, including official documents, leaders' speeches, history textbooks, and newspaper editorials will be studied. The purpose of this analysis is to examine how ideas of history and memory have played the role of road maps in China's approaches to the three crises with the United States—the only three hot external conflicts since the recent institutionalization of historical memory.

FRAMES, ANALOGIES, AND INTERPRETATION: HOW CHINA VIEWED THE THREE INCIDENTS

In the eyes of many Americans and international observers, the following assumptions can be made:

1. Issuing Taiwanese president Lee a visa to deliver the graduation address at his alma mater was innocuous.
2. The 1999 embassy bombing was merely a technical mistake, and the U.S. government offered official apologies fully and quickly.
3. The 2001 plane collision was an accident outside Chinese territorial waters.

These observers would not consider any of these incidents to be intentional or to suggest any kind of bullying or aggression toward China or the Chinese people. However, as discussed in the previous sections, the majority of the Chinese people, including the majority of the CCP Politburo, saw both the embassy bombing and the spy plane collision as clear signs of American aggression. Many of them even viewed these events as new humiliations of China, yet two more to add to the long line of humiliations that China has suffered on the international stage since the Opium Wars.

Historical memories provide individuals with a reservoir of shared symbols and analogies that may be enlisted to define contesting social groups.[45] These analogies often help reconcile conflicting incoming information in ways consistent with the expectations of the analogy. In China's case, these analogies form a victimization narrative that pervades the Chinese consciousness. The century of humiliation has provided the current Chinese leadership with plenty of historical analogies to use, and it often draws parallels between current and historical events. For example, in 1990 Chinese leader Deng Xiaoping drew a parallel between seven Western industrialized countries' decision to impose economic sanctions on China in response to the 1989 Tiananmen Square Massacre and the invasion of China by allied forces of eight powers in response to the 1900 Boxer Rebellion:

> I am a Chinese, and I am familiar with the history of foreign aggression against China. When I heard that the seven Western countries, at their summit meeting, had decided to impose sanctions on China, my immediate association was to 1900, when the allied forces of the eight powers invaded China.[46]

Zhu Wenli's research referenced the same mentality when NATO bombed Yugoslavia, suggesting "the historical precedent the Chinese referred to was not the ethnic cleansing against the Jews by Hitler, as in the West, but the allied military intervention during the Boxer Rebellion."[47] Clearly, historical analogies function as important information processors that define current situations as analogous to previous crises.

During the embassy bombing crisis, Chinese state media incited public outrage by drawing parallels between the current U.S. military actions and the "gunboat diplomacy" of the nineteenth and early twentieth centuries. For instance, a *People's Daily* opinion article entitled "China, Not in 1899" compared the 1999 embassy bombing to the Eight Nation Alliance's invasion one hundred years earlier:

> This is 1999, not 1899 in the era when the United States demanded the spheres of influence held by various countries in China had to be open to the United States; they had the so-called equal share of profits without the need to ask whether China agreed or not. It is not the era when

> Western powers willfully plundered the Imperial Palace, burned down Yuanming Palace and raced to occupy Hong Kong and Macao, nor is it the era when China was under the rule of the corrupt government of the Qing Dynasty and Chiang Kai-shek. China is a country that has stood up, which has defeated the Japanese fascists, which has had a trial of strength with the United States in the Korean battlefield and won victory. The Chinese people are not to be bullied; encroachment upon China's sovereignty and dignity is intolerable. In the veins of the Chinese people circulate the blood of the anti-imperialist patriots over a period of 150-plus years. US-led NATO should bear this in mind.[48]

It is important to note that the *People's Daily* is the mouthpiece of the Chinese Communist Party, and this newspaper's opinion articles represent the party's official viewpoint.

Historical memory can be easily activated when an out-group's mischievous behavior causes suffering of the in-group. The three Chinese killed by the U.S. "satellite-guided near-precision weapon" in Belgrade on May 8, 1999, quickly activated the Chinese memory of past suffering, reminding them of a time when Western invaders had more advanced weapons. The political slogan "Backwardness incurs beatings by others" (*luohou jiuyao aida*) has been used as a political theory to explain China's national experience during the century of humiliation. The Chinese "suspicion syndrome" was activated in such an emergent and urgent occasion. Conspiracy theories about imperialist powers have a long history in China, so it is not surprising that this history of conspiracy mentality would shape current crises.

The May 4th Movement, China's first nationalist movement in modern history, was touched off in 1919 by what the Chinese called the "Versailles conspiracy." Early that year, the victorious nations of World War I convened a peace conference in Paris. Britain and the United States dominated the meeting and rejected the Chinese representatives' demands, which included taking back the privileges in Shandong that Japan had taken from Germany during World War I. The Chinese warlord government nevertheless yielded to the pressure exerted by the foreign powers and signed the Versailles Treaty. Many Chinese believed that there were schemes among the Western countries to divide China, and even secret agreements between the Chinese government and the foreign powers. On May 4th, more than 3,000 students from Peking University and other schools gathered together and held a demonstration. They shouted out such slogans as "Struggle for sovereignty externally" and "Get rid of national traitors at home." The May 4th Movement became a significant frame for the Chinese, as they viewed a grand conspiracy among the Western powers and a conflation between enemies and traitors. Such ideas have since become China's worst national security scenario.

Since the days of U.S. secretary of state John Foster Dulles, the Chinese leadership has perceived an American campaign to undermine the political authority and rule of the CCP through a combination of sanctions and "peaceful evolution" tactics. In the 1990s, the U.S. emphasis on human rights, the battles over the extension of most-favored nation trading status, and the opening of Radio Free Asia were all seen in Beijing as proof of an American conspiracy to undermine CCP rule. From the Chinese leadership's perspective, the U.S. threat to the CCP's political survival was precisely equated with a threat to national security.

With this historical background, it is easier to understand why some Chinese leaders believed that the embassy bombing was intentional and that the United States aimed to "sound China out" and to "create internal chaos in China." As Li Ruihuan said in the Politburo meeting, "The Americans hope for nothing better than to provoke contradictions between the [Chinese] government and the broad masses of people, especially young students, and thereby shift the crisis."[49] With the inundation of state-sponsored media provoking such ideas, many ordinary Chinese people subscribed to the same belief. According to a CNN report on May 12, 1999, one student demonstrator in front of the U.S. Embassy said: "It's the same old story, when hegemonist powers unite to bully China, it's always the same. They are afraid of China and want to keep us down."[50] Likewise, as Rebecca MacKinnon and Mike Chinoy observed, "The intensity of those demonstrations illustrated how the days of Western intervention in China during the colonial era are sorely remembered by many Chinese."[51] Thus, the institutionalized memory of conspiracy against China has become so ingrained in the collective psyche that it was the first explanation for American actions in the three crises. Without this memory and the propagation of the CCP's master narrative of national history, the Chinese interpretation may have been very different.

The life-and-death struggle for national survival that China experienced in the early part of the twentieth century has left a deep impression on the Chinese collective memory. A very strong sense of crisis and insecurity has become an important theme of the national political discourse in China. As a result of the patriotic education campaign, many Chinese have begun to confront rather than avoid their past humiliation. The new focus on Chinese misery during the century of humiliation has given rise to an outpouring of victim consciousness among the Chinese public. All three of the crises that are the focus of this chapter fed into a renowned "Chinese sense of victimization," having once been the world's greatest nation only to be humiliated in the nineteenth and early twentieth centuries.[52] The government reeducation campaign has reinforced this memory of humiliation, and therefore it has become ingrained in the consciousness of the Chinese public. The three U.S.-China crises only served to reactivate these feelings of humiliation, causing the Chinese to see themselves as the injured party, victims of U.S. aggression.

The lens of historical memory has been shown to influence both the masses and the elites to interpret the present and make decisions on policy. Due to this heightened sense of historical memory, what appeared to be an isolated or accidental event to Americans was considered by Chinese leaders to be yet another in a long line of humiliations. The three incidents thus easily touched on sensitive Chinese feelings about Western imperialist nations taking advantage of a weakened China in the late 1800s and early 1900s. A deep historical sense of victimization by outside powers, a long-held suspicion about foreign conspiracies against China, and the powerful governmental education and propaganda campaigns on historical humiliation have worked together to construct a special Chinese "culture of insecurity." Thus, this culture of insecurity has become the frame by which the Chinese interpret present-day events and influences their reactions and demands to rectify perceived humiliation.

FILTERS AND OPTIONS: HOW CHINA DECIDED WHAT TO DO

For all three crises, there existed other options for response, including diplomatic practices for handling these kinds of incidents. Such practices are in place to ensure cooler heads of reason prevail when tensions arise. While China reacted to escalate tensions in these crises, it is important to understand how the other diplomatic options were ruled out during the decision-making processes.

A normal response for handling the EP-3 plane collision would have been for the twenty-four American crew members to be released in the first several days, with China retaining the plane; only then would the two countries start to negotiate compensation and settlement. China's holding of the U.S. crew members was a clear choice to escalate tension.

In the case of the embassy bombing, if the same incident had happened between the United States and another country, it would certainly have aroused a very strong response. Even if the country of the embassy bombed was a U.S. ally, emotional demonstrations would almost certainly be expected to happen. However, for most countries, the demonstrations would be spontaneous; the government would certainly not organize them, but instead would step in to try to prevent the protesters from destroying U.S. property or besieging the U.S. ambassador and staff. As Simon Shen observed:

> Although the anti-American demonstrations in response to the bombing were overwhelmingly voluntary, they were still indirectly endorsed by the government: in a single-party regime, only the government would be able to provide transportation, to loosen security procedures allowing the masses to apply for demonstration permits, and to tacitly tolerate physical damage to the U.S. Embassy in Beijing.[53]

Similarly, if a sixteen-year policy practice regarding an issue sensitive to another country were reversed, as in the case of the Clinton administration's decision to issue the Taiwanese president a visa, diplomatic protests and actions such as recalling an ambassador could be expected of an angry government, but the responses would be kept within the diplomatic sphere. China's responses in 1995 and 1996, on the other hand, were three rounds of large-scale, live-ammunition military exercises with ballistic missiles flying over Taiwan.

The historical-memory variable helps explain why Chinese leaders did not choose to resolve the embassy bombing incident through cool diplomacy. When most Chinese leaders and many Chinese citizens viewed the incident as an intentional, carefully crafted plot, "cool diplomacy" would not pass the domestic test and therefore was dismissed as a nonoption. Through the lens of historical memory, isolated or accidental events were magnified and rendered emotional. Diplomacy between the two states therefore quickly became a zero-sum game. The historical memory context is the key to understanding Beijing's behavior during the three crises.

What made the Chinese leaders especially angry in these situations was that they had no other measures at their disposal to exact revenge or punish the United States. In 1999, Beijing did move to cancel scheduled high-level visits, halt bilateral dialogues over human rights and arms control issues, and suspend the negotiations over China's WTO entry.

However, these actions did not serve as a real punishment to the United States; in fact, some of these actions would end up hurting China. In light of this situation, one can see why Beijing would choose to send students to the U.S. Embassy in Beijing during the Belgrade bombing crisis. When the emotional young people pelted U.S. diplomatic facilities with rocks and debris, besieging the U.S. ambassador and his staff, the Chinese felt that the United States was finally physically punished for its previous aggression.

Rejecting America's repeated apologies became another way for the Chinese government to punish the Americans. Immediately after the bombing, the Clinton administration offered an official apology. President Clinton also tried twice to use the bilateral hotline to talk with President Jiang—a hotline that had been established after the Taiwan Strait Crisis in 1996 as a confidence-building measure between the two nations. However, in this incident, Jiang refused to take Clinton's calls or accept his apology. Seeking direct communication between top leaders is a normal and proper diplomatic action after a serious bilateral issue or incident, and it seems inexplicable that the Chinese government would cut off such routine diplomatic channels of communication. But as Gries comments on the Chinese behavior: "Like a father refusing his son's repeated prostrations of forgiveness, rejecting America's repeated apologies was one of the few ways China's leadership could seek to restore Chinese self-esteem in the eyes of the Chinese people."[54]

Historical memory helps explain why Chinese leaders did not choose to resolve the three incidents diplomatically. In the early morning of May 8, 1999, top Chinese leaders were discussing whether the American attacks were intentional or accidental. If they accepted the U.S. explanation that it was a tragic technological mistake, then there would be no crisis between the two countries, or at least between the two governments. Because historical memory was acting as a filter, however, the government did not consider diplomatic reactions acceptable, which limited their response choices.

PRIDE, FACE, AND NATIONALISM: WHAT MOTIVATED CHINA'S AGGRESSION

The EP-3 incident began on April 1, 2001. However, Chinese president Jiang Zemin left Beijing on April 4 to conduct a scheduled visit to five Latin American countries. Many people thought that he would postpone this visit due to the crisis, but as a show of strength, Jiang proceeded with the visit. Before departing Cuba, he presented Fidel Castro with a poem he had written the night before. The poem was written in Chinese calligraphy on a large page of folded paper.[55]

> In the bright dawn cloud
> I left China
> Ten thousand kilometers to Latin America
> Only takes ten days
> And I heard
> The fierce wind and the storm from the opposite shore
> The pine trees
> Stand still,
> With the pride and strength of the mountain.[56]

Written just one day after the end of the EP-3 standoff, what Jiang wanted to say in this poem is clear. In Chinese literature, the pine is a common metaphor used to represent steadfast revolutionaries and great leaders who are unafraid of foreign pressures. The poem can be interpreted this way: For Jiang, the crisis is a test (the "fierce wind" and the "storm from the opposite shore") of China's and his own pride, strength, honor, and courage. As Jiang hints in this poem, he is the winner of the test (the pine trees standing still), has saved face, and won pride ("the pride and strength of the mountain").

The collision between the Chinese fighter plane and the U.S. spy plane developed into an unexpected clash of face and pride. For Beijing, a form of apology from the U.S. president, above all, was the gesture of abasement that would give China face. A *People's Daily* article of May 19 particularly praised Jiang's "staunch and mature leadership" during the embassy bombing incident: "The leadership of the Party with comrade Jiang Zemin at the core has demonstrated its courage and ability to control complicated internal and international situations, and to handle major breaking events."[57]

When an incident is perceived as an act of bullying and humiliation, because the central myth and the legitimacy of the government are highly dependent upon maintaining China's "national face" it becomes natural and understandable that the government needs to be tough. The legitimacy of China's current rulers is highly dependent upon successful performance on the international stage. The Chinese political elites are responsible for maintaining China's national *mianzi* (face) in its dealings with other nations.[58] Because the CCP has built its legitimacy on a reputation as the righter of past wrongs, it cannot afford to allow the country to be humiliated again.

Interpretations of history often force unprepared and caught-off-guard governments to deal with internal and external challenges to conventional views of memory and history, especially when dealing with sensitive issues of national pride and international honor.[59] Conflict resolution can be made profoundly difficult in these situations. To Beijing, each of the three crises was much more than a simple violation of Chinese sovereignty; each was seen as a test for the party—not just a test of wills but a test of the ruling party's legitimacy and political credibility. The Chinese government needed to be able to show the public that it had successfully obtained some kind of victory over the United States. If the government could not obtain a victory, leaders felt that they would appear weak and lose face in the eyes of the public. The zero-sum nature of face and China's history of victimization at the hands of the West combine to make many contemporary Chinese people view diplomacy as a fierce competition between leaders who win or lose face for the nations they embody.[60] For them, a public apology meant admitting a fault. Clinton's full apologies and Bush's two "sorrys"—translated by the Chinese as full apologies—were skillfully posed by Chinese official media as diplomatic victories for Beijing.

The American apologies were also used by Beijing to promote itself to the moral high ground—"We are right" and "You owe us." As Lucian Pye explains:

> When the Chinese have the moral high ground, they can be unrelenting in exploiting the situation. It goes back to the Confucian tradition, in which the ruler is morally superior, and therefore when your opponent apologizes it proves they are morally inferior and cannot be the legitimate ruler.[61]

As discussed in the previous chapters, the new focus on Chinese historical misery during the patriotic education campaign has given rise to an outpouring of victim consciousness among the Chinese public. More and more Chinese people have come to hate Western countries, especially the United States and Japan. All three of these U.S.-China crises fit perfectly into the victimization narrative in China and thus provided the means necessary to touch off Chinese popular nationalism. The crises should be understood in the context of the rising nationalism in China after the tragedy in Tiananmen Square in 1989 and the end of the Cold War. In chapter 4, I discussed how the state-led campaign of patriotic education has promoted national humiliation education and contributed to the rise of nationalism in China, which helped Beijing to regain its ethical and moral legitimacy. The Communist Party masked itself as a nationalist party following the end of the Cold War and the collapse of Communism in Eastern Europe.

The rise of nationalism, however, is a double-edged sword. It can help authorities consolidate their power and promote political solidarity in Chinese society by focusing animosity on external opponents, rather than domestic leaders. On the other hand, it can also put pressure on government policy making. During all three crises, the government not only negotiated with the U.S. government but also had to deal with its domestic audiences, particularly China's new generation of nationalists. As Jeffrey Wasserstrom suggests, the government was somehow "riding the tiger" of nationalist outrage and succeeded in 1999 without much direct criticism. However, it must be understood that this will not always be the case.[62]

Feelings of shame surrounding past traumas can lead victims to overexaggerate current threats and incite strong feelings of desire for revenge. The beliefs of history and memory in China thus motivated the escalation of conflict and the course of its development. For the Chinese, taking a hard-line approach indicated their moral superiority. This helps to explain why many of the Chinese government's actions in external affairs are regarded as harsh by foreigners but perceived as soft by much of its domestic audience.

In a case study of the Cuban Missile Crisis, Himadeep Muppidi states that the 1962 standoff was a "cultural production": The official U.S. state narrative of American Cold War identity—by which it was intolerable for the United States to accept Soviet weapons on nearby land in the Western Hemisphere—both constituted the events of October 1962 as a crisis and marginalized alternative understandings of these events.[63] Using the same concept, the three U.S.-China crises were also cultural productions. The Chinese official state narrative of past humiliation, the sense of victimization, and the suspicion syndrome led the Chinese to view the three incidents as crises and marginalized alternative understandings. The long-held beliefs of historical memory acted to intensify reactions based on nationalism, pride, and the importance of China's face.

The beliefs of historical memory justified the escalation of the conflict and the course of its development for the Chinese because being tough and aggressive had an ethical and moral correctness. Through the three crises, we can see how powerful historical memory has been in providing the moral motivation for people's conflict actions, and how political leaders can use history and memory to mobilize mass support and justify hostility against another group. This usage of history and memory as a means to an end could affect the escalation and deescalation of a conflict.

HISTORICAL MEMORY AS FOCAL POINTS

As discussed in chapter 1, when political actors must choose between sets of outcomes, ideas or identity can act as causal factors in influencing policy behavior by coordinating cooperation and group cohesion. In situations where there are no objective criteria on which to base one's choices, political elites may settle on courses of action on the basis of shared cultural, normative, religious, ethnic, or causal beliefs.[64] However, ideas and beliefs can also contribute to outcomes in an opposite—even negative—way, thus causing conflict and disorder.

In this section, we will compare the three U.S.-China crises with two groups of cases involving conflict or tension with China. In the first group, we will examine China's actions with regard to three U.S.-related incidents that did not involve actual conflict, including U.S.-China WTO negotiations and arms control negotiations. The second group of cases will explore China's conflict behavior with three non-U.S. countries—hereinafter referred to as the "non-U.S. conflicts." The analysis presented in this section further examines the activation of historical memory and its effect on Chinese foreign affairs by comparing the three hot conflicts with nonconflict U.S.-China incidents and with conflicts China had with other countries. In doing so, we can pinpoint the issues that made these hot conflicts unique and delve deeper into our analysis of memory and crises in foreign affairs.

COMPARISON WITH THREE NONCONFLICT U.S.-CHINA INCIDENTS

Since the end of the Cold War, especially during the course of the three crises, China's leadership actually tried hard to avoid direct conflict with the West, particularly with the United States. The collapse of Communism in Eastern Europe and the overthrow of the Romanian regime had a particularly chilling effect on Chinese leaders. In the midst of the anguish following the end of the Cold War, the subsequent sanctions and pressures from the West further added to Beijing's anxiety and nervousness.

China's leaders have adopted a moderate stance on many occasions, at times even submitting to what they considered insulting demands. For example, China allowed the United States to publicly search the vessel *Yinhe* for chemical weapons in 1993, although there were no such weapons on board. China also began to cooperate with the United States in the field of arms control, agreeing to join the Nuclear Nonproliferation Treaty in 1991, acceding to the Missile Technology Control Regime in 1992, and agreeing to join the Comprehensive Test Ban Treaty in 1996. China has steadfastly attended multilateral negotiations on arms control and disarmament and has signed or ratified almost all of the multilateral arms control treaties, making a positive contribution to the progress of international arms control and disarmament.

China also signed the World Trade Organization entry agreements with the United States despite the parallels many of its domestic critics drew between the WTO treaties and the unequal treaties the Qing dynasty signed with the Western powers a hundred years before. It is important to note that this was the same period of time during which three hot conflicts threatened U.S.-China relations. By comparing these issues, we can identify why China cooperated on certain issues and yet escalated conflict on others.

To put these three cases—the *Yinhe*, arms control negotiations, and WTO entry—into the "nonconflict" category does not mean there were no disputes or confrontations. The WTO negotiations, for example, took thirteen years and experienced many setbacks and serious disputes during the process. However, China's main approach toward these three incidents was cooperative, trying hard to avoid the escalation of conflict. By contrast, in all three U.S.-China crises discussed earlier, China intentionally escalated the conflict. A careful review of the six cases indicates that the conflict and nonconflict incidents have major differences in three aspects: emergency, public awareness, and negotiation modes.

Emergency

All three U.S.-China crises were sudden emergencies. The Belgrade bombing, the airplane collision, and the visa issue set off immediate predicaments for U.S.-China relations. On the other hand, two of the three nonconflict cases—the WTO negotiations and the arms control negotiation—involved lengthy processes. The *Yinhe* incident, however, was also an emergency. On July 23, 1993, the CIA alleged that a Chinese container ship, the *Yinhe*, was carrying chemical weapons material to Iran and sent three U.S. military ships to pursue the *Yinhe* in international waters. Meanwhile, U.S. pressure persuaded Persian Gulf countries not to permit the ship to dock, unload cargo, or take on fresh food and water for twenty days.

Public Awareness

The Chinese Communist Party maintains tight control of all the media in China. Public awareness of a particular international incident therefore is largely dependent on whether the party allows the media to report the event or not. However, some international crises or emergencies are difficult for the party to hide. This is especially true of events with casualties, despite the CCP's attempts at controlling the flow of information and filtering of the news.

The embassy bombing happened at midnight on May 8, but the Chinese official media did not report it until approximately 12 hours later. The media did not report President Clinton's first apology on May 8 because the government needed to enflame the public's hatred during the early stages of the crisis. During the 1996 Taiwan Strait Crisis, Beijing actually carried out a media blitz against the United States and the Taiwanese leader. The EP-3 incident was negatively labeled the "spy plane incident" in the Chinese media. The official media gave detailed reports about the accident and explanations as to why it was the EP-3's fault, as well as documentation of the humanitarian treatment that China was providing to the U.S. crew members.

The nonconflict events, however, did not require such comprehensive media coverage. For example, the Chinese people were aware that talks were taking place between the two countries during the thirteen-year WTO and six-year arms control negotiations; however, they were not told any details of these negotiations. Even today, the average Chinese person does not have access to the WTO treaties that the two countries signed. For most Chinese people, the *Yinhe* incident is a nonevent; it is almost unheard of in China. There were hardly any official reports about this event for numerous reasons. First, the incident did not happen inside

China, so the government could easily hide it from public awareness. Second, for the first few weeks, the government itself was not quite sure whether there were chemical weapons materials in this container ship or not. Third, if the media were allowed to report it, the public might think it was a humiliation to China for allowing the United States to conduct an open inspection of this Chinese ship. This type of logic on the part of the CCP is and has been used as grounds for keeping certain news from the common Chinese person.

Negotiation Modes

While all six cases ultimately involved negotiations to settle the conflicts, there are differences in the negotiation methods that distinguish the three nonconflict cases from the three cases of escalation. The negotiations of the three nonconflict cases were conducted mainly among professional experts from the two countries. For example, the Chinese team participating in the arms control negotiations was composed of nuclear experts, officials from the Arms Control Bureau of the Foreign Affairs Ministry, and scholars of arms control issues from government think tanks. The *Yinhe* incident was negotiated solely by officials of the Arms Control Bureau. The negotiations conducted during the three conflict crises, however, were mainly political and very public. Not only were the diplomats of the two countries involved, but also the military, the U.S. Congress, and even the media were indirectly involved in the talks. The leaders of the two countries made numerous open statements and exchanged letters during the processes.

The similarities and differences of the six cases are represented in table 7.1. As we can see, the six cases are comparable because they all concerned sovereignty issues. However, the three conflict cases (U.S.-China crises) shared similarities:

1. Emergency and urgency: Each was an accident or unexpected event.
2. There was a high degree of public awareness.
3. Settlement negotiations were conducted under the high degree of public attention with involvement of various domestic constituencies of both sides.

Contrasting with the three crises, the three nonconflict cases all involved a low degree of public awareness and were negotiated by professionals

TABLE 7.1 COMPARATIVE CASE STUDIES: THREE NONCONFLICT INCIDENTS

	Approach			Public		Negotiation mode	
Events	Conflict	Cooperation	Sovereignty	awareness	Emergency	Professional	Political
WTO negotiations (1986–2001)		√	√	Low	√	√	
Arms control negotiations (1991–1996)		√	√	Low	√	√	
Yinhe incident (1993)		√	√	Low	√	√	
Taiwan crisis (1995–1996)	√		√	High	√		√
Embassy crisis (1999)	√		√	High	√		√
EP-3 incident (2001)	√		√	High	√		√

in a relatively undisturbed environment. The average Chinese people did not know much about the incidents and had very limited access to the negotiation information. Two of the nonconflict cases were not emergencies. The *Yinhe* incident was the exception, but although the incident was sudden and unplanned, it is not considered a true emergency. Since the incident was unknown to most Chinese people and the negotiation was conducted secretly, the Chinese government was not under pressure to settle it in a certain way.

HANDLING CONFLICTS WITH OTHER COUNTRIES

During this period of time, China had territorial disputes with some ASEAN countries, especially with the Philippines and Vietnam. And in 1998, there were massive anti-Chinese riots in Indonesia. Comparing these non-U.S. conflicts with the three U.S.-China crises, the six cases share three important distinctions:

1. Each of them involved Chinese casualties. Compared with the three U.S.-China crises, the Chinese casualties in the non-U.S. cases were much larger.
2. All six cases were emergencies, meaning the leaders had to make decisions quickly.
3. Each of the cases was related to sovereignty issues. The South China Sea disputes were directly about territory. In the Indonesian case, even though the Indonesian ethnic Chinese are no longer citizens of the People's Republic of China (China does not accept dual citizenship), this was an anti-Chinese riot. The ethnic Chinese were targeted in the bloody Jakarta unrest in May 1998. According to Indonesian government sources, more than 1,000 Chinese people died, many women were raped, and over 4,000 buildings were destroyed during these riots.[65]

Table 7.2 provides comparisons between the three non-U.S. cases and the three U.S.-China crises.

Given the important similarities, it seems as though China treated various countries differently when dealing with conflicts, and this factor affected China's approach to conflicts and disputes. If the situation were reversed—the United States or Japan had anti-Chinese riots, say, or seized and attacked Chinese fishermen and fishing boats—the response would

TABLE 7.2 COMPARATIVE CASE STUDIES: THREE NON-U.S. CASES

Events	Approach		Memory of past conflict	Public awareness	Emergency	Casualty and injury
	Conflict	Cooperation				
Indonesia anti-China riots (1998)		√	Low	Medium	√	√
South China Sea disputes with the Philippines (1990s)		√	Low	Medium	√	√
South China Sea disputes with Vietnam (1990s)		√	Medium	Medium	√	√
Taiwan crisis (1995–1996)	√		High	High	√	√
Embassy crisis (1999)	√		High	High	√	√
EP-3 incident (2001)	√		High	High	√	√

likely be very different: One would expect huge waves of nationalism to touch off zero-sum conflict behavior from both the state and the people.

One likely explanation for this different outlook could be the view that China has of the Philippines, Vietnam, and Indonesia, which are considered China's Asian neighbors and Third World "brothers." They are smaller than China and have never invaded China. As discussed in chapter 5, for many Chinese, the countries of the world can be divided into two groups: those who have historically been the bully—mainly the Western countries—and those who have been bullied—the Third World countries. The Chinese government's handling of the disputes with Indonesia, the Philippines, and Vietnam indicate that the Chinese were not that sensitive and tough compared with their approach in handling the three U.S.-China crises.

Another factor that distinguished the two groups of cases was the degree of public awareness. The Chinese official media reported about the South China Sea disputes and the Indonesia riots, but did not provide details of the conflicts. During the Indonesia riots, many photos were spread on the Internet, and some Chinese people, mainly students and intellectuals having access to Internet, became aware of the riots and therefore strongly criticized the government for being cold and detached toward the overseas Chinese. The differences in degree of public awareness indicated that the Chinese government was less likely to overreact when the event was not the focus of domestic attention and when the issue had not activated Chinese people's sensitive historical memory.

THE ACTIVATION OF HISTORICAL MEMORY

During the three U.S.-China crises, history and memory served as road maps. It is evident that memory influenced the leaders' interpretation and judgment regarding the conflict situations. Memories of past injustice functioned as filters that limited choices by excluding other variables and contrary interpretations. Because of these memories, the Chinese leadership was restricted in its policy options. The Chinese had no choice but to demand an apology because it symbolized not only an admittance of wrongdoing but also a boost in status for China. Finally, memory provided motivation and mobilization for conflict actions. Without the emphasis on historical memories, the Chinese people would not have been so easily spurred into taking action.

The beliefs of history and memory also served as focal points by causing conflict and constituting difficulties to the settlement of the conflict.

The historical memory variable explains why China cooperated with the United States on some issues but turned aggressive on other issues at the same time. It also helps us understand why China treated the United States differently from other countries when dealing with conflicts. While it is true that identity and beliefs have the effect of bringing a group closer, emphasizing cooperation and cohesion, it is also true that this sense of identity and history can equally cause conflict and disorder.

This research indicates that the cognitive content of history and memory, especially the sense of victimization and suspicion syndrome, deeply affected Chinese people's attitudes, interpretation, and judgment regarding the conflict situations. International confrontations are often perceived and experienced by the Chinese as assaults on fundamental identity, dignity (face), authority, and power. A deep historical sense of victimization by outside powers and long-held suspicions about foreign conspiracies against China had a far-reaching effect on Chinese people's attitudes, strategies, and policies concerning conflict and reconciliation. Sensitivity to old grievances (closely connected with this nation's historical memory and its chosen traumas) renders the country prone to tantrums at even the slightest international offense, real or imagined. This effect on perception and sensitivity wreaked havoc on the three hot crises between the United States and China, almost causing irreparable damage to U.S.-China relations.

This research has also compared the three U.S.-China crises with three nonconflict U.S.-China events (WTO negotiations, arms control negotiations, and the *Yinhe* incident) and three non-U.S. cases (territory disputes with Vietnam and the Philippines and the 1998 anti-Chinese riots in Indonesia). Based on the analysis of these comparative cases, this research shows that the following factors very often activate Chinese historical memory:

1. Emergency (e.g., accident or unexpected events) and urgency
2. Incidents that cause Chinese suffering (e.g., casualties and injuries)
3. A dispute with a country that historically has had troubles with China

In conclusion, the historical memory variable helps explain why China generally cooperated with the United States during the same period of time it turned aggressive on the three crisis incidents, and why China treated the United States differently from other countries when dealing with conflicts. Chinese people's collective historical consciousness about the country's traumatic national experiences and the state's political use of the past constitute a powerful force in the way the Chinese conceptualize, manage, and resolve external conflict. In crisis situations of confrontation and conflict, especially when confrontation is perceived by the Chinese as an assault on fundamental identity, face, and authority, historical memory very often serves as a major motivating factor.

Numerous books and articles have been produced by authors of both policy and academic communities in attempting to interpret Chinese conflict behavior during these crises. This study argues that, even though existing theories and explanations illuminate certain aspects of the three U.S.-China crises, full explanatory pictures emerge only after this phenomenon is also analyzed through the lens of historical memory.

8

MEMORY, TEXTBOOKS, AND SINO-JAPANESE RECONCILIATION

PRISONERS OF HISTORY?

Chongqing, one of China's southwestern cities, hosted the 2008 East Asian Soccer Federation Championship in February 2008. The four participants in this championship were the national teams from the major countries of East Asia: China, Japan, North Korea, and South Korea. The opening game was between China and Japan on February 20. Before this game, Xie Yalong, the chief of China's Soccer Association, gave a half-hour pep talk to the Chinese players. According to a report from *Sina.com*, a leading Internet news website in China, Xie talked first about Chongqing's role during the Anti-Japanese War.

As China's provisional capital during the war, Chongqing became a main target of Japanese terror bombing. The bombing campaigns lasted for more than five years, from 1938 to 1943. A conservative estimate places the number of bombing runs at over 5,000, with more than 11,500 bombs dropped. A recent study shows that about 23,600 people were killed and 31,000 wounded in the bombings. On June 5, 1941, alone, the Japanese flew more than twenty sorties in a bombing raid on Chongqing that lasted for three hours; some four thousand residents hiding in a tunnel were asphyxiated.[1]

Xie told his players about the Japanese bombing of Chongqing and the trauma the local people suffered during the war. At the end of his talk, Xie said: "In this place Chongqing, we can lose to any team, but we definitely can't lose to Japan. Today must be the day recorded in history. The Chinese team must defeat the Japanese!" Because of his lengthy pep talk, the Chinese team was a bit late to the game.[2] That night China lost the game 0–1.

During the Anti-Japanese War, more than 900 Chinese cities were occupied by the Japanese. Many places in China, like Chongqing, have tragic memories of the war. Today's younger generations, including the members of the 2008 soccer team, have heard many stories about the war from various sources, such as their grandparents and people like Xie Yalong. They have also learned this part of history from history classes and from official patriotic education campaigns. In many Chinese cities, there are numerous museums, monuments, and historical sites that were established in memory of this war. All these sources of memory have made forgetting impossible. We can understand why, more than sixty years after the end of World War II, the ghosts of war still haunt Chinese-Japanese relations. Although more than three decades have passed since relations were normalized, the enmity of the past remains alive.

For people of the two countries, this part of history not only exists in the present day through stories and monuments but can also be revived at any time today through the casual remarks of a politician, the release of a new movie, or the publication of a new history book. That war has left many sensitive historical symbols between the two countries, and these symbols can be "reactivated" deliberately or unintentionally and can cause major tensions or even conflicts between the two countries.

On April 5, 2005, the Japanese Education Ministry approved a new junior high school textbook titled *Atarashii rekishi kyōkasho* (New history textbook), written by the Japanese Society for History Textbook Reform (JSHTR). This move ignited immediate outrage in some Asian countries, especially China and South Korea, where critics charged that this organization has been using history textbook revision to minimize Japan's culpability for its wartime actions.[3] According to critics, the textbook provides a distorted and self-serving account of Japan's colonial and wartime activities. One example is its description of the invasion of the Korean Peninsula as an unopposed annexation necessary for Japan's security.[4]

Four days later, on April 9, an estimated 10,000 to 20,000 Chinese demonstrators marched to the Japanese Embassy in Beijing, throwing stones at the facility. The next day, 20,000 demonstrators marched in two cities in southern Guangdong Province, and protestors attacked a Japanese department store in Shenzhen.[5] Two weeks after the textbook was approved, anti-Japanese protests broke out in more than ten Chinese cities. In each case, protesters chanted slogans and burned Japanese flags. People carried banners with slogans reading: "Japan Must Apologize to China," "Never Forget National Humiliation," and "Boycott Japanese Goods."[6] The protests were the largest anti-Japanese demonstrations in China since the two countries normalized diplomatic relations in 1972 and the largest protests against any country since 1999, when the United States destroyed the Chinese Embassy in Belgrade during the conflict in Kosovo.

Outrage was also fierce in South Korea, where the spokesman for the Foreign Ministry said the newly approved textbooks were still "far from sufficient when universal values and historic truth are taken into account." The new textbook emphasized the legitimacy of Japan's claim to a group of desolate islands that South Korea insists are part of its territory.[7] In Seoul, two South Koreans, Park Kyung-ja and Cho Seung-kyu, used weed clippers and a knife to chop off their fingers outside the Japanese Embassy to protest Japan's claims to these islands.

In many deep-rooted conflicts, past relationships and problems become the ghosts haunting current realities and frequently affect normal communication. Historically, a poor relationship and suspicion between two nations initially impede constructive discussion. Very often, people in entrenched human conflict do not communicate their identities, historic grievances, memories, or alienation. Therefore, most of these intractable conflicts are not ready for formal conflict intervention (e.g., mediation) or negotiation.

Indeed, historical issues and the interpretation of the past have been the major barriers for a real reconciliation among China, Japan, and South Korea. The controversy surrounding history education and the adoption of history textbooks in East Asia has been an issue of much debate among scholars of many different disciplines.[8] In this chapter, I address the issue from the perspective of conflict resolution.

To a great extent, the memories of past conflicts have come to shape international relations in East Asia.[9] However, no country should be a prisoner of its past. As Johan Galtung comments, "We are not handcuffed to history, but a high level of consciousness about the nature of those handcuffs is needed, as well as a willingness to become liberated."[10] In this regard, it is important for the three East Asian countries to take advantage of the ideas and methods pioneered by experts in the rapidly growing field of conflict analysis and resolution.

I have thus far laid down an account of how China uses history and memory in patriotic education, in foreign relations, and during times of crisis. Although I have focused on history as a tool of the CCP, history can also be used as a tool of those who wish to heal these old wounds. What if history, rather than being used as a tool to provoke animosity, were used as a tool of reconciliation? Do the Chinese and Japanese people, especially elites, have the consciousness and willingness to become liberated? What strategies and methods can be used to overcome the shadow of the past? In this chapter, I focus on these questions.

FROM "DISCOURSE ON HATRED" TO "DISCOURSE ON FORGIVENESS"

In her book *Discourses on Violence*, Vivienne Jabri challenges the "orthodox" theories on the sources of conflict and war. She believes orthodox theories are inadequate to fully understand violent conflict, as they focus too much on how such conflicts break out rather than the social conditions that promote them. According to Jabri, the phenomenon of violent conflict cannot be understood simply through analyses of leadership and decision making; it is necessary to uncover the continuities in society that enable conflict and give it legitimacy.[11] She argues that violent conflict is a social institution that is reproduced through social and political discourses, which convey legitimacy to it. When a collective identity is defined through exclusionist language, under certain circumstances, this might provide grounds for stereotyping. The implications of constructing group identity based on opposition to another group are of central importance in understanding the processes that legitimize violence. The enemy created through this process becomes the legitimized target of discrimination and violence. The point that Jabri makes is that exclusionist discourse of violent conflict is not confined to the battlefield but also occurs prior to fighting.

History textbooks have been regarded as a major component in the construction and reproduction of national narratives. History education is not purely for distributing the different "scholarships" of history, nor is it entirely free of political influence. Studies on how China, Korea, and Japan deal with historical issues in their education systems have yielded uneasy messages. History textbooks and history education in these three countries have become a source of the same type of exclusionist discourse that Jabri has described.

Although textbooks masquerade as a neutral and legitimate source of information, political leaders as well as citizens often have a vested interest in retaining simplistic narratives that flatter their own group. The assumption that history is about "our ancestors" is also quite common in East Asia, which is certainly different from conceiving of history as being about how people in the past—whoever they may have been—lived and coped. However, when history textbooks are compiled based on the assumption that they should be about one's ancestors, they are often imbued with ethnocentric views, stereotypes, and prejudices, making it difficult to avoid the glorification or demonization of particular groups. History textbooks have thus become sources of controversy and conflict.

To account for a group's past conflicts with other groups, the history textbooks of all three countries adopt a mix of both "victor narratives" and "victim narratives." While the Chinese and Korean textbooks provide detailed descriptions of the wartime atrocities committed by the Japanese, such content is downplayed in most Japanese textbooks. Instead, the Japanese versions tend to associate the war with the atomic bombings of Hiroshima and Nagasaki and the air raids on Tokyo. According to Saburo Ienaga, since the 1920s, Japan's textbooks have taught generations of its children that war is glorious and, consequently, have concealed many of the sad truths about war.[12] Takashi Yoshida agrees that the Japanese government has been reluctant to portray the wartime events in a detailed and critical manner.[13]

In his attempt to understand this, Tomoko Hamada compared the portrayal of Japan's colonization of Asia (1937–1945) in three Japanese middle school history textbooks and one Chinese government-approved textbook. The results of his study indicated that the Japanese textbooks tend to employ formulas for describing the nobility of failure, while Chinese textbooks adhere to the conventional heroic folktale with such functional units as endurance, struggle, and ultimate victory.[14] According to the research of Chunghee Soh, Koreans harbor a deep sense of victimization in their memories of their checkered historical relationship with Japan, which has generated a nationalist sentiment toward Japan's ethnocentric representations of bilateral and regional events in its history textbooks. Soh believes that this is the reason a new Japanese history textbook could create such vehement "national furor" in South Korea.[15]

In Japan, many people connected China's anti-Japanese sentiments with Chinese history education. For example, Japanese foreign minister Nobutaka Machimura accused Beijing of indoctrinating China's students with an unbalanced view of the past, claiming that "Chinese textbooks are extreme in the way they uniformly convey the 'our country is correct' perspective." Some Japanese lawmakers proposed that Tokyo ask Beijing to remove all exhibits from the Chinese People's Memorial Hall of the Anti-Japanese War in Beijing that did not represent facts.[16] A *Kyodo News* article notes that the Chinese government introduced "patriotic education" in 1994 to raise anti-Japanese sentiment in students by emphasizing Japanese atrocities conducted in China before and during World War II.[17]

When people use different criteria and approaches toward their own national experiences as compared with the histories of other groups, this inevitably creates inconsistent historical narratives. Two countries may describe the same historical event very differently in their respective history textbooks, which can lead to misunderstandings in their bilateral relations. Countries with a long history of conflict between them are particularly sensitive about how specific parts of their history are narrated and taught in the other country. More specifically, people fight over the accuracy of history textbooks in telling what they perceive to be the truth. History textbooks thus become the source of new conflicts between old enemies.

One of the most debated historical issues between China and Japan is the Nanjing Massacre. For Chinese people, the "Rape of Nanjing" is a national trauma they will never forget. Chinese people believe that there were more than 300,000 people executed by the Japanese military after they conquered the city in December 1937. The figure of 300,000 victims is the official Chinese estimate and the number that Chinese students have been taught in their history textbooks. The official middle school history textbook uses many photos, statistics tables, eyewitness accounts, and personal anecdotes to recount this incident. It provides very detailed accounts of how people were executed on a massive scale at various execution sites and how their bodies were disposed of by the Japanese military. Numerous films, novels, historical books, and newspaper articles about the Rape of Nanjing have been produced in China, especially in the 1990s after the patriotic education campaign began.

However, if you have a copy of the 2005 version of the history textbook published by the JSHTR, you will find no mention of the Nanjing Massacre. Indeed, there is only one passage that refers to this event:

> In August 1937, two Japanese soldiers [and] one officer were shot to death in Shanghai. After this incident, the hostilities between Japan and China escalated. Japanese military officials thought Chiang Kai-shek would surrender if they captured Nanking [Nanjing], the Nationalist capital; they occupied that city in December. But Chiang Kai-shek had moved his capital to the remote city of Chongqing. The conflict continued.[18]

The editors of the book did add a footnote here that makes the only direct reference to the Massacre: "At this time, many Chinese soldiers and civilians were killed or wounded by Japanese troops (the Nanking Incident). Documentary evidence has raised doubts about the actual number of victims claimed by the incident. The debate continues even today."[19] According to Yoshida's research, only two of the seven middle school textbooks used in Japan in 2002 gave numbers for the controversial death toll of the Nanjing Massacre, while others used more ambiguous terms such as "many" and "massive" to describe the casualties in an effort to avoid the domestic challenges from Japan's right wing.[20]

When the same historical event receives such different treatments in the textbooks of the two countries, it is not difficult to understand why history textbooks could trigger massive protests. As Laura Hein and Mark Selden put it, history lessons not only shape behavior for citizens within one's own society but also "chronicle relations with others." People argue over the contents of such textbooks because education is tied to the future, reaches deep into society, and is most often directly dictated by the state.[21]

Indeed, there is a feedback loop in China and Japan whereby the nationalistic history education stimulates the rise of nationalism, and the rise of nationalism provides a bigger market for nationalistic messages. At the same time, top-level leaders not only are locked into their individual positions but also frequently use historical grievances as resources for political mobilization.

The controversy surrounding history education and the adoption of school history textbooks in East Asia raises the question of why history education and history textbooks in particular are important enough to fight over. In fact, the battles over history education and textbooks are certainly not limited to Asia. Studies have indicated that these are "common" phenomena in many countries engaged in deep-rooted conflicts. Manipulation of the past often entails the use of stereotypes and prejudice in describing the other. Carried to the extreme, stereotyping and prejudice foster what Elie Podeh calls "delegitimization"—the "categorization of groups into extreme negative social categories which are excluded from human groups that are considered as acting within the limits of acceptable norms and/or values."[22] Textbooks can disseminate hatred between two civilizations. But are people doomed to be locked into this kind of feedback loop? Are there any tools or strategies that people can use to get past the discourse of hatred?

Going back to Vivienne Jabri's theory, she proposes that preventing conflict means preventing the exclusionist discourse and symbolic politics by limiting opportunities in the short run and changing hostile myths and attitudes in the long run.[23] The best strategy for countries to become liberated from the past chosen trauma, if we follow Jabri's recommendation, is to introduce a new "peace discourse"—a dialogue on tolerance, forgiveness, and reconciliation—to replace the current discourses on hatred and struggle. According to Jabri, since structure and actor are mutually constitutive, actors can work to change the conflict structure in which they operate. Actors can emancipate themselves from structure and enable the possibility of the creation of new discourses on peace, which could serve to institutionalize an environment of peace as a social continuity. As for conflict resolution and transformation strategies, she implies that the traditional conflict resolution approach to violent conflict will not yield success until it deals with these long-term social causes of conflict.

JOINT HISTORY TEXTBOOK WRITING AS A PEACEBUILDING METHOD

If textbooks and other narratives of history become the source of conflict between different countries, then revision of these through joint authorship presents a viable method of reconciliation and conflict resolution. According to John Burton, a founding figure of conflict resolution studies, what is needed in resolving deep-rooted conflict is a method wherein the cause of conflict can be analytically understood, and a method wherein traditional power bargaining does not take place.[24] This is referred to as a "joint problem-solving approach." Cooperative efforts to solve shared problems might be a guiding principle for the reconciliation of relations in all of the bilateral relationships plagued by ingrained conflict in the Asia-Pacific area.

In May 2005, the first joint history textbook in East Asia, *The Modern and Contemporary History of Three East Asian Countries*, was simultaneously published in China, South Korea, and Japan (in the respective languages of each country), after three years of preparation.[25] This nongovernmental project, in which some fifty independent teachers, historians, and members of civic groups from the three nations participated, aimed to establish a jointly recognized interpretation of history.

The project began in March 2002 when historians from China, Japan, and South Korea attended a conference on history education in China. During this meeting, the participants reached a consensus that the transcription of a unified historical interpretation of past conflicts would play a vital role in the reconciliation between the three countries. Immediately after the conference, three national history textbook writing committees were formed, and in August 2002 the first project meeting was held in Seoul.[26] The trilateral history textbook writing committee was composed of fifty-three members: seventeen from China, thirteen from Japan, and twenty-three from the Republic of Korea. Most of them were history professors or senior researchers affiliated with historical research institutes or museums in their home nations. Among the Japanese and South Korean committee members, there were also middle school history teachers and members of nongovernmental organizations and civic groups. All participated as independent scholars, as the project was nongovernmental in nature and began without any sponsors or subsidies.[27] After eleven meetings and six revisions over the course of three years, the joint history textbook was finally published in 2005.

This is not the first instance that the multilateral writing of a history textbook has been used as a method of peacebuilding and reconciliation. For example, bilateral history textbooks have been published jointly by Germany and Poland and by Germany and France. These efforts have contributed to the reconciliation of these countries after World War II and later during the integration of the European Union.[28] Jeffrey Wasserstrom has argued that the publication of the trilateral history textbook in East Asia could, in retrospect, mark "another watershed moment in Asian relations: the point at which Japan, China, and South Korea finally began to accept a shared story of the past."[29] This statement might be too optimistic, but the efforts of this project deserve acknowledgment. Both the resulting book and the project itself are a rich case for analyzing the role of history education in intergroup conflict and reconciliation.

There are several characteristics of the joint history textbook that distinguish it from other history textbooks that have been produced in these three countries. First, *The Modern and Contemporary History of Three*

East Asian Countries does not present history from a single country's perspective but rather makes special efforts to introduce a jointly recognized interpretation of history among the three nations. History textbooks are often written from a single point of view; that is, they are based on domestic interpretations of the past. These texts are most commonly the basis for national narratives of history. By contrast, this first joint history textbook in East Asia primarily focuses on the interactions between the three East Asian countries. As the preface of the book states, these nations have very close geographical and historical ties, and their histories cannot be understood separately.[30]

Second, this book uses an "introspective narrative" to replace the victor and victim narratives that were used by traditional national history textbooks in the three countries to account for past conflicts and violence. It encourages its readers to explore the deep roots and causes of historical tragedies, to reflect on past mistakes, and to learn from history. In the preface, the editors ask readers to consider the following question: What are the lessons we can learn from studying the history of East Asia?[31] Indeed, throughout the textbook, the focus is placed on exploring the sources of the Asia-Pacific War. The editors' stated guideline for compiling this book was: "By remembering past mistakes, we can avoid repeating the same mistakes and can become wiser. We study history in order to remember the past experiences and lessons and to open up the future."[32] Instead of just telling people what happened in the past, introspective narratives of history encourage readers to think for themselves about *why* events occurred and even go further to ponder how to prevent the same events from happening again.

Third, the editors of *The Modern and Contemporary History* made extensive use of archival photos, statistics, eyewitness accounts, and personal anecdotes to introduce events. These contents occupy about one-third of the total space of the book. The inclusion of such a large number of photos and eyewitness reports may be a way the editors used to redress nationalist bias and minimize their own comments in order to avoid disagreements on the presentation of sensitive historical events. However, the accounts of historical events in this book sometimes are fairly brief and simple. Compared with previous national textbooks, the descriptions of each country's domestic affairs and foreign relations are fairly brief. For example, while presenting China's Anti-Japanese War, the book makes no mention of the internal conflicts between the Chinese Communist Party and the Nationalist Party, to which official history textbooks in mainland

China have always devoted a large part of their content. Given that this is the first time the three countries have worked together on a joint account of history, it is understandable that the editors were very cautious to avoid controversy; they sought maximum common ground between the three countries. The lack of information about domestic politics and the sparse details, however, make this book supplementary reading rather than the primary reading material for middle school history classes.

Finally, this textbook introduces students to the difficult and complicated process of reconciliation. Students will be able to learn that the three countries have differences over the interpretation of some historical events and that the historical issues have been barriers to establishing healthy relations. The trilateral textbook covers the nation-building processes of the three countries after the war and the thorny processes of reconciliation. It also addresses several controversial issues that currently affect relations between Japan and its East Asian neighbors: individual compensation, the use of "comfort women" during the war, problems over history textbook content, and Japanese leaders' visits to the Yasukuni Shrine in Tokyo.[33]

All three versions of the trilateral history textbook have been well received in the markets of their respective countries. The first print run of the Chinese version was 20,000 copies, and it sold out within two days. The Korean and Japanese versions also sold 20,000 copies each in the first week, a remarkable number for a social science book in these countries. The Japanese publisher decided to publish second and third editions and added another 15,000 copies as a supplement to the first edition.[34] The three versions of this book had sold more than 230,000 copies by May 2006, one year after it was first published. A new Chinese version was published in May 2006 with some minor revisions and new pictures, but no major changes to the integrity of the original work.[35]

The original objective of the editors was to make a textbook for middle school students, yet, strictly speaking, the trilateral history book is not yet a textbook. Textbooks have to go through a rigorous process to gain official approval, which this book has not yet received in any of the countries, nor has the book become required reading for students as a supplementary text.[36] But even though this book has not yet entered the classrooms, its relative success in the markets indicates that there is considerable interest in new narratives of history in these three countries.

The publication of the book has also received extensive media attention, especially in China and Korea. It received favorable comments and endorsements from Chinese official newspapers and websites, but was also criticized in scholars' personal blogs and online discussion forums. For example, one writer observed that the editors had had to make compromises and therefore sometimes used very brief narratives to avoid disagreement.[37] Dissident Chinese writer Yu Hua wrote a review of this textbook under the title "No Truthful History Under Monopoly" claiming that the book basically contains nothing that contradicts Beijing's official narrative on history. For example, it still gives much credit to the Chinese Communist Party for China's success in the war against Japan even though the CCP in fact did not play an active role fighting the Japanese. The book also fails to identify the North Koreans as the instigators of the Korean War.[38]

In Japan, much of the discussion on the trilateral textbook has focused on the Japanese participants in the project. Of the thirteen Japanese editors, six were from two organizations—Children and Textbooks Japan Network 21 (Kodomo to Kyōkasho Zenkoku Netto 21) and the Asian Network for History Education (Rekishi Kyoiku Ajia Nettowaku)—both of which are strongly opposed to the content of the history textbook written by the JSHTR. Indeed, both these organizations were established with the specific aim of discouraging Japanese regional school district boards from adopting the JSHTR textbooks. Precisely because most of the Japanese historians involved in this trilateral textbook project are portrayed as representing the Japanese left, no right-wing historians participated in the project, leaving some Japanese to see this book as simply another left-wing book in cahoots with the Chinese and Koreans.

In most societies, history and civics textbooks present an "official" story or a master narrative of national experiences. The creation of such books is fairly simple as there are few, if any, competing points of view. However, the creation of the trilateral textbook was naturally a very different case, and the writers and publishers acknowledged the prevalence of "fierce disputes" during the writing process.[39] As all three countries had already established their own perspective on this part of history, it was difficult to come to an agreement. Nonetheless, the publication of this book is an important first step. It will be the first of many to approach the controversy and sensitive historical issues of East Asia with an awareness of multiple perspectives.

People fight over the accuracy of history textbooks in telling the truth. Such "truth" is also an important factor in the process of reconciliation. According to John Paul Lederach, reconciliation involves the identification and acknowledgment of what happened (i.e., the truth), along with an effort to "right" the wrongs that occurred (i.e., justice) and forgive the perpetrators (i.e., show mercy).[40] Reconciliation also involves the creation of the social space where both truth and forgiveness are validated and joined together, rather than being forced into an encounter in which one must win out over the other or both become fragmented. This is the approach taken by the South African Truth and Reconciliation Commission, for instance.[41] According to James L. Gibson's research, the truth-telling or discussion process has significantly aided the process of reconciliation and democratization in South Africa.[42]

To put it simply, how well the new textbooks reflect the critical truths of the past conflict becomes the critical factor in determining how much of a contribution history education can make to the process of reconciliation. Confronting the past has become an established norm for reconciliation and for countries undergoing transitions from violence to peace, from authoritarianism to democracy. According to Tristan Borer, truth-telling contributes to reconciliation, human rights, gender equity, restorative justice, the rule of law, the mitigation of violence, and the healing of trauma, all of which are deemed to be constitutive of sustainable peace.[43]

However, for many historical events, restoring historical truth is not an easy task, and reconciliation does not mean unprincipled compromise. After sincere efforts to find consensus, the different sides may still hold opposing viewpoints and interpretations of a past event. Still, it is the collaborative effort between countries or groups that contributes to the process of reconciliation. As an essential step, the cooperative writing of history should provide opportunities for two or more sides to confront their common past. Instead of providing only one side's story, history textbooks can present two or more narratives of past events and let students choose for themselves which they are willing to accept. By doing so, history textbooks can introduce students to the complicated process of reconciliation itself and enhance their critical thinking skills. As Elizabeth Cole and Judy Barsalou suggest:

> Revisions in the methodology, as well as the content, of history textbooks and programs can promote long-term reconciliation by enhancing critical thinking skills, willingness to question simplistic models, empathy skills, and the ability to disagree about interpretations of the past and their implications for present social issues without resorting to violence.[44]

By providing multiple perspectives, history education can avoid marginalizing or demonizing particular groups. Education can encourage students to explore the variegated experiences of different groups affected by violence. Teaching history can therefore help students become engaged, responsible citizens. The process of joint history writing can also involve historians from previously conflicting regions to engage in honest discussion. This is an essential step for the two groups in seeking truth, justice, and mercy.

In terms of teaching history, it is not inappropriate to tell students that some historical events are interpreted differently in other countries. Understanding differing judgments can be empowering. This approach can also provide students with a more distanced view of the exclusive nationalist description of history. Instead of providing only their own country's story, textbooks can provide differing opinions, allowing students to interpret events for themselves. In this way, textbooks can convey not only historical events but also the long road to reconciliation and can encourage students to use critical-thinking skills in reading about historical and current events alike.

The trilateral history-writing project of *The Modern and Contemporary History* makes an effort to promote understanding and tolerance in East Asia. Although there may be disagreement on the exact account of history or point of view expressed in the book, its publication has contributed to promoting a new approach that is now part of the political discourse in each of the three countries. Preventing conflict means preventing exclusionist discourse and symbolic politics by limiting opportunities for disagreement and changing the myths and attitudes that lead to hostility. A true reconciliation in East Asia will be contingent on whether people can utilize a new peace discourse, using tolerance, forgiveness, and reconciliation to replace the current use of historical hatred and trauma. The trilateral history-writing project is an important effort in East Asia to initiate such a discourse.

FROM "TOP-DOWN" TO "MIDDLE-OUT"

As Canadian member of Parliament Irwin Cotler observes: "Where there is no remembrance, there is no truth; where there is no truth, there will be no justice; where there is no justice, there will be no reconciliation; and where there is no reconciliation, there will be no peace."[45] History education is no longer a domestic issue in East Asia. Historical narratives and the interpretation of the past have always been the major barriers for a real reconciliation and have evoked popular nationalism throughout the region. At the same time, the top-level leaders are often locked into their individual positions or party politics. Some of them even use historical grievances as resources for political mobilization. Considering this dynamic, a "middle-out" approach should be considered an essential step for reconciliation and conflict resolution in East Asia.

Conflict resolution practitioners such as John Paul Lederach emphasize the importance of midrange leadership and what they call a "middle-out approach" for building peace. This approach recognizes that midlevel leaders—"unofficial but influential" social and political groups as well as individuals—are a natural bridge for influencing both national- and local-level leaders. These midlevel leaders can be highly respected individuals (e.g., Nobel laureates and prominent scholars), leaders of civic groups and institutions, or leaders of identity groups. Such individuals are likely to have connections with people at both the top and grassroots levels, and their position does not depend on political or military power.

Values and beliefs rooted in the history of parties' relationships and reinforced by a sense of victimization are resistant to change. But empirical evidence shows that new information from reliable sources can alter the parties' beliefs, even if this information contradicts past perceptions.[46] The task of changing public opinion is more complicated than changing a single person's opinion, of course. There are many barriers in the way of its transformation: societal factors such as social networks or political leaders, and psychological factors such as family and friends who reinforce negative stereotypes. However, these barriers can be susceptible to new information, if it comes from reliable sources, is disseminated through mass media and personal networks, and includes both sides of the issue.

The middle-level leaders can act as channels through which new perceptions and ideas are filtered to ordinary citizens, and they can also communicate with authoritative decision makers. They are the reliable sources for new information and new concepts. The middle-out approach can therefore communicate new concepts to the upper echelons of leadership as well as to the general public. Each single book, public speech, and dialogue of the midlevel leadership of two countries can make a difference.[47]

For example, a widely circulated article, "New Thinking on Sino-Japanese Relations," published in 2002 in the Beijing-based journal *Strategy and Management*, has actually triggered a major debate in China about the China-Japan relationship. The article, written by Ma Licheng, a noted editorial writer for the *People's Daily*, suggests that China should get rid of its sense of victimization and become a confident big state with a healthy psychology. In the essay, Ma made a rare public call for China to bury wartime grievances and presented a scathing criticism of China's strongly nationalist anti-Japanese sentiment. Ma believed the issue of getting Japan to apologize for its war crimes had already been resolved. "The most important thing," he wrote, "is to look ahead."[48] Ma's view has drawn criticism from scholars and the public at large, but it has also gained some support.

The essay "Japan-China Rapprochement and Diplomatic Revolution" by Shi Yinhong, an international relations expert, has attracted great attention as well. Shi warns that mutual hatred and antagonistic sentiments could aggravate Sinophobia in Japan and lead to a vicious cycle that is potentially dangerous for China. Shi recommends that China put historical baggage aside, express understanding for Japan's military buildup, and even support Tokyo's bid to become a permanent member of the UN Security Council.[49]

Major Chinese foreign affairs journals, as well as Internet news services, have published articles or even set up special forums for this debate. Many arguments for and against have been published on the topic. This is quite unusual, since open debate over Chinese foreign policy decision making has been forbidden in China and most Chinese media and international relations experts habitually toe the party line. The appearance of Ma's and Shi's articles in openly published journals is a positive change. Although the majority do not yet agree with the points of view they expressed and some personal attacks on the two authors have also appeared on the Chinese Internet, the new thinking has already spread and become part of the political discourse in China.

The trilateral history textbook writing project is another good example of the middle-out approach. The fifty-three editorial participants are all renowned historians and educators. Although they are from different countries, they received similar academic training in history and came together because they all share a strong commitment to the social responsibility of historians. Through their book, they have transmitted new information about the historical events and new perspectives on reconciliation. Its popularity shows that there is indeed interest in these countries in learning about different perspectives and new information.

It is not easy to evaluate the impact of history education on individual students and the larger society.[50] Whereas peacemaking and peacekeeping happen during and immediately after conflict, peacebuilding is a process that is intended to affect the underlying causes of conflict. Moreover, unlike peacekeeping, which can be implemented relatively quickly, and peacemaking, which can occur over a period of a few months, peacebuilding is a long, slow political and social process that in a sense is never completed. It is unrealistic, therefore, to expect a joint history-writing project to bring about dramatic changes in bilateral relations, especially in a short period of time. However, some positive changes have been witnessed since the publication of this trilateral book.

Japanese prime minister Shinzo Abe visited China in October 2006. This was the first time in five years that a Japanese prime minister had received an invitation to visit Beijing. Abe's predecessor, Junichiro Koizumi, had upset Beijing by repeatedly visiting the Yasukuni Shrine. As a result, both China and South Korea had refused to meet with Koizumi either at home or in Japan, and there had not been any mutual visits between the Chinese and Japanese leaders since October 2001. During the meeting, Abe and Chinese premier Wen Jiabao reached an unusual agreement in bilateral relations: They agreed to establish a joint historical study group to conduct research on historical issues between the two countries in order to find similarities in their perceptions of history and analyze the differences between them.

In accordance with this agreement, each country appointed a ten-member team to participate in the project.[51] On December 26, 2006, the twenty Chinese and Japanese historians gathered in Beijing for the first-ever government-sponsored joint historical research project. Bu Ping, a participant in the nongovernmental trilateral history textbook committee, was appointed head of the Chinese team. Shinichi Kitaoka, head of the Japanese team, had previously participated in a joint history study between Japan and South Korea and is the former deputy permanent representative of Japan at the United Nations. During the meeting, the two sides agreed on the work process, scope, and topics for joint research.[52]

This initiative on the part of the two governments deserves encouragement. In many deep-rooted conflicts, past relationships and problems become sticking points during current events and impede the reconciliation process. Because of these sticking points, countries are ill equipped to deal with intractable conflicts, and formal conflict management techniques are not very useful. Harold Saunders argues that in such conflicts "sustained dialogue" is a more appropriate response to underlying causes.[53] Indeed, a growing number of conflict resolution practitioners have been utilizing dialogue to transform deep-rooted, value-based conflicts, as well as ethnic conflicts such as those between the Palestinians and the Israelis and among groups in Northern Ireland. Unlike debate, which seeks to score points and to persuade, the goal of dialogue, in which small groups of people who hold opposing views on highly divisive and emotional issues are brought together to have a conversation is to create mutual understanding and respect—essentially the recognition of the validity of opposing viewpoints.[54] Although this does not directly lead to a resolution of the conflict, it can lead to a transformation in the way the conflict is pursued. Evidently, the top leaders of China and Japan have also realized that joint history research and dialogues are necessary and effective steps for rebuilding relationships.

Bu Ping's appointment is also a good example of how a nongovernmental project can prepare for formal dialogue between two governments. History teachers and historians alike can play an important role in the reconciliation of deep-rooted conflicts. History education and school history textbooks can serve as "agents of memory." They shape our identity in dynamic ways—not only in how we understand ourselves but also in how we are understood by others. Without meaningful educational reform, other political mechanisms—such as diplomatic meetings between political leaders and other official exchanges between countries—are likely to be top-down and will have only a limited impact on building peace and understanding.

However, dialogues between historians are not enough. The three East Asian countries should promote a dramatic increase in contact and exchange between government officials and key civilian counterpart groups. For example, Chinese and Japanese representatives, including those considered hard-liners on each side, should begin meeting behind closed doors with competent facilitators. These meetings should continue at regular intervals for a period of several years. Considering the tendency of each country's media establishment to demonize the other, a journalists' exchange program should also be implemented to permit reporters and commentators to spend time living among the people in the other country.

As Podeh suggests, controversies over textbooks reveal one important way "societies negotiate, institutionalize, and renegotiate nationalist narratives."[55] In each of the East Asian countries, there are internal debates and controversies over historical issues, especially regarding which historical facts the younger generation should learn in history classes. The lack of internal consensus indicates uncompleted nation building and an ongoing search for identity in these countries. As a *Newsweek* article commented on China's history education: "To face the future confidently, China must be able to face its past truthfully."[56] This comment holds true for each of the East Asian countries.

9

MEMORY, NATIONALISM, AND CHINA'S RISE

IN AN article in *Forbes* in 2008, former Singapore premier Lee Kuan Yew quoted a Chinese poem.[1] Reading this poem, Lee, as one of the few world leaders knowledgeable about both Western and Eastern culture, said that he was sad to see the "gulf in understanding" between Chinese and Westerners. This poem, "What Do You Really Want from Us?" illustrates the obvious Chinese frustration at not being understood, and the great perceptional divide between Chinese and Westerners.

When we were the Sick Man of Asia,
We were called the Yellow Peril.
When we are billed to be the next superpower,
We are called The Threat.
When we closed our doors,
You smuggled drugs to open markets.
When we embrace free trade,
You blame us for taking away your jobs.
When we were falling apart,
You marched in your troops and wanted your fair share.
When we tried to put the broken pieces back together again,
Free Tibet, you screamed. It was an Invasion!
When we tried Communism,
You hated us for being Communist.

When we embrace Capitalism,
You hate us for being Capitalist.
When we had a billion people,
You said we were destroying the planet.
When we tried limiting our numbers,
You said we abused human rights.
When we were poor,
You thought we were dogs.
When we loan you cash,
You blame us for your national debts.
When we build our industries,
You call us polluters.
When we sell you goods,
You blame us for global warming.
When we buy oil,
You call it exploitation and genocide. . . .
What do you really want from us?
Think hard first, then answer.[2]

While this anonymous Chinese poem has been widely distributed and discussed in Internet chat rooms, many say it precisely reflects Chinese sentiment. Westerners may perceive the incidents listed in this poem as independent and incomparable events that happened over an extended period of time. Many Chinese, however, view these events as current and feel closely connected with what happened one hundred years ago. The "century of humiliation" has provided the Chinese with plenty of historical analogies to use, and they often draw parallels between current and historical events.

Over the past three decades, China has been undergoing a tremendous transformation. In addition, the Chinese people have experienced a series of dramatic changes—both domestically and internationally. China is not only changing but also rising on the world stage. Given these facts, surely it is time for the West to rethink its perceptions about China.

Recent media images of people standing in front of tanks in Egypt have conjured comparisons with the "tank man" in Tiananmen Square in 1989. Twenty years ago, as that man stood up to the procession of tanks, many people, both Chinese and foreigners, believed that the government was on the brink of collapse. In this book, I have answered questions about how Beijing survived and even regained popular support after the shameful

1989 crackdown. Prosperity and development are not the only explanatory factors. The preceding discussion has demonstrated the power of historical memory in political transition and national identity formation. By reemphasizing and reopening China's chosen trauma, Beijing was able to make a successful transition from a bankrupt communist ideology to one of nationalism based on historical memory. During the past twenty years, historical memory has been an effective tool for the Chinese Communist Party (CCP) to maintain its political strength.

Historical memory is the prime raw material for constructing China's national identity. A thorough understanding of Chinese historical consciousness is essential to Chinese politics and foreign policy behavior analysis. It helps to understand what goes on in the minds of China's young patriots who will lead this rising power in the remainder of this century. In this concluding chapter, I review and further integrate the findings from the previous chapters, especially regarding how the lenses of history and memory facilitate a better understanding of China's national identity, Chinese nationalism, and China's rise and intentions.

HISTORICAL MEMORY AND NATIONAL IDENTITY

Historical memory has been a subject that many political scientists usually avoid, despite the fact that it continues to be a hot topic in daily newspapers, novels, and performing arts.[3] This is because it is much easier to tell stories about history than to measure the effects of historical memory in a society. It is hard to find direct correlations between perceptions and behavior; likewise, it is also extremely difficult to measure how identities and perceptions influence decision-making behavior.

In this book, I have conducted a systematic examination of the function of historical memory in the national identity formation of contemporary China. In meeting the challenge of addressing historical memory as a causal factor behind action, I have used two analytical frameworks as road maps and tools of analysis. The first framework, as discussed in chapter 1, is a method of measuring historical memory as a collective identity. This framework is based on the theory that a collective identity has four types of identity content: constitutive norms, relational content, cognitive models, and social purpose. Each of the four types implies an alternate causal pathway between this collective identity and policy behaviors or practices.

Constitutive norms specify rules that determine group membership and putative attributes—who a group member is and what it means to be a group member. Earlier discussions have described how the Communist government, especially its top leaders, used the content of historical memory to construct the rules and norms of the ruling party in the post-Tiananmen and post–Cold War eras. As discussed in chapter 5, the leaders of the CCP have creatively used the content of historical memory to generate new theories and explanations to redefine the party's membership and mission in the post-Tiananmen era. No longer is the CCP the "vanguard of the Chinese working class"; it is now "the firmest, most thoroughgoing" patriot, the newest categorization the party has found for itself. After deleting the words "realization of a communist society" from its mission statement, the CCP has made the "great rejuvenation of the Chinese nation" its grand mission.

Historical memory also provides relational content to compose comparisons and references to other groups. Beijing's new emphasis on historical trauma has significantly increased the sensitivity for the government handling relations with countries that have had historical troubles with China. Chapters 7 and 8 particularly concentrated on why China treated the United States and Japan differently from other countries in dealing with disputes and conflicts.

Not only does historical memory facilitate intergroup comparisons as relational content, but it also provides a source of social mobility and social change. As noted in chapter 4, the basic purpose of the patriotic education campaign is twofold: It seeks to improve China through the promotion of positive "social change," with the realization of the "rejuvenation of Chinese nation" as the goal; and it aims to prevent the spread of "social mobility"—people leaving the party or even emigrating as a consequence of negative social identity.

Historical memory has also provided political leaders with special resources for social mobilization of mass support. From Sun Yat-sen to Chiang Kai-shek and Jiang Zemin to Hu Jintao, I have illustrated how different generations of Chinese leaders have all used China's traumatic national experiences to mobilize popular support. Each of these leaders emphasized that his work was to restore China to its former position and glory. Each also asked his subjects to be ready to sacrifice personal interests in order to better serve the grand collective mission of the country. Throughout different political situations, the grand mission of national rejuvenation has been used as an important justification for political dictatorship and various imposed limitations on civil rights, from freedom of speech to the Internet. Chinese people have been told that all of these controls are necessary steps for achieving the ultimate grand mission of the country.

Further, historical memory has profoundly influenced the Chinese people's perception and understanding of the external world. As discussed in chapter 1, the cognitive content of historical memory provides a source of frames, lenses, and analogies to interpret the outside world. I have provided many examples of how policy makers in Beijing have used historical analogies to perform specific cognitive and information-processing tasks deemed essential to political decision making. Chapter 7 particularly focused on how the constructed memory of the century of humiliation affected China's diplomatic handling of three U.S.-China crises in 1996, 1999, and 2001. A deep historical sense of victimization by outside powers, combined with the powerful governmental education campaigns on historical humiliation, has constructed a special Chinese "culture of insecurity" and long-held suspicions about foreign conspiracies against China.

In summation, historical memory has defined modern-day China in numerous ways. It has specified norms or rules for the ruling party's new membership; constituted references and comparisons to other countries, especially China's old foes; affected the way Chinese leaders and people interpret and understand the world; and provided the government and the people with socially appropriate roles to perform. Findings of this research suggest that China's unique national experiences—both China's chosen glory over its ancient civilization and its chosen trauma resulting from the century of humiliation—have played a crucial role in shaping Chinese national identity. Through a systematic examination of the role of historical memory in the processes of identity construction of the Chinese nation, this research has also provided new perspectives in understanding China's new nationalism and China's rise.

CHINA'S "MYTH-TRAUMA" NATIONALISM

Nationalism is a complex phenomenon. There are different types of nationalism, which can be expressed along civic, ethnic, cultural, religious, or ideological lines. Compared with other countries, Chinese nationalism is neither religiously, ethnically, nor ideologically based; it is tied to China's national experiences and strong historical consciousness. The concept of a Chosenness-Myths-Trauma (CMT) complex is a useful tool for understanding Chinese nationalism. As proud citizens of the Central Kingdom, the Chinese feel a strong sense of chosenness, and their experience of Western and Japanese incursions and degeneration into a semicolony is what Chinese people refer to as their "national humiliation." It is this experience that forms China's national trauma. Clearly, understanding the politics of historical memory is essential to comprehending several debates about China's new nationalism in the post–Cold War era.

BETWEEN STATE AND SOCIETY

Recent arguments about nationalism in China have been focused on the debate as to whether Chinese nationalism is a top-down imposition by the state or a bottom-up phenomenon from the people. A point of view that I presented in this research is that any single approach to Chinese nationalism—be it a primordial, constructivist, or instrumentalist explanation of Chinese nationalism or any other either-or debate on this topic—is an oversimplification of a complex reality.

It is true that the Chinese people's special historical consciousness has not only been derived from the country's traumatic national experiences but has also been constructed by the Communist regime for instrumental motives. Chapter 4 discussed how China's nationwide patriotic educational campaign enabled Beijing to creatively use history education as an instrument for the glorification of the party and for the justification of the CCP's single-party rule. This new narrative also means that the discourse of national humiliation has become an integral part of the construction of Chinese nationalism.

For a long time, many China watchers have considered anything coming from the Communist government to be propaganda. Such propaganda is normally taken to be based not on truth but on false, made-up stories. While the patriotic education campaign is certainly part of the government's propaganda apparatus, the actual historical events—such as the foreign invasions and unequal treaties introduced in China's new history textbooks and the articles displayed in those patriotic education museums—are not made up. It is true that the government very often does not provide the complete, unbiased account of historical events in school textbooks and official publications, but the narratives of the official history textbooks are still based on the historical facts, not invented or imagined events. Strategically, the Chinese government incorporates these actual historical events into the message they wish to propagate.

While the patriotic education campaign is a top-down history education project, it is not the Chinese people's only source of knowledge on national humiliation. Just like Premier Wen Jiabao's family, many Chinese suffered great losses during the century of humiliation. The loss of family members, homes, and land all contributed to these traumas, which have been passed from one generation to another in the telling and retelling of the horrors these people endured. Today's youth feel strongly connected to this history that their parents or grandparents witnessed and experienced. They have learned these painful memories through old family photos, diaries, and treasured articles passed down through the generations. Given this large and sympathetic audience, it is difficult to suggest that the patriotic education is merely propaganda. Without comprehension of the primordial background of Chinese nationalism, we would not be able to fully understand why an elite-led, top-down propaganda campaign could have realized its objectives of enhancing the regime's political legitimacy and improving social solidarity.

Indeed, this research suggests that the linkage between the top-down approach and the bottom-up response is historical consciousness. A state's "official nationalism" is often largely dependent on the degree of "social nationalism" shared by all citizens. States must become social nations if they are to successfully mobilize nationalist behavior among the population.[4] Many Chinese share a strong collective historical consciousness regarding the country's century of humiliation, and this is a central element in shaping Chinese national identity. As an integral part of the CCP's reform package, the government abandoned the communist ideology and began to stress the shared sense of Chinese national identity, history, and culture. The party's turn to nationalism can be seen as an indication of its failure to re-create a Chinese community. The CCP feared that it could be excluded from a community the people might create themselves and, as a result, incited nationalistic fervor.[5]

The patriotic education campaign represented a major shift in Beijing's identity politics. The CCP leaders have transformed China from an ideological nation to a social nation. In doing so, the regime has attempted to regain its political legitimacy and power of mobilization—two things the party had lost after the government's brutal crackdown on the student pro-democracy movement in June 1989.

Chinese nationalism has long proved to be an extremely effective device for providing a sense of solidarity in times of social unrest and political uncertainty. As I have illustrated, there is strong historical precedent for the current emphasis on national pride rather than socialist ideology in Chinese political education and party-line campaigns. Patriotic propaganda has an emotional appeal to the more broadly and deeply felt Chinese nationalism. This nationalism is centered on ethnic identity and on the attachment to historical territorial boundaries.[6]

BETWEEN INTERNAL AND EXTERNAL REASONS

Another debate about Chinese nationalism is about whether internal or external factors were the main source that fueled the rise of nationalism in post–Cold War China. Some China observers believe that there were direct connections between the state patriotic education campaign and the rise of anti-Western nationalism. However, others contend that Chinese nationalism arose as a *response* to the increasing Western pressures and hostility toward China after the crackdown at Tiananmen Square in 1989.[7]

I have drawn on the activation of historical memory to explain the ignition of nationalism in recent years. As discussed in chapters 7 and 8, historical consciousness is often buried in deeply held thinking patterns and remains dormant until something causes it to ignite. Understanding its activation is one of the most intriguing phenomena in studying historical memory. During times of radical change in a nation's history, political leaders or social elites often choose to reactivate the group's chosen traumas and glories, which become the fuel to ignite nationalism and further exacerbate the existing conflicts between the group and other nations.[8] Historical memory can also be activated by external factors, such as hostile behavior or dialogue from foreign countries. Whether deliberate or unintentional, memory can be easily reactivated during particular events, especially in moments of crisis.

Chapter 4 highlighted how China's patriotic educational campaign can be viewed as an intentional activation of historical memory by political leaders. When the official communist ideology lost credibility, the regime became incapable of enlisting mass support behind a socialist vision of the future. Under these circumstances, the CCP leaders chose to launch the campaign of patriotic education to reactivate and reinforce people's historical consciousness about national humiliation. The various activities of this campaign, from the revision of history textbooks to the construction of memory sites, aimed to make the young generation of Chinese confront the country's past humiliations. The real purpose of this campaign was to redefine the legitimacy of the CCP's post-Tiananmen leadership and to fill the "spiritual vacuum" after the failure of the official Marxist and Maoist ideologies.

Historical memory makes a useful explanatory model for understanding Chinese conflict behavior during several international crises, in particular why the Chinese reacted so strongly in some international incidents yet remained calm in dealing with others. In chapter 7, I presented three conditions that very often activate Chinese historical memory: emergency or urgency; incidents that involve Chinese suffering; and disputes with a country that has historically had problems with China. In crisis situations of confrontation and conflict—especially when confrontation is perceived by the Chinese as an assault on fundamental identity, face, and authority—historical memory often serves as the major motivating factor. Through the lens of historical memory, an event that might otherwise be viewed as isolated or accidental can be perceived by Chinese leaders as a new form of humiliation. The accidental or mischievous behavior of the United States during the three crises discussed in chapter 7 caused casualties, thus reopening sensitive Chinese feelings about Western imperialism and the exploitation of a weakened China in the nineteenth and early twentieth centuries.

Historical experience has shown that Western pressure on Beijing often backfires; such tactics have proven to offend Chinese patriotic sensibilities, resulting in the activation of Chinese historical memory. Although many Chinese chafe at the current regime's corruption and maladministration, they believe that foreign governments have no business telling China what is right or wrong and should not interfere in Chinese affairs. Thus, any Western unfriendliness in attitude or policy toward Beijing is taken to be aimed at the Chinese people. While Westerners may regard their comments on China affairs as firm and straightforward, the average Chinese citizen perceives such statements as rude and bullying.

External pressure all too often ends up getting exploited by the CCP leaders to cement internal solidarity, undermine political opposition, and mobilize popular support. It is difficult, if not impossible, to foster patriotism without incurring or facing enemies and opponents. China's official media have heavily criticized Western (especially American) foreign policies, with the intent that popular animosity toward opponents will enhance internal solidarity and mobilize domestic support. The rise of nationalism and anti-Western propaganda reinforce each other and together serve the regime's domestic needs in increasing internal cohesion and solidarity.

A thorough understanding of the conditions and circumstances that may activate historical memory can assist us in comprehending the sources and dynamics of nationalism in China. Additionally, such an understanding can provide us with an ability to predict the danger of crisis and conflict in future situations.

BETWEEN POLITICS AND CULTURE

The research presented in this book has made it apparent that historical memory is a large and complicated topic with many diverse aspects. While focused mainly on the political aspects of collective memory—the state use of memory and elite history making—I have also introduced the concept of historical memory as an element of national deep culture. An important characteristic of China's patriotic education is the idea that national history and collective historical memory are a group's national "deep culture." As pre- and subconscious patterns of thinking and feeling, deep culture is not objective knowledge, and very often cannot be explicitly learned. Rather, it is our "collective unconscious" and generally functions out of awareness at the intuitive level. Thus, deep culture remains dormant until confronted with a need to interact.[9]

In the deep culture of each society are the shared narratives of a community such as the cultural knowledge, beliefs, or teachings from community sages. These shared narratives dictate how to act in different circumstances, influencing various practices from how a group of people worship to how they celebrate, and even informing their responses to defeat and humiliation. Many cultures share this trait of having a special "culture of humiliation."

There is a Chinese folk story that has to be mentioned when talking about China's culture of humiliation. This is the story of King Goujian—a story from the fifth century b.c. that has been passed down from one generation to another and has become one of the most famous stories in China. During the Spring and Autumn Period of Chinese history, the kingdom of Wu, led by King Fuchai, attacked the kingdom of Yue. The attack resulted in the capture of the king of Yue, Goujian. Goujian was forced into servitude for Fuchai for several years. Upon being granted his freedom, Goujian returned to Yue and rebuilt his military. To never forget the humiliation he suffered during his defeat, Goujian exchanged his soft silk-padded bedding for a pile of brushwood and hung a gall bladder from the ceiling in his room; he forced himself to taste the gall-bladder every day before having dinner and going to bed. By imposing such measures of suffering upon himself, Goujian reinvigorated his strength and ultimately conquered Wu twenty years later. Historian Paul Cohen believed that the Goujian story is "terribly important," because it tells us about "the interior of the Chinese world at particular moments in time."[10]

Education on the Goujian story has a long history in China. *Woxin changdan* (卧薪尝胆), meaning "sleeping on brushwood and tasting gall," is a four-word idiom derived from the Goujian story that all schoolchildren learn in primary school. The main theme of the lesson on *Woxin changdan* is to teach the younger generation how to respond to defeat and humiliation. The emphasis is not placed on the humiliation itself, but on the way one responds to this humiliation. Throughout China's history, the education on the Goujian story has not been limited to the individual level of encouraging people to accomplish their personal goals through hard work and persistence; more importantly, the education is applicable for the entire community, as it teaches the whole country the importance of remembering their group's past defeat and humiliation and how to rectify the collective humiliation.

Through the ancient Goujian story, we can better understand the way in which the Chinese responded to their national experiences in the century of humiliation, the period from the First Opium War to the Anti-Japanese War. We have also cultivated a greater understanding of the Chinese outlook through three other examples of China's past and present leaders mentioned in this book:

- The tale of Chiang Kai-shek, who wrote the two Chinese characters *Xuechi* ("Avenge Humiliation") in his diary as a daily routine every day for more than twenty years.
- The story of Wen Jiabao, who always used his childhood war memories to introduce his political beliefs: "I can tell you clearly and definitely, I myself and my people will use our own hands to build my country well."[11]
- The example of Hu Jintao, who always ends his public speeches with a call for people to "strive harder for the great rejuvenation of the Chinese nation."

From King Goujian twenty-five centuries ago to Chiang seventy years ago to the present-day Hu and Wen, Chinese leaders of different time periods all had the same attitude toward defeat and humiliation, and they shared the same unwavering determination to rid the country of shame. Each of these stories illustrates the power not only of historical memory but also of deep national culture.

While history and memory can be used as tools for political purposes, the influence of politics is often short lived. For instance, there is no way of telling how long the patriotic education campaign of today will last, as there are so many factors influencing political maneuvers. However, we can be sure that the Goujian story will continue to pass from one generation to another in the Chinese community. This is a difference between politics and culture. From high-profile politics to subconscious national deep culture, from raw materials for constructing identity to tools for ideological campaigning, the multifaceted dimensions of history and memory issues in China help us understand the complexity of Chinese society.

BETWEEN MEMORY AND CYBERSPACE

A common view of collective memory is that, as time passes, the younger generation's memory and attitude toward the group's past traumas gradually diminish. In the case of China, however, the country's post–Cold War popular nationalism is essentially a youth nationalism, as the most active participants are young people who did not directly experience national humiliation. According to Minxin Pei, young, urban, educated Chinese are more nationalistic and are the ones using the Internet to promote nationalistic fervor.[12] Some China observers have also found that highly connected and Internet-savvy Chinese youths today have emerged as virulent nationalists.[13]

When the Internet first emerged as an important communication tool, many Western observers believed that it would play a significant role in democratizing opinion among authoritarian societies such as China. However, the Internet has now been exploited as the new media for nationalistic rhetoric. In a 2002 *Weekly Standard* article entitled "Who Lost China's Internet?" Ethan Gutmann argued that the Internet in China has been "a tool of the Beijing government, not a force for democracy."[14]

China has seen a boom in Internet usage in recent years. The number of Internet users reached about 253 million by the end of 2008, putting it ahead of the United States as the world's biggest Internet market.

Additionally, a survey found that nearly 70 percent of China's Internet users were age 30 or younger.[15] The emergence of the Internet in the last two decades has given nationalists more power to express themselves following particular incidents. Various Internet chat rooms played important roles in organizing the 2005 anti-Japanese protests in China, for example. Shinzo Abe, the secretary general of Japan's ruling Liberal Democratic Party, commented, "Because of the anti-Japanese education in China, it is easy to light the fire of these demonstrations and, because of the Internet, it is easy to assemble a lot of people."[16] The Internet has revolutionized the way the Chinese protest in the streets, facilitating larger and more decentralized demonstrations.[17]

The Internet has also made studying history easier by providing today's young people with a wealth of readily accessible information about historical events online. Internet chat rooms have provided a forum for facilitating dialogue about past historical traumas and events. Whenever there is an important anniversary coming up, Chinese Internet users post their comments and initiate discussions about these events. According to Gerrit Gong, modern digital and Internet technologies enhance memory and the implications of history and memory.[18] Gong sees the new technologies, which allow images and sound to be played repeatedly and over great distances, as enhancing people's memories of past events. With an expanding global network and an intimately personal reach, such technological advances have made strong contributions to historical memory, because "they bring together images and sounds that give remembering and forgetting issues surprising intensity, speed, scope, and emotional resonance."[19] Forgetting past traumas may become even more difficult.

BETWEEN GLOBALISM AND NATIONALISM

Today, Beijing is facing a dilemma between globalism and nationalism. The manipulation of history and the rise of nationalism reinforce each other and together serve the regime's domestic needs to increase its legitimacy and internal cohesion. As noted earlier, there is a feedback loop in China whereby nationalistic history education stimulates the rise of nationalism, and the rise of nationalism provides a bigger market for nationalistic messages. However, the same two elements have also constituted major obstacles to the government's further opening up and pursuit of China's national interests in a globalized world.

Clearly, nationalism is a two-edged sword. On the one hand, as Paul Cohen notes:

> Chinese leaders welcomed popular nationalism to the extent that it served as a substitute form of political validation and had a genuine interest in reminding the Chinese people of past humiliations at the hands of the West and Japan and in celebrating all instances (such as the Hong Kong reversion and the victory over Japanese aggression in 1945) in which these humiliations were "wiped clean."[20]

But on the other hand, the rise of nationalism has also increased pressure on the government's policy-making abilities. The government also fears a completely unfettered popular nationalism that might imperil the stability of the regime, undermine China's modernization efforts, and interfere with the government's foreign policy.[21]

China has been one of the greatest beneficiaries of globalization, bringing the nation unprecedented wealth and power. As China embraced globalization, millions of jobs were created and wealth among all people in China continues to increase. Compared with just twenty years ago, even the lowest class in China has seen its standard of living vastly improve. However, it is dangerous, if not impossible, for a big power like China to embrace both globalism and nationalism simultaneously.

A *YaleGlobal* article by James Farrer presents a good example of how the 2005 anti-Japanese protests put the Shanghai city government in a difficult situation. According to Farrer, the city government was under conflicting pressures between national and local interests during the nationalist protests against Japanese history textbooks and Japanese ambition of becoming a permanent member of the UN Security Council. While the Beijing leadership saw no need to address affected business owners, the city government was unwilling to further endanger its cosmopolitan ambitions in order to appease nationalist sentiments.

> The day after the protest, the municipal government went into damage control mode, contacting shop owners whose property was destroyed and providing forms to claim compensation. The head of Shanghai's Foreign Affairs Office met with the Japanese consulate general and expressed regret for property damage. Therefore, while the Chinese national government publicly denied any need to apologize or compensate for the protests, the Shanghai city government moved quickly.[22]

It is interesting to note that during all of the recent popular anti-foreign nationalism incidents—from the Belgrade bombing and the U.S. spy plane incident to the Japanese textbook and Yasukuni Shrine controversies—the Chinese government not only negotiated with foreign governments but also had to negotiate with its domestic audiences, especially China's new nationalists. As Kenneth Pyle put it, "The government struggles to maintain its version of the master narrative, but the effort to both promote and contain nationalism is fraught with danger."[23] By the same token, Gong commented that China's "overreliance on history to provide national legitimization could challenge the ability of any Chinese government to satisfy its own people or to engage internationally."[24]

For China to break the feedback loop of nationalism reactivating historical memory and historical memory feeding nationalism, it must change its historical narrative. In light of this notion, I recommend a "middle-out approach," recognizing the important role that midlevel leaders—academics, historians, bureaucrats—play in the process of nation building and peacebuilding. China adopted this tradition of a middle-out approach when new intellectuals in the early twentieth century, such as Lu Xun, reached out to summon both the common people and the top Chinese elites for national salvation, as discussed in chapter 3.

During the last few decades, China has undergone an extraordinary transformation. A new middle class is on the rise, and a civil society has emerged. Remarkably, many of these changes have been initiated not from the top down, but from the middle out. China's ever-growing, influential intellectual and business elites—of which Ma Licheng, Shi Yinghong, and Yuan Weishi are representative—are working to transmit new concepts to the upper echelons as well as to the general public. As illustrated in chapter 8, there are ways history and memory can be used to reverse negative discourse. Through a middle-out approach, changes can be made to the national narrative, allowing it to confront its past. Without a new approach to national history, however, the Chinese are doomed to remain in this dilemma between nationalism and globalism. Indeed, China needs more people to participate in the new discourse of peace and reconciliation.

An enduring tenet of the post–Cold War era is that globalization can be a catalyst for democratization and a means of opening up closed or semiclosed societies. However, we must also understand that globalization and marketization may contribute to the development of nationalism and chauvinistic social discourse among these societies for a given period of time. I am a personal acquaintance of several well-known Chinese journalists and scholars reporting and commenting on global issues. They are frequent international visitors, with plenty of sources of information. It is interesting to observe how the points of view of journalists and scholars vary when they are speaking to different crowds. For instance, when they talk with friends, their opinions are rather objective. However, they suddenly become "anti-U.S. heroes" when they are directly facing the public. The only explanation for this type of behavior is that there is a huge market in Chinese society for anti-U.S. and nationalist discourse. Under the current social context of China, nationalistic voices are far more marketable than those calling for peace and rationality.

There is another tendency that can be seen as a consequence of globalization. China's embrace of globalization has aligned once fractious elites behind a banner of shared economic interest. China's globalization dividends, including its trade surplus and the world's highest reserves of foreign currency, have provided the government with ample resources to buy the loyalty of the intellectual and economic elites. Scholars, entrepreneurs, and government officials, who just two decades earlier stood divided in Tiananmen Square, are now allies and have become the stakeholders and co-owners of the new "China, Inc." For example, professors in China's top universities now regularly receive generous state funding for research. In addition, government officials and military officers have received frequent salary raises, and their incomes have doubled in the last five years. It appears that those in China on the top are content in sharing the dividends of their prosperity while harmoniously singing the praises of globalization and the stability of single-party rule.

The empirical core of this book is concentrated on decoding one of the most misunderstood and least addressed elements in Chinese politics today—historical memory. Without directly addressing Chinese nationalism, I have used historical memory to explain the cultural and historical foundations of that nationalism. As this analysis has indicated, an understanding of the politics of historical memory is essential to comprehending the linkage between the top-down state nationalism and popular social nationalism, the conditions and circumstances that ignite nationalist movements, and the controversies between globalism and nationalism in today's China.

HISTORICAL MEMORY AND CHINA'S RISE

While the whole world is talking about China's "rise," the Chinese like to use another word—*rejuvenation* (*fuxing*). Through this term, the Chinese emphasize their determination to restore themselves to their former position and glory. As discussed in chapter 5, the word *rejuvenation* is deeply rooted in China's history and historical memory. Although China was once the mightiest empire and is the oldest civilization in the world, its modern history beginning from the middle of the nineteenth century has been full of humiliation. For this reason, the Chinese have aspired to revive their historical glory. In response to this popular desire, the CCP has replaced the wording of the party's mission since the end of the Cold War from its emphasis on the "realization of communism" to "the great rejuvenation of the Chinese nation."

Indeed, this is the most profound transition in the history of the Chinese Communist Party. The CCP has become less ideologically based since the 1980s, evolving from a revolutionary party of worker-peasants into a nationalist party of elites in recent years. Any person interested in the study of Chinese foreign policy should pay particular attention to this background. CCP leader Hu Jintao is an enthusiastic proponent of the "great rejuvenation" of China, often ending his public speeches by calling for the people to "strive harder for the great rejuvenation of the Chinese nation." Hu has even said that his personal dream is to "achieve the rejuvenation of the Chinese nation."[25] For many Chinese, the rejuvenation of China simply means to be *fuqiang* (富强)—prosperous and strong. While this may seem like a goal all countries strive toward, the particular usage of the word *fuqiang* indicates how important this goal is to the Chinese, as it is deeply rooted in people's historical memory.

The Chinese collective memory is full of memories of poverty, starvation, and famine. Throughout China's long history, wealth had always been concentrated among a few groups of people, while most citizens lived in poverty and owned very little individual property. As discussed in chapter 6, frequent natural disasters exacerbated the poverty and famine. Moreover, Confucianism—the most important system of moral, philosophical, and quasi-religious thought in ancient China—actually discourages people to strive for wealth and personal property. For this reason, Chinese leader Deng Xiaoping's remarks in 1992 were considered revolutionary when he said, "China has been poor for thousands of years. It is time to prosper." He also said, "To get rich is glorious." Deng's famous remarks launched a full-scale revolution in China. His economic reform did more than just unleash economic drive; it also overturned the millennia of ordinary Chinese setting aside their personal welfare for emperors, warlords, and interest groups.

The characters *fu* and *qiang* are deeply connected with one another, as the Chinese realized that a poor country cannot be a strong country. In China, the saying "Backwardness incurs beatings by others" (*luohou jiuyao aida*) has been used as a political theory to explain China's national experiences during the one hundred years of national humiliation. Many Chinese believe that China has been bullied by foreign powers in modern times only because China was poor and weak during that specific period. As mentioned in chapter 5, the CCP has been drawing upon this theory to justify its arms, nuclear, and manned space programs. The idea of building a strong army has also been very popular among common people. While those outside of China debate whether the national goal of achieving a "rich country and strong army" (*fuguo qiangbing*) could turn aggressive and upset the status quo, for the Chinese this is merely a humble goal. It is the utmost goal of the collective society that their country is strong enough to protect itself and therefore that the national humiliation of the past will never return.

In the CCP's new constitution that was amended in 2007, the ruling party pictured a "well-off society" (*xiaokang shehui*) by 2021 (the CCP's centenary):

> The strategic objectives of economic and social development at this new stage in the new century are to consolidate and develop the relatively comfortable life initially attained, bring China into a moderately prosperous society of a higher level to the benefit of well over one billion people by the time of the Party's centenary and bring the per capita GDP up to the level of moderately developed countries and realize modernization in the main by the time of the centenary of the People's Republic of China.[26]

According to this goal, China's per capita gross domestic product (GDP) is projected at around $10,000 by 2021, and the country's GDP per capita in 2000 was about $800.

While a country can set achievable goals to quantify its wealth and strength, there is also an important nonmaterial objective in China's discourse of rejuvenation: respect. For the Chinese, rejuvenation can only be achieved by being respected and free from foreign invasions by other countries. This idea of respect is deeply related to the people's historical memory. Foreign ridicule of Chinese backwardness and physical differences (such as the "Sick Man of East Asia" idea) has been an integral part of the Chinese collective memory of national humiliation, and this mentality has affected Chinese people's attitudes, interpretation, and behavior in interacting with other countries.

While the ruling party in China is willing to tell people about its dreams and mission, it is often difficult for the outside world to interpret China's intentions. As mentioned, the current debates tend to focus on two competing arguments that suggest either that China's rise will upset the balance of power or that interdependence will cause China to become more pacific and to integrate with the world. Iain Johnston posed the question this way: Is China a status quo power or revisionist power?[27]

Since no country's intentions can be articulated in such simple terms, I do not offer a direct answer to this question. However, I believe Jeffrey Legro put it best when he said that existing answers to this question generally lack the very thing needed: "a general explanation of contingent change in the intentions of China."

> Even if we had access to the inner workings of the Chinese government today, it is unlikely that information would tell us about future aims. Even if China today has some secret plan for world hegemony or world harmony, those aims will be subject to change by China's very growth and the process by which it unfolds.[28]

Indeed, it is nearly impossible to predict China's true intent, even with one-on-one interviews with top Chinese leaders. Chinese leaders insist that China will rise peacefully and will never seek hegemony. In a speech at Cambridge University in February 2009, Premier Wen Jiabao made it very clear that the political science theory of hegemony does not apply to China:

> The argument that a big power is bound to seek hegemony does not apply to China. Seeking hegemony goes against China's cultural tradition, as well as the will of the Chinese people. China's development harms no one and threatens no one. We shall be a peace-loving country, a country that is eager to learn from and cooperate with others. We are committed to building a harmonious world.[29]

We can quote Wen's statement, but that is not real evidence that China will actually rise peacefully, as some already maintain that this is just Beijing's propaganda. Even if the current leaders of China are truly genuine in their rhetoric, there is no way of predicting whether the next generation of leaders will follow suit. The debate over China is not about what China wants today, but rather what it might want tomorrow.

Any judgment on national intentions should be based on a good understanding of the country's national identity and national interest. For that reason, I have focused this book on understanding China's national identity. I argue that historical memory is the key element in China's national identity formation, because without understanding this element, we cannot fully comprehend Chinese people's perceptions, attitudes, and intentions. I would suggest that the Chinese people's historical consciousness and the myth-trauma complex are the dominant ideas in China's public rhetoric and bureaucratic procedures.

Understanding a country's foreign policy, especially its future intentions, is a significant and critical challenge for scholars and policy makers. Traditional methods of studying foreign policy and national intentions have focused on the target state's political, economic, and social background—institutions, policies, and people (leaders, leadership, and decision making)—all of which are visible. After years of relative neglect, theorists and practitioners finally recognize culture and other ideational factors are keys to understanding state behavior and international politics. Culture, as Raymond Cohen reflected, is "the hidden dimension," unseen, yet exerting a pervasive influence on the behavior of individuals, groups, and society.[30]

From the visible institutions to the hidden dimensions of culture, ideas, and historical memory, our understanding of state behavior and foreign policy also goes deeper and broader and is much more comprehensive. However, researchers also need to proceed with caution when using ideational factors as variables. Such factors cannot be treated as relatively fixed sets of psychological traits, as static values or orientations. Since culture and ideas themselves are dynamic, adaptive, and open, researchers must be keen to the notion that they can—and often do—change.

I have employed China's history education and the top-down ideological education campaigns to explain the rise of nationalism in China in the 1990s and 2000s. However, following the same constructivist approach, to know China's intentions and what Chinese nationalism will look like in 2020, it is also necessary to pay attention to China's identity education and social discourses in the next several years.

We must also be aware that the patriotic education campaign is only one facet of China's education system. Today, 300 million Chinese children are learning English, and over a million Chinese young people are studying abroad.[31] In 2009 alone, 98,510 Chinese graduate and undergraduate students poured into U.S. colleges and universities, and these numbers are increasing with every new term. According to a report by the Institute of International Education, an 11 percent growth in undergraduate enrollments in 2009 was driven largely by a 60 percent increase from China.[32]

Through this research, it is evident that historical memory has become institutionalized and embedded in China's educational system, popular culture, and public media. However, at the same time, diverse cultures and information from various parts of the world, especially the West, are also featured daily on China's television, radio, and print media. Hollywood movies, Japanese cartoons, and Korean TV shows are all extremely popular among Chinese young people. It is obvious that two tendencies are developing at the same time. While there may be controversies between humiliation education and learning English, both will play large roles in the identity formation of China's next generation, thus influencing China's intentions in the future.

Much of the recent discussion regarding China has revolved around the government's national strategy of a "peaceful rise." For many, China can rise peacefully only after it has changed from a Communist dictatorship to a multiparty democracy, where officials are chosen in regular elections. However, without liberation from the powerful complex of historical myth and trauma, a multiparty democracy could lead China into a dangerous development, because history and memory issues can be easily used by nationalist leaders as tools for mobilization or in generating conflicts between the new democratic China and its old enemies.

The Chinese are pursuing a national rejuvenation. However, in this process, China should modernize not only its financial system and highway network but also its political system and citizen education. Chinese leaders and elites should recognize that their dream of restoring China's long-lost glory should actually be geared more toward a realistic, and less nationalistic, goal of nation building.

Certainly not every member of a community, especially one as large and diverse as China's, shares the same historical memory. The collective memory of a community in a rural area in China might emphasize famine and domestic violence more than the events of the century of humiliation. But I have focused on what I refer to as the "master historical narrative" in China. Since the education system and foreign policy making both come from the state, this master narrative is a major force in Chinese society.

However, we should not forget the brutal internal conflicts the Chinese have experienced during the recent centuries, including civil wars, revolutions, mass violence, and famines. Many of the historical truths of these domestic conflicts and violence are still concealed in the official explanations. In today's China, the master narrative of national history is still based on official statements rather than public consensus. Despite the fact that party leaders have made an effort to teach Chinese people to "never forget national humiliation," they have always avoided discussing the tremendous failures and catastrophes that have been caused by the party.

The ruling party's legitimacy has been built upon distorted "historical contributions" that have effectively infiltrated the Chinese people's historical consciousness. The politics of such historical memory has provided China's ruling party with the instrument for its mass mobilization and social cohesion. Given these facts, China's democratization might finally begin from the point of disclosure of these historical truths. In this sense, we can better understand the importance of history and memory issues for China's domestic politics and international orientation, and the significance of studying China's current affairs through the lens of historical memory.

ACKNOWLEDGMENTS

THIS BOOK was completed through the support of many people. I first want to extend my warm appreciation to the U.S. Institute of Peace. I completed the final revision of this book while serving as a senior fellow at the institute's Jennings Randolph Program for International Peace. I would like to thank my colleagues at Seton Hall University, particularly in the John C. Whitehead School of Diplomacy and International Relations. I also want to express my gratitude to my advisors, Kevin Avruch, Carol Hamrin, John Paden, and Richard Rubenstein, at the Institute for Conflict Analysis and Resolution at George Mason University.

Thank you to Andrew Berry, Vance Crowe, Chandra DeNap, Joseph Imbriano, Heather Martino, Lauren Reed, and Francis Tanczos. Not only were they my first readers, but they also provided valuable feedback, suggestions, and revisions, many of which have been absorbed in this book. I would also like to thank the anonymous reviewers for their thorough and detailed comments. I have incorporated substantial revisions throughout the manuscript based on the suggestions I received from them.

This book is dedicated to my wife Xiaojuan. Without her love, support, and encouragement, this work would not have been started or completed. And to my little daughter Anya, who was born while I was occupied with this book: Anya, now that this book is completed, Daddy looks forward to spending more time with you.

NOTES

PREFACE

1. David Shambaugh, "China at 60: The Road to Prosperity," *Time*, September 28, 2009.
2. Shirk, *China: Fragile Superpower*, 10.
3. Legro, "What China Will Want," 515.

INTRODUCTION: FROM "TANK MAN" TO CHINA'S NEW PATRIOTS

1. Matthew Forney, "China's Loyal Youth," *New York Times*, April 13, 2008.
2. Barmé, "Anniversaries in the Light, and in the Dark."
3. Smith, *The Ethnic Origins of Nations*, 383.
4. Callahan, "History, Identity and Security," 184.
5. Pennebaker, *Collective Memory of Political Events*, vii.
6. Eller, *From Culture to Ethnicity to Conflict*.
7. Gong, *Memory and History*, 26.
8. Gries, "Face Nationalism," 15.
9. Unger, *Using the Past*, 1.
10. Thurston, "Community and Isolation," 170.
11. Minxin Pei, "China's Fragile Mindset," *Christian Science Monitor*, April 9, 2001.
12. PEP, *Quanrizhi putong gaoji zhongxue jiaokeshu*, 42–47.
13. Lind, "Regime Type and National Remembrance."

14. Fukuyama, "The New Nationalism," 38–41.
15. Shaules, *Deep Culture*, 12.
16. Markovits and Reich, *The German Predicament*, 9.
17. Cohen, *Speaking to History*, 232–33.
18. This definition was given by the journal *History & Memory*, published by the Indiana University Press.

1. HISTORICAL MEMORY, IDENTITY, AND POLITICS

1. T. H. R., "Uses of the Past," 5.
2. McBride, *History and Memory in Modern Ireland*, 1.
3. Roudometof, *Collective Memory*, 5.
4. Gong, *Memory and History*, 26–27.
5. Jedlicki, "Historical Memory," 226.
6. Roudometof, *Collective Memory*, 6–7.
7. Ibid.
8. Goldstein and Keohane, "Ideas and Foreign Policy," 4.
9. George, "The Causal Nexus," 95.
10. Bruland and Horowitz, "Research Report," 1.
11. George, "The Causal Nexus."
12. Wang, *Limited Adversaries*, 28.
13. Callahan, "History, Identity and Security," 184.
14. See, for example, Halbwachs, *On Collective Memory*. See also Eller, *From Culture to Ethnicity to Conflict*.
15. Smith, *The Ethnic Origins of Nations*.
16. Volkan, *Bloodlines*, 48.
17. Galtung, "The Construction of National Identities."
18. Volkan, *Bloodlines*, 48.
19. Volkan, "Large Group Identity," 6.
20. Volkan, *Bloodlines*, 48.
21. Ibid., 81.
22. Volkan, "Large Group Identity," 6.
23. Smith, *The Ethnic Origins of Nations*.
24. Gong, *Memory and History*, 26–27.
25. Halbwachs, *On Collective Memory*, 224.
26. Anderson, *Imagined Communities*.
27. Hutchinson, *Ethnicity*, 8–9.
28. Kaufman, *Modern Hatreds*.
29. Kammen, *The Mystic Chords of Memory*, 5.
30. Apple and Christian-Smith, *The Politics of the Textbook*, 10.
31. Ibid.

32. Tajfel, *Human Groups and Social Categories.*
33. Khong, *Analogies at War.*
34. Putnam and Holmer, "Framing, Reframing, and Issue Development."
35. Avruch, *Culture and Conflict Resolution.*
36. Markovits and Reich, *The German Predicament*, 9.
37. Khong, *Analogies at War*, 101.
38. Ibid.
39. Record and Terrill, *Iraq and Vietnam.*
40. Griffin, *The New Pearl Harbor.*
41. Gong, *Memory and History*, 28.
42. Ibid., 36.
43. Volkan, *Bloodlines.*
44. Bell, *Memory, Trauma and World Politics*, 6.
45. Jedlicki, "Historical Memory," 226.
46. Smith, *Myths and Memories of the Nation*, 9.
47. Kaufman, *Modern Hatreds.*
48. Zerubavel, *Recovered Roots.*
49. Bell, *Memory, Trauma and World Politics*, 20.
50. Zajda and Zajda. "The Politics of Rewriting History."
51. Bar-Tal, *Shared Beliefs in a Society.*
52. A group of scholars at Harvard University formed an interdisciplinary research team to study how to overcome the problems that hamper the more systematic incorporation of identity as a variable in helping to explain political action. The Harvard Identity Project's main publications include Abdelal et al., "Identity as a Variable."
53. Abdelal et al., "Treating Identity as a Variable," 3.
54. Abdelal et al., "Identity as a Variable," 696.
55. Ibid., 698–99.
56. Abdelal et al., "Treating Identity as a Variable," 8.
57. Tajfel and Turner, "Social Identity Theory."
58. Mercer, "Anarchy and Identity."
59. Tajfel and Turner, "Social Identity Theory," 9.
60. Goldstein and Keohane, "Ideas and Foreign Policy."
61. Katzenstein, "Alternative Perspectives," 24.

2. CHOSEN GLORY, CHOSEN TRAUMA

1. Teng and Fairbank, *China's Response to the West*, 266–69.
2. Jiang, *Zhongguo jindaishi*, 17. Unless otherwise stated, all translations performed by the author.
3. Mitter, *A Bitter Revolution*, 30.

4. Ebrey, *The Cambridge Illustrated History of China*, 257.
5. Jiang, *Zhongguo jindaishi*, 15–16.
6. Volkan, *Bloodlines*, 81.
7. Galtung, "Construction of National Identities," 244–45.
8. Galtung, *Globe Projections*, 9–10.
9. Chiang, *China's Destiny*, trans. Wang Chung-hui, 9.
10. Liu, *The Clash of Empires*, 94.
11. Von Falkenhausen, "The Waning of the Bronze Age," 544.
12. Dikötter, *The Discourse of Race in Modern China*, 2.
13. Ibid.
14. Volkan, "Large Group Identity," 6.
15. Madeleine Brand and Howard Berkes, "China Celebrates Opening of Summer Olympics," *National Public Radio*, August 8, 2008.
16. "Beijing Olympic Games Open in Passion as Quake-Affected China Hosts World with Pride," *Xinhua*, August 9, 2008, available at http://news.xinhuanet.com/english/2008–08/09/content_9067226.htm.
17. "Ancient Chinese Music at Beijing Olympics Opening," *Xinhua*, August 8, 2008, available at http://news.xinhuanet.com/english/2008-08/08/content_9052538.htm.
18. Tamura, *China*, 70.
19. PEP, *Chuji zhongxue jiaokeshu zhongguo gudaishi*, 139.
20. Xu, *China and the Great War*, 21.
21. Wade, "The Zheng He Voyages," 1.
22. Wen, "Turning Your Eyes to China."
23. Mitter, *A Bitter Revolution*, 26.
24. Callahan, "National Insecurities," 206.
25. Wireman, "The People's Republic of China Turns 50," 19.
26. Gries, "Face Nationalism,"14.
27. Hu, "Dui lishi xu xinhuai qianjing."
28. Volkan, *Bloodlines*, 48.
29. Fairbank and Goldman, *China*, 201–5.
30. Schoppa, *Revolution and Its Past*, 120.
31. Jiang, *Zhongguo jindaishi*, 6.
32. Ibid, 9.
33. Ebrey, *The Cambridge Illustrated History of China*, 257.
34. Spence, *The Search for Modern China*, 155.
35. Ebrey, *The Cambridge Illustrated History of China*, 239.
36. PEP, *Putong gaozhong kecheng biaozhun shiyan jiaokeshu lishi*, 52.
37. Kataoka, *Resistance and Revolution in China*, 5.
38. Based on the museum brochure purchased by the author from the Opium War Museum in Humen, Guangdong Province. Translated by the author.

39. Hanes and Sanello, *The Opium Wars*, 176.
40. Ibid., 223–28.
41. Barmé, "Yuanming Yuan."
42. Ibid.
43. Callahan, *China*, 16.
44. Ibid.
45. PEP, *Putong gaozhong kecheng biaozhun shiyan jiaokeshu lishi*, 52.
46. See, for example, "China Says Christie's Auction of Looted Relics a Lesson to World," Xinhua, March 2, 2009.
47. Ebrey, *The Cambridge Illustrated History of China*, 253.
48. Fairbank and Goldman, *China*, 221.
49. The conflict description in this section was based on Fairbank and Goldman, *China*, 220; Ebrey, *The Cambridge Illustrated History of China*, 252–54; and the "Sino-Japanese War" entry in the *Encyclopedia Britannica*.
50. See, for example, "MIT Web Page Upsets Chinese Students: Image Depicting Sino-Japanese War Removed After Complaints," Associated Press, April 28, 2006; and Peter C. Perdue, "Open Letter to Chinese Students at MIT," April 28, 2006, http://web.mit.edu/history/Open%20Letter%20to%20Chinese%20Students%20at%20MIT.pdf.
51. Fairbank and Liu, *The Cambridge History of China*, 115–23.
52. Ibid., 125–30.
53. Mitter, *A Bitter Revolution*, 34.
54. Ebrey, *The Cambridge Illustrated History of China*, 285.
55. Ibid.
56. Ibid.
57. Chang, *The Rape of Nanking*, 51–52.
58. Askew, "The Nanjing Incident."
59. Fairbank and Liu, *The Cambridge History of China*, 533–40.
60. Ibid., 540.
61. See PEP, *Quanrizhi putong gaoji zhongxue jiaokeshu zhongguo jinxiandaishi*, 43, and Higher Education Press, *Zhongguo jixiandaishi*, 519–20.
62. Chiang, *China's Destiny*, 17–55.
63. Ibid., 39.
64. Ibid., 40.
65. Fairbank and Goldman, *China*, 200.
66. Hsu, *The Rise of Modern China*, 190.
67. Fairbank and Goldman, *China*, 201.
68. Wang, *China's Unequal Treaties*, 11.
69. Ibid.
70. Chiang, *China's Destiny*, 31.
71. Treaty of Shimonoseki, 1895, translation available at http://www.taiwandocuments.org/shimonoseki01.htm.

72. Ibid.
73. Xu, *China and the Great War*, 174.
74. Chiang, *China's Destiny*, 31.
75. Boxer Protocol, Article 6, September 7, 1901, translation available at http://www.international.ucla.edu/asia/article.asp?parentid=18133.
76. Spence, *The Search for Modern China*, 235.
77. Boxer Protocol, Article 9.
78. Chiang, *China's Destiny*, 43.
79. Mitter, *A Bitter Revolution*, 40.
80. Michael Duffy, ed., "'21 Demands' Made by Japan to China, 18 January 1915," August 22, 2009, http://www.firstworldwar.com/source/21demands.htm.
81. Hsu, *The Rise of Modern China*, 494–502.
82. Callahan, "National Insecurities," 203.
83. Ibid., 210.
84. Chiang, *China's Destiny*, 54.
85. PEP, *Putong gaozhong kecheng biaozhun shiyan jiaokeshu lishi*, 61.
86. Chiang, *China's Destiny*, 59.
87. "Chiang Kai-shek: Death of the Casualty," *Time*, April 14, 1975.
88. Gries, *China's New Nationalism*, 47.
89. Volkan, "Large Group Identity."
90. Mitter, *A Bitter Revolution*, 40.
91. Ebrey, *The Cambridge Illustrated History of China*, 258.
92. Fairbank and Goldman, *China*, 205.

3. FROM "ALL-UNDER-HEAVEN" TO A NATION-STATE: HUMILIATION AND NATION-BUILDING

1. Morse, *The International Relations of the Chinese Empire*, 223.
2. Kim, "The Evolving Asian System," 37–38.
3. Xu, "Internationalism, Nationalism, National Identity," 102.
4. Townsend, "Chinese Nationalism."
5. Ibid., 12.
6. Duara, "De-constructing the Chinese Nation," 34.
7. Townsend, "Chinese Nationalism," 2.
8. Xu, "Internationalism, Nationalism, National Identity," 102–3.
9. Duara, "De-constructing the Chinese Nation," 31.
10. Hsu, *China's Entrance*, 13.
11. Pye, "International Relations in Asia," 9.
12. Xu, "Internationalism, Nationalism, National Identity," 103.
13. Kohn, "The Nature of Nationalism," 1001–21.
14. Xu, "Internationalism, Nationalism, National Identity," 102.

15. Kohn, "The Nature of Nationalism," 1001.
16. Liang, *Wuxu zhengbian ji*, 44.
17. Xu, "Internationalism, Nationalism, National Identity," 103.
18. Fitzgerald, "The Nationless State," 66.
19. Xu, "Historical Memories of May Fourth."
20. Levenson, *Confucian China*.
21. Townsend, "Chinese Nationalism," 1–30.
22. Cohen, "Remembering and Forgetting," 1.
23. Ibid., 20.
24. Ibid., 23.
25. Lu, *Nahan*, 23.
26. Wang, *China's Unequal Treaties*, 63.
27. Barmé, "Anniversaries."
28. Wang, *China's Unequal Treaties*, 78–80.
29. Jayshree Bajoria, "Nationalism in China," *Newsweek*, April 24, 2008.
30. Wang, *China's Unequal Treaties*, 67.
31. Ibid., 72.
32. Fitzgerald, *Awakening China*.
33. Quoted in Wang, *China's Unequal Treaties*, 65.
34. Ibid.
35. Wang, *China's Unequal Treaties*, 70.
36. Huang, "Chiang Kai-shek's Politics," 11–12.
37. Ibid. This diary entry was quoted from Wang Yugao, *Shilue Gaoben* [Shilue Manuscripts]. Archives of President Chiang Kai-shek, Academia Historica, Hsintien, Taiwan, May 9, 1928.
38. Ibid., 29.
39. Chiang, *China's Destiny*, 46.
40. Wang, *China's Unequal Treaties*, 78.
41. Ibid., 74.
42. Fitzgerald, "The Nationless State," 73.
43. Cohen, "Remembering and Forgetting," 23.
44. Yick, *Making of Urban Revolution in China*, 185.
45. "China: Crisis," *Time*, November 13, 1944, available at http://www.time.com/time/magazine/article/0,9171,801570-4,00.html.
46. Chiang, *China's Destiny*, 46.
47. Callahan, "History, Identity and Security," 185.
48. Ibid., 210.
49. Cohen, "Remembering and Forgetting," 9.
50. Wang, *China's Unequal Treaties*, 63.
51. Xu, "Historical Memories of May Fourth."
52. Mao, "The Chinese People Have Stood Up!"
53. Weber, *Essays in Sociology*.

54. Xu, "Internationalism, Nationalism, National Identity," 102.
55. Mao, *Selected Works*, 2:224.
56. Guo, "Political Legitimacy and China's Transition," 8.
57. Coble, "China's 'New Remembering,'" 397.
58. Ibid., 396.
59. Callahan, "History, Identity and Security," 185.
60. Denton, "Heroic Resistance and Victims of Atrocity."
61. Buruma, "The Joys and Perils of Victimhood," 4.
62. Ding, *The Decline of Communism*, 164.
63. Ibid.
64. Mao, *Selected Works*, 2:337.
65. Barmé, "To Screw Foreigners Is Patriotic," 234.
66. Buruma, "The Joys and Perils of Victimhood," 3–4.
67. As quoted in Barmé, "Mirrors of History."
68. "Chinese National Anthem," *China Travel Discovery*, n.d., http://www.chinatraveldiscovery.com/china-facts/national-song.htm.
69. Chen, "The China Challenge."
70. Chen, "The Impact of Reform," 22–34.
71. Zhao, *A Nation-State by Construction*, 288.
72. Sullivan, "Discarding the China Card," 3–4.
73. Kennedy and O'Hanlon, "Time to Shift Gears on China Policy," 52.

4. FROM VICTOR TO VICTIM: THE PATRIOTIC EDUCATION CAMPAIGN

1. Podeh, "History and Memory in the Israeli Educational System," 65.
2. See, for example, Podeh, "History and Memory in the Israeli Educational System"; Hein and Selden, "The Lessons of War, Global Power, and Social Change"; and Cole and Barsalou, *Unite or Divide?*
3. Evans, "Redesigning the Past," 5.
4. See also Merridale, "Redesigning History in Contemporary Russia."
5. See, for example, the *Journal of Contemporary History*'s special issue "Redesigning the Past: History in Political Transitions," vol. 38, no. 1 (2003).
6. Harrison, "Communist Interpretations of the Chinese Peasant Wars," 92.
7. Deng Xiaoping, "Address to Officers at the Rank of General and Above in Command of the Troops Enforcing Martial Law in Beijing," June 9, 1989, in Deng, *Selected Works*, available at http://english.peopledaily.com.cn/dengxp/vol3/text/c1990.html.
8. CCCPC (Central Committee of the Communist Party of China), "Guanyu chongfeng liyong wenwu."
9. Jiang, "Jiang Zemin zongshuji zhixin Li Tieying," 1.
10. Ibid.

11. National Education Council, "Zhongxiaoxue jiaqiang jindai xiandaishi."
12. Zhao, *A Nation-State by Construction*, 218.
13. CCCPC, "Aiguo zhuyi jiaoyu shishi gangyao," 1.
14. Pyle, "Nationalism in East Asia," 31.
15. Cohen, "Remembering and Forgetting," 18.
16. Callahan, "History, Identity and Security," 186.
17. Cohen, "Remembering and Forgetting," 18–19.
18. Unger, *Using the Past to Serve the Present.*
19. Thurston, "Community and Isolation," 150.
20. Barmé, "History for the Masses," 260.
21. Respectively, PEP, *Chuji zhongxue jiaokeshu zhongguo lishi*, and PEP, *Gaoji zhongxue keben zhongguo jixiandaishi.*
22. Gries, "Face Nationalism," 80–81.
23. Gries, *China's New Nationalism*, 73.
24. Ibid., 70.
25. Ministry of Education, *Lishi jiaoxue dagang.*
26. CCCPC, "Aiguo zhuyi jiaoyu shishi gangyao," 1
27. CCCPC, "Guanyu chongfeng liyong wenwu," 1.
28. Ibid.
29. See http://cn.netor.com/m/box200106/m6373.asp?BoardID=6373.
30. See the website of the Chinese People's Memorial Hall of Anti-Japanese War, http://www.1937china.com.
31. "Zhongxunbu fuze tongzhi tan dierpi aiguozhuyi jiaoyu jidi" [Cadre in charge of the Department of Propaganda talks about the patriotic education bases], *PLA Daily*, June 13, 2001.
32. "Beijing aiguozhuyi jiaoyu jidi 12 nian cangan renshu yu 2.5 yi renci" [More than 250 million people visited Beijing's patriotic education bases in recent 12 years], Xinhua, October 12, 2004, available at http://news.xinhuanet.com/newscenter/2004-10/12/content_2081385.htm.
33. "Hebei aiguozhiyi jiaoyu jidi jianshe xunli" [The development of patriotic education bases in Hebei Province], *Zhongguo hongse luyou wang* [*China Red Tourism*], July 14, 2004, accessed July 6, 2005, http://www.crt.com.cn/98/2004-7-14/news200471411931.htm.
34. "Jiangsu 189 ge aiguozhuyi jiaoyu jidi mianfei kaifang" [Jiangsu Province's 189 patriotic education bases free of charge to the whole society], Xinhua, October 1, 2004, accessed July 6, 2005, http://internal.northeast.cn/system/2004/10/01/017350497.shtml.
35. "Jiangxi xiang weichengnianren mianfei kaifang ziguozhuyi jiaoyu jidi" [Jiangxi Province opens its patriotic education bases to the minors free of charge], Xinhua, June 23, 2004, available at http://www.edu.cn/20040623/3108703.shtml.
36. "Wu Linhong, yu aiguo qing, li baoguo zhi, anhuisheng aiguozhiyi jiaoyu jidi xunli," [The development of patriotic education in Anhui Province], *Anhui*

News, June 13, 2005, accessed July 6, 2005, http://ah.anhuinews.com/system/2005/06/13/001282026.shtml.

37. CCCPC, "Guanyu jingyibu jiaqiang he gaijing weichengnianren sixiang daode."
38. Zhao, "A State-Led Nationalism," 298.
39. CCCPC, "Guanyu jiaqiang aiguozhuyi jiaoyu jidi gongzuo de yijiang."
40. *Mo wang guochi* [Never forget our national humiliation] was published by Haiyan Press in 2002.
41. "China Boosts 'Red Tourism' in Revolutionary Bases," *Xinhua*, February 22, 2005, available at http://www.china.org.cn/english/government/120838.htm.
42. Ibid.
43. "'Red Tourism' Booming in China," *Reuters*, December 21, 2007.
44. Zhao, *A Nation-State by Construction*, 220.
45. Cohen, "Remembering and Forgetting," 18.
46. "China's Family Planning Policy Helps Prevent 400 Million Births by 2005," Xinhua, May 3, 2006, available at http://english.people.com.cn/200605/03/eng20060503_262703.html.
47. Markovits and Reich, *The German Predicament*, 9.
48. Cole and Barsalou, *Unite or Divide?* 13.
49. Goldstein and Keohane, "Ideas and Foreign Policy."
50. Ibid.
51. White, "Postrevolutionary Mobilization in China," 55.
52. Ibid. White quotes this definition from a 1959 article in *Hongqi* [Red flag], the official magazine of the Central Committee of the CCP.
53. White, "Postrevolutionary Mobilization in China," 58–59.
54. Ibid., 59.
55. "Professionals, Entrepreneurs New Pillar of China," *Xinhua*, July 26, 2006, available at http://www.chinadaily.com.cn/china/2006-07/26/content_649812.htm.
56. Rupert Wingfield-Hayes, "China's Rural Millions Left Behind," *BBC News*, March 6, 2006.
57. Yuan, "Xiandaihua yu lishi jiaokeshu."
58. Joseph Kahn, "China Shuts Down Influential Weekly Newspaper in Crackdown on Media," *New York Times*, January 25, 2006.
59. Yuan, "Xiandaihua yu Lishi Jiaokeshu." The textbook that Yuan commented on is the *Chinese History, Third Volume* (*Zhongguo lishi disance*), edited by the People's Educational Press (PEP). It is the official text for the first year of middle school and covers history of the "century of humiliation" from 1840 to 1949.
60. Yuan, "Xiandaihua yu Lishi Jiaokeshu."
61. Philip P. Pan, "Leading Publication Shut Down in China," *Washington Post*, January 25, 2006.

62. CCCPC, "Aiguo zhuyi jiaoyu shishi gangyao."
63. See the official website of Chinese Ministry of Education for related policy documents, accessed January 22, 2012, http://www.moe.gov.cn/publicfiles/business/htmlfiles/moe/moe_772/201001/xxgk_80672.html.
64. Guo, "Patriotic Villains and Patriotic Heroes."
65. CCCPC, "Aiguo zhuyi jiaoyu shishi gangyao."
66. Lovell, "It's Just History."
67. Zhao, "A State-Led Nationalism," 288.
68. Ibid.
69. Geoffrey Crothall, "Patriotic Patter Winning Students," *South China Morning Post*, July 10, 1994.
70. "Japan Glosses, China Distorts," *Asian Wall Street Journal*, April 11, 2005.
71. Mark Magnier, "Like Japan's, Chinese Textbooks Are Adept at Rewriting History," *Los Angeles Times*, May 8, 2005.

5. FROM VANGUARD TO PATRIOT: RECONSTRUCTING THE CHINESE COMMUNIST PARTY

1. Christensen, "Chinese Realpolitik," 46.
2. Ibid.
3. Barmé, "To Screw Foreigners Is Patriotic," 211.
4. Ibid., 211–12.
5. Jiang, "Aiguo zhuyi he woguo zhishi fenzi de shiming."
6. Mercer, "Anarchy and Identity."
7. Cohen, "Remembering and Forgetting," 18.
8. Barmé, "To Screw Foreigners Is Patriotic," 213.
9. Deng, *Selected Works*, 3:372.
10. Miller, "The Road to the 16th Party Congress."
11. Renwick and Qing, "Chinese Political Discourse."
12. Miller, "The Road to the 16th Party Congress."
13. For the drafting process for the political report of the Fourteenth Party Congress, see He Husheng, "Zhongguo xing naojing" [China's new ideas], Section 5, accessed May 15, 2008, http://www.tianyabook.com/zhexue/newbrain/index.html.
14. For the drafting process for the political report of the 16th Party Congress, see "Guanfang meiti pilou shiliuda baogao yinian lingershitian de qicao guochen" [Official sources disclose the one year and twenty days' drafting process of the report of the 16th Party Congress], *Xinhua*, November 20, 2002, available at http://www.chinanews.com.cn/2002-11-20/26/245383.html.
15. Miller, "The Road to the 16th Party Congress."
16. The Constitution of the CCP is available in translation at http://news.xinhuanet.com/english/2007-10/25/content_6944738.htm.

17. Jiang, "Speech at the 6th Plenary Session," translated by *Xinhua*. Emphasis added.
18. Jiang, "Report at the 16th CCP National Congress," translated by *Xinhua*.
19. Jiang, "Speech at the 6th Plenary Session."
20. CCCPC, "Aiguo zhuyi jiaoyu shishi gangyao."
21. Hu, "Report at the 17th CCP National Congress," translated by *Xinhua*.
22. Jiang, "Speech at the Meeting Celebrating the 80th Anniversary."
23. Zerubavel, *Recovered Roots*.
24. Jiang, "Speech at the Meeting Celebrating the 80th Anniversary."
25. Jiang, "Report at the 15th CCP National Congress."
26. Thurston, "Community and Isolation."
27. Bell, *Memory, Trauma and World Politics*, 20.
28. Renwick and Qing, "Chinese Political Discourse," 111–43.
29. Yan, "The Rise of China in Chinese Eyes."
30. Jiang, "Speech at the Meeting Celebrating the 80th Anniversary."
31. Hu, "Report at the 17th CCP National Congress."
32. Ibid.
33. Jiang, "Speech at the Meeting Celebrating the 80th Anniversary."
34. "Hu Jintao Meets with New Party Delegation," Xinhua, July 13, 2005, available at http://english.china.org.cn/english/China/134789.htm.
35. Cummings, "PRC Foreign Policy Responsiveness," 1.
36. Rose Brady, "A New Face on China's Foreign Policy," *BusinessWeek*, August 4, 2003, available at http://www.businessweek.com:/print/magazine/content/03_31/b3844142.htm.
37. Song, Zhang, and Qiao, *Zhongguo keyi shuo bu*.
38. Yan, *Zhongguo guojia liyi fenxi*.
39. "Chinese Foreign Minister Tang Jiaxuan Gives a Press Conference During the 1st Session of the 10th NPC," Ministry of Foreign Affairs, March 6, 2003, accessed June 14, 2005, http://www.mfa.gov.cn/eng/wjdt/zyjh/t24953.htm.
40. "Statement by Foreign Minister Tang Jiaxuan at the 54th Session of the UN General Assembly," Ministry of Foreign Affairs, November 19, 1999, available at http://www.china-un.ch/eng/ljzg/zgwjzc/t85884.htm.
41. Brady, "A New Face on China's Foreign Policy."
42. Gries, *China's New Nationalism*, 102.
43. Wen Jiabao, "Turning Your Eyes to China," speech given at Harvard University, Cambridge, MA, December 10, 2003, available at http://www.news.harvard.edu/gazette/2003/12.11/10-wenspeech.html.
44. "Wen Jiabao zai huanying yanhui shang zhici" [Wen Jiabao addresses at the welcoming dinner], *China Daily*, December 9, 2003, accessed July 24, 2005, http://www.chinadaily.com.cn/gb/doc/2003-12/09/content_288689.htm.

45. "Premier Wen Jiabao Held a Press Conference," Ministry of Foreign Affairs, March 18, 2003, accessed July 24, 2005, http://www.fmprc.gov.cn/eng/topics/3696/t18867.htm.
46. Ibid.
47. "Washington Post Interview with Premier Wen Jiabao," *People's Daily*, November 24, 2003, available at http://english.people.com.cn/200311/23/eng20031123_128838.shtml.

6. FROM EARTHQUAKES TO OLYMPICS: NEW TRAUMA, NEW GLORY

1. Economy and Segal, "China's Olympic Nightmare," 48.
2. "Chinese Students Say Huge Crowds Made for Successful Relay," Xinhua, April 24, 2008, available at http://www.chinadaily.com.cn/olympics/torch/2008-04/24/content_6642166.htm.
3. Shaila Dewan, "Chinese Student in U.S. Is Caught in Confrontation," *New York Times*, April 17, 2008.
4. Henry Sanderson, "China Protests French Retailer Carrefour," Associated Press, April 19, 2008, accessed May 22, 2008, http://www.msnbc.msn.com/id/24218173.
5. Translated from a photo on Chinese online forum, accessed October 5, 2008, http://www.xcar.com.cn/bbs/viewthread.php?tid=7882759&page=1.
6. "'One World, One Dream' Selected as the Theme Slogan for Beijing 2008 Olympic Games," press release, Beijing Organizing Committee for the Olympic Games, December 25, 2005, available at http://en.beijing2008.cn/75/66/article211996675.shtml.
7. Houlihan and Green, *Comparative Elite Sport Development*, 46.
8. Jo Kent, "The Pressure's on as China Rushes for Gold: Chinese Athletes Face High Expectations to Win Big in Beijing," *ABC News*, July 24, 2008.
9. "Zoukai huo zhongguo Aoyun guanjun danbi zuigao jiangjin," *Yahoo Sports*, September 18, 2008, available at http://sports.cn.yahoo.com/08-09-/357/2aq8i.html.
10. Ibid.
11. Xu, *Olympic Dreams*, 203.
12. "China's Darling Liu Xiang Prepares to 'Fly' at Bird's Nest," *China Daily*, August 2, 2008.
13. Ibid.
14. "Fame Holds No Attraction for Liu Xiang," *Times* (London), May 27, 2008.
15. "China Mourns as Liu Xiang Pulls Out of Hurdles," *Times* (London), August 18, 2008.
16. Yang, "Imaging National Humiliation."
17. Xu, *Olympic Dreams*, 19.

18. Zhai Hai, "Dongya binfu shuofa de lailongqumai" [The origin and development of the phrase "Sick Man of East Asia"], Sina Blog, http://blog.sina.com.cn/s/blog_48670cb201008rtk.html.
19. Yang, "Imaging National Humiliation."
20. Brownell, *Beijing's Games*, 34.
21. Yang, "Imaging National Humiliation."
22. "*Cong dongya bingfu dao jingji daguo*," Beijing Organizing Committee for the Olympic Games, April 29, 2004, accessed May 17, 2008, http://www.beijing2008.cn/37/67/article211986737.shtml.
23. Zhai, "Dongya binfu shuofa de lailongqumai."
24. "*The One Man Olympics* premieres in Beijing," May 16, 2008, China Internet Information Center, http://www.china.org.cn/culture/2008-05/18/content_15311813.htm.
25. "Fame Holds No Attraction for Liu Xiang," *Times* (London), May 27, 2008.
26. "It's Pride of Asia, Liu Xiang Says," Xinhua, August 27, 2004, available at http://news.xinhuanet.com/english/2004-08/28/content_1902300.htm.
27. Translation quoted from Xu, *Olympic Dreams*, 19.
28. "Hu Jintao Receives a Group Interview with Foreign Journalists," August 1, 2008, accessed August 5, 2008, http://www.fmprc.gov.cn/eng/zxxx/t463165. See also "Stay Out of Politics, Hu Tells the Media," *Australian*, August 2, 2008, accessed August 5, 2008, http://www.theaustralian.com.au/news/stay-out-of-politics-hu-to-media/story-e6frg6t6-1111117086099.
29. "Coming Distractions: Speaking to History" [interview with Paul A. Cohen], *China Beat*, September 26, 2008, http://thechinabeat.blogspot.com/2008/09/coming-distractions-speaking-to-history.html.
30. Mercer, "Anarchy and Identity."
31. Woods Hole Oceanographic Institution, U.S. Geological Survey, and American Geophysical Union, "May 2008 Earthquake in China Could Be Followed by Another Significant Rupture," press release, September 10, 2008, available at http://www.whoi.edu/page.do?pid=45697&cid=49386&c=2.
32. "The World's Worst Natural Disasters: Calamities of the 20th and 21st Centuries," *CBC News*, August 30, 2010, http://www.cbc.ca/world/story/2008/05/08/f-natural-disasters-history.html.
33. "Flood—Data and Statistics," *Prevention Web*, accessed March 29, 2009, http://www.preventionweb.net/english/hazards/statistics/?hid=62.
34. Ibid.
35. David Crossley, "10 'Worst' Natural Disasters," Department of Earth and Atmospheric Sciences, Saint Louis University, October 18, 2005, http://www.eas.slu.edu/hazards.html.
36. "Wenchuan Earthquake Has Already Caused 69,196 Fatalities and 18,379 Missing," *Sina*, July 6, 2008, available at http://news.sina.com.cn/c/2008-07-06/162615881691.shtml.

37. Liu Yunyun, "The PLA Shoulders the Load," *Beijing Review*, May 23, 2008.
38. "The World's Worst Natural Disasters."
39. Galtung, *Peace by Peaceful Means*, 254.
40. Merkel-Hess et al, *China in 2008*, 215.
41. You Nuo, "Words of Wisdom from Distant Past," *China Daily*, June 2, 2008.
42. Yang, "A Civil Society."
43. Brownell, *Beijing's Games*, 191.
44. Xu, *Olympic Dreams*, 268.

7. MEMORY, CRISES, AND FOREIGN RELATIONS

1. For scholarly works on China's conflict behavior after the end of the Cold War, see Bernstein and Munro, *The Coming Conflict with China*; Christensen, "Chinese Realpolitik"; Gries, *China's New Nationalism*; Gilpin, *War and Change in World Politics*; Johnston, *Cultural Realism*; Mearsheimer, *The Tragedy of Great Power Politics*; and Shulsky, *Deterrence Theory and Chinese Behavior*.
2. William Arking, "Q&A on Chinese Embassy Bombing," *Washington Post*, May 8, 2000.
3. Zong, "Zhu Rongji in 1999 (2)," 74–75.
4. Rebecca MacKinnon, "Protesters Attack U.S. Embassy in Beijing," *CNN*, May 8, 1999.
5. The descriptions of the crises are based on official statements, speeches, letters, and press conference briefings of the two sides during the negotiation process. A collection of China's official statements on this incident is available at the website of the Chinese Ministry of Foreign Affairs, http://www.fmprc.gov.cn/eng/topics/3755/3756/3778/default.htm.
6. Shambaugh, "The United States and China" 241.
7. See Ching Cheong, "China Debates Its Foreign Policy," *Straits Times*, May 24, 2001.
8. For example, Tong Zeng published a book that speculated that SARS could be a biological weapon developed by the United States against China. This book immediately stimulated dialogue on many Chinese Internet discussion boards and chat rooms.
9. According to this journal's introduction, *Chinese Law and Government* "contains unabridged translations of scholarly works and policy documents in the field of politics and government published originally in China. The emphasis is on translation of material that has lasting value for research." Published six times a year by M. E. Sharpe, the journal is listed among the Social Sciences Citation Index's Political Science and Law journal list.
10. Craig S. Smith, "Tell-All Book Portrays Split in Leadership of China," *New York Times*, January 17, 2002.

11. Zong, "Zhu Rongji in 1999 (2)," 76–81.
12. "One center" means putting economic construction at the center of all party work, and "two basic points" means upholding reform and openness, on the one hand, and the "four cardinal principles"—upholding the socialist path, the people's democratic dictatorship, the leadership of the Communist Party of China, and Marxist-Leninist-Maoist thought—on the other.
13. "Commentary on Awareness, Power of Chinese People," *People's Daily*, May 19, 1999.
14. Zong, "Zhu Rongji in 1999 (2)," 78.
15. See, for example, Gries, *China's New Nationalism*; Shen, "Nationalism or Nationalist Foreign Policy?"; and Zhao, "An Angle on Nationalism in China Today."
16. Zhao, "An Angle on Nationalism in China Today."
17. According to Zhao, the research was conducted in Beijing in the summer of 1999. Beijing was chosen for the study because the city has always been the center of political activism in China. Students were chosen as the sample population because they have played a very important role in China's national politics.
18. Zhao, "An Angle on Nationalism in China Today."
19. *Duowei Times* is a New York City–based Chinese-language newspaper. This interview is also available at John Holden's personal blog: http://blog.sina.com.cn/s/blog_4ee219e301000a82.html.
20. John Sweeney and Jens Holsoe, "NATO Bombed Chinese Deliberately," *Observer*, October 17, 1999.
21. "Albright Apologizes for Accidental Bombing of China Embassy," U.S. State Department, May 8, 1999, http://usembassy-israel.org.il/publish/press/state/archive/1999/may/sd3511.htm.
22. Clinton, "Bombing of Chinese Embassy in Belgrade," May 10, 1999, 733.
23. Ibid.
24. "Spokesman Zhu Bangzao Gives Full Account of the Collision between US and Chinese Military Planes," Chinese Foreign Ministry, April 4, 2001, http://www.fmprc.gov.cn/eng/topics/3755/3756/3778/t19301.htm; emphasis added.
25. "Diary of the Dispute," *BBC News*, May 24, 2001, http://news.bbc.co.uk/2/hi/asia-pacific/1270365.stm.
26. "Secretary Colin L. Powell Briefing for the Press Aboard Aircraft En Route to Andrews Air Force Base," U.S. State Department press release, Washington, DC, April 3, 2001.
27. "US-China Ties Hinge on Connotation of Single Word," *Reuters*, April 10, 2001.
28. "Ambassador Joseph W. Prueher's Letter to Foreign Minister Tang Jiaxuan," United States Embassy in Beijing, Beijing, China, April 11, 2001. http://www.usembassy-china.org.cn/press/release/2001/0113letter-en.html.

29. See Avruch and Wang, "Culture, Apology, and International Negotiation." Chinese Foreign Ministry's translation of the letter is available at its website, http://www.fmprc.gov.cn/chn/9704.html.
30. "US Spy Plane Crew Leaves Haikou, South China," *People's Daily*, April 12, 2001, http://english.people.com.cn/english/200104/12/eng20010412_67543.html. The Chinese version of this statement is available at http://www.people.com.cn/GB/paper39/3163/417194.html.
31. Shulsky, *Deterrence Theory and Chinese Behavior.*
32. Bernstein and Munro, *The Coming Conflict with China.*
33. Brookes, "Strategic Realism."
34. Gilpin, *War and Change in World Politics.*
35. Avruch and Wang, "Culture, Apology, and International Negotiation," 345.
36. Melinda Liu and Leslie Pappas, "How Low Would He Bow?" *Newsweek International*, June 28, 1999; William Safire, "Cut the Apologies," *New York Times*, May 17, 1999; Henry Kissinger, "Chinese Behavior Is Excessive and Really Unacceptable," *CNN*, May 11, 1999.
37. Robert Kagan and William Kristol, "National Humiliation," *Weekly Standard*, April 9, 2001.
38. Gries and Peng, "Culture Clash?", 176
39. Yee, "Semantic Ambiguity."
40. Avruch and Wang, "Culture, Apology, and International Negotiation."
41. Gries, *China's New Nationalism*, 156.
42. Huntington, *Clash of Civilizations*, 34.
43. Johnston, *Cultural Realism.*
44. See, for example, Chen and Ma, *Chinese Conflict Management and Resolution.*
45. Tidwell, *Conflict Resolved?*
46. Deng, *Selected Works.* Available at http://www.cpcchina.org/2010-10/26/content_13918429.htm.
47. Zhu, "How Chinese See America."
48. Zhongkun Han, "China, Not in 1899," *People's Daily*, May 12, 1999.
49. Zong, "Zhu Rongji in 1999 (2)," 79.
50. MacKinnon, "Protesters Attack U.S. Embassy in Beijing."
51. Rebecca MacKinnon and Mike Chinoy, "Chinese Embassy Bombing Exposes Raw Historical Nerve," CNN, May 12, 1999.
52. Fox Butterfield, "China's Demand for Apology Is Rooted in Tradition," *New York Times*, April 7, 2001.
53. Shen, "Nationalism or Nationalist Foreign Policy?"
54. Gries, *China's New Nationalism.*
55. "Jiang Gives Castro Gift of Words," *Miami Herald*, April 16, 2001.
56. Xinhua News Agency provided the Chinese original version of the poem. This English version was translated by the author.

57. "Chinese People's Awareness and Strength," *People's Daily*, May 19, 1999.
58. Gries, *Face Nationalism*, 102.
59. Gong, *Memory and History*, vii.
60. Gries, *Face Nationalism*, 199.
61. Quoted in Fox Butterfield, "China's Demand for Apology Is Rooted in Tradition," *New York Times*, April 7, 2001.
62. Wasserstrom, *China's Brave New World*, 93.
63. Muppidi, "Postcoloniality."
64. Goldstein and Keohane, "Ideas and Foreign Policy," 18.
65. "Ethnic Chinese Tell of Mass Rapes," *BBC News*, June 23, 1998, accessed on July 5, 2005, http://news.bbc.co.uk/2/hi/events/indonesia/special_report/118576.stm.

8. MEMORY, TEXTBOOKS, AND SINO-JAPANESE RECONCILIATION

1. "Chongqing Bombing Victims Sue," *Japan Times*, March 31, 2006, available at http://search.japantimes.co.jp/text/nn20060331a6.html.
2. See Kanji et al., *Atarashii rekishi kyōkasho*. The Japanese Society for History Textbook Reform (Atarashii Rekishi Kyōkasho o Tsukuru-kai) was founded by a group of conservative scholars in 1997 to promote a revised view of Japanese history. An earlier version of the society's textbook met with widespread protests in 2001 in China and North and South Korea, as well as in Japan.
3. Japanese history textbook controversies have been issues of considerable debate among scholars. See Barnard, *Language, Ideology and Japanese History Textbooks*; Hein and Selden, *Censoring History*; and Hamada, "Constructing a National Memory."
4. Phillip J. Cunningham, "Japan's Revisionist History," *Los Angeles Times*, April 11, 2005.
5. "China's Anti-Japan Rallies Spread," BBC, April 10, 2005, available at http://news.bbc.co.uk/2/hi/asia-pacific/4429809.stm.
6. "Japan Seeks China Talks on Riots," CNN, April 16, 2005, accessed March 12, 2008, available at http://www.cnn.com/2005/WORLD/asiapcf/04/16/china.japan.ap/index.html.
7. "S. Koreans Chop Off Fingers in Anti-Japan Protest," Reuters, March 14, 2005.
8. See, for example, Ienaga, "The Glorification of War in Japanese Education"; Lee, "Textbook Conflicts"; and Rose, *Interpreting History in Sino-Japanese Relations*.
9. Gong, *Memory and History.*
10. Galtung, "Construction of National Identities."
11. Jabri, *Discourses on Violence.*
12. Ienaga, "The Glorification of War in Japanese Education."

13. Yoshida, "Advancing or Obstructing Reconciliation?" 55.
14. Hamada, "Constructing a National Memory."
15. Soh, "Politics of the Victim/Victor Complex."
16. "Japan Urges China to 'Improve' Education on History," *Kyodo News*, March 5, 2005.
17. "Anti-Japan Mood Seen Keeping Japan, China Apart," *Kyodo News*, September 15, 2004, available at http://www.thefreelibrary.com/TokyoNow%3A+Anti-Japan+mood+seen+keeping+Japan,+China+apart.-a0122269102.
18. Kanji et al., *Atarashii rekishi kyōkasho*, 49. The English translation here and below is that of the Japanese Society for History Textbook Reform (available at http://www.tsukurukai.com/05_rekisi_text/rekishi_English/English.pdf). The quality of the translation is not good, but it provides a literal translation of the original Japanese version.
19. Ibid.
20. Yoshida, "Advancing or Obstructing Reconciliation?" 68–69.
21. Hein and Selden, "The Lessons of War, Global Power, and Social Change," 3–4.
22. Podeh, "History and Memory in the Israeli Educational System," 68.
23. Jabri, *Discourses on Violence*.
24. Burton, *Conflict Resolution*.
25. The Chinese version, *Dongya sanguo de jinxiandaishi* (Modern and contemporary history of three East Asian countries), was published by Social Sciences Academic Press (Shehui Kexue Chubanshe) in Beijing in 2005; a version in traditional Chinese characters was also published in Hong Kong by Joint Publishing (Sanlian Chubanshe). The Japanese version, *Mirai o hiraku rekishi: Higashi Ajia sankoku no kingendaishi* (A history that opens the future: Modern and contemporary history of three East Asian countries), was published by Kôbunken in Tokyo, and the Korean version was published by Hani Book.
26. Based on the Xinhua interview with Zhu Chengshan, July 5, 2007, http://www.js.xinhuanet.com/xin_wen_zhong_xin/2005-07/05/content_4569047.htm.
27. Ibid.
28. See Horvat, "Overcoming the Negative Legacy of the Past."
29. Wasserstrom, "Asia's Textbook Case," 80.
30. *Dongya sanguo de jinxiandaishi*, 2.
31. Ibid., 1–2.
32. Ibid., 1.
33. Ibid., 214–15. The Shintoist Yasukuni Shrine, dedicated to the spirits of those who died fighting on behalf of the emperor of Japan, is viewed by the Chinese as a symbol of Japanese imperialist aggression. Visits to the shrine by Japanese Cabinet members and prime ministers, in particular, have been the cause of protests at home as well as by Japan's neighbors, including China and North and South Korea.

34. Raymond Zhou, "East Asia History Book Sets Facts Right," *China Daily*, June 10, 2005, available at http://www.chinadaily.com.cn/english/doc/2005-06/10/content_450083.htm.
35. "*Dongya sanguo de jinxiandaishi* chuban xiudingban," *People's Daily*, May 16, 2006.
36. Zhou, "East Asia History Book Sets Facts Right."
37. These readers' reviews are available at http://comm.dangdang.com/review-list/9000330.
38. Yu Hua, "Zhuanzhi zhixia wu xingshi," *Baidu Blog*, accessed December 22, 2008, http://tieba.baidu.com/f?kz=246558051.
39. Zhou, "East Asia History Book Sets Facts Right."
40. Lederach, *Building Peace*, 23–35.
41. Cole and Barsalou, *Unite or Divide?*
42. Gibson, *Overcoming Apartheid.*
43. Borer, *Telling the Truths.*
44. Cole and Barsalou, *Unite or Divide?* 21.
45. Irwin Cotler, "Beyond Annapolis: Rectifying an Historical Injustice," *JPost.com*, December 10, 2007, http://cgis.jpost.com/Blogs/guest/entry/beyond_annapolis_rectifying_an_historical.
46. See, for example, Brito et al., *Politics of Memory*, 1–39; and Christie, *The South African Truth Commission.*
47. Lederach, *Building Peace*, 46.
48. Ma, "Dui ri gaunxi xin siwei."
49. Shi, "Zhongri jiejing ju waijiao geming."
50. Cole and Barsalou, *Unite or Divide?* 13.
51. "China, Japan End First Joint Study Session on History," Associated Press, December 27, 2006, available at http://www.chinadaily.com.cn/china/2006-12/27/content_769169.htm.
52. Ministry of Foreign Affairs of Japan, "The First Meeting of the Japan-China Joint History Research Committee (Summary)," December 2006, http://www.mofa.go.jp/region/asia-paci/china/meet0612.html.
53. Saunders, "Sustained Dialogue in Managing Intractable Conflict."
54. See Burgess et al., *Transformative Approaches to Conflict.*
55. Podeh, "History and Memory," 68.
56. Zakaria, "The Virtue of Learning Vices."

9. MEMORY, NATIONALISM, AND CHINA'S RISE

1. Lee Kuan Yew, "Two Images of China," *Forbes*, June 16, 2008.
2. The full text of this poem can be read at http://www.washingtonpost.com/wp-dyn/content/article/2008/05/16/AR2008051603460.html.

3. Markovits and Reich, *The German Predicament*, 9.
4. Kellas, *The Politics of Nationalism and Ethnicity*, 196.
5. Thurston, "Community and Isolation," 171.
6. Hamrin and Wang, "The Floating Island," 343.
7. See, for example, Li, "China Talks Back"; and Zhang Ming, "The New Thinking of Sino–US Relations."
8. Volkan, "Large Group Identity."
9. Shaules, *Deep Culture*, 12.
10. Cohen, *Speaking to History*, 240.
11. "Wen Jiabao zai huanying yanhui shang zhici" [Wen Jiabao addresses at the welcoming dinner], *China Daily*, December 9, 2003, accessed July 24, 2005, http://www.chinadaily.com.cn/gb/doc/2003-12/09/content_288689.htm.
12. Jayshree Bajoria, "Nationalism in China," *Newsweek*, April 24, 2008.
13. See, for example, Paul Mooney, "Internet Fans Flames of Chinese Nationalism," *YaleGlobal*, April 4, 2005, available at http://yaleglobal.yale.edu/content/internet-fans-flames-chinese-nationalism.
14. Ethan Gutmann, "Who Lost China's Internet?" *Weekly Standard*, February 15, 2002.
15. David Barboza, "China Surpasses U.S. in Number of Internet Users," *New York Times*, July 26, 2008.
16. Erich Marquardt, "The Price of Japanese Nationalism," *Asia Times*, April 14, 2005.
17. Gries, "Face Nationalism," 252.
18. Gong, *Memory and History*, 32.
19. Ibid.
20. Cohen, "Remembering and Forgetting," 22.
21. Ibid.
22. Farrer, "Nationalism Pits Shanghai Against Its Global Ambition."
23. Pyle, "Nationalism in East Asia," 33.
24. Gong, *Memory and History*, 42.
25. "Stay Out of Politics, Hu Tells the Media," *Australian*, August 2, 2008.
26. A Xinhua translation of the CCP constitution is available at http://news.xinhuanet.com/english/2007-10/25/content_6944738.htm.
27. Johnston, "Is China a Status Quo Power?"
28. Legro, "What China Will Want."
29. "Full Text of Chinese Premier's Speech at University of Cambridge," Xinhua, February 3, 2009, available at http://news.xinhuanet.com/english/2009-02/03/content_10753336_1.htm.
30. Cohen, *Negotiating Across Cultures*.
31. "Full Text of Chinese Premier's Speech at University of Cambridge."
32. Mary Beth Marklein, "Chinese College Students Flocking to U.S. Campuses," *USA Today*, December 8, 2009.

BIBLIOGRAPHY

Abdelal, Rawi, Yoshiko M. Herrera, Alastair Iain Johnston, and Terry Martin. "Treating Identity as a Variable: Measuring the Content, Intensity, and Contestation of Identity." Paper presented at the annual convention of the American Political Science Association (APSA), San Francisco, August 30–September 2, 2001.

Abdelal, Rawi, Yoshiko M. Herrera, Alastair Iain Johnston, and Rose McDermott. "Identity as a Variable." *Perspectives on Politics* 4, no. 4 (2006): 695–711.

Anderson, Benedict. *Imagined Communities: Reflections on the Origin and Spread of Nationalism*. London: Verso, 1991.

Apple, Michael W., and Linda K. Christian-Smith. *The Politics of the Textbook*. New York: Routledge, 1991.

Askew, David. "The Nanjing Incident: Recent Research and Trends." *Electronic Journal of Contemporary Japanese Studies* (2002). http://www.japanesestudies.org.uk/articles/Askew.html.

Avruch, Kevin. *Culture and Conflict Resolution*. Washington, DC: U.S. Institute of Peace Press, 1998.

Avruch, Kevin, and Zheng Wang. "Culture, Apology, and International Negotiation: The Case of the Sino-U.S. 'Spy Plane' Crisis." *International Negotiation* 10 (2005): 337–53.

Barmé, Geremie R. "Anniversaries in the Light, and in the Dark." *China Heritage Quarterly*, March 19, 2009.

Barmé, Geremie R. "History for the Masses." In *Using the Past to Serve the Present: Historiography and Politics in Contemporary China*, edited by Jonathan Unger, pp. 260–86. Armonk, NY: M. E. Sharpe, 1993.

Barmé, Geremie R. "Mirrors of History on a Sino-Japanese Moment and Some Antecedents." *Japan Focus*, May 11, 2005.

Barmé, Geremie R. "To Screw Foreigners Is Patriotic: China's Avant-Garde Nationalists." *China Journal* 34 (1995): 209–34.

Barmé, Geremie R. "Yuanming Yuan, the Garden of Perfect Brightness." *China Heritage Quarterly*, December 2006.

Barnard, Christopher. *Language, Ideology and Japanese History Textbooks*. London: Routledge Curzon, 2003.

Bar-Tal, Daniel. *Shared Beliefs in a Society: Social Psychological Analysis*. Thousand Oaks, CA: Sage, 2000.

Bell, Duncan S. A. *Memory, Trauma and World Politics: Reflections on the Relationship Between Past and Present*. New York: Palgrave, 2006.

Bernstein, Richard, and Ross H. Munro. *The Coming Conflict with China*. New York: Knopf, 1997.

Borer, Tristan Anne, ed. *Telling the Truths: Truth Telling and Peace Building in Post-Conflict Societies*. Notre Dame, IN: Notre Dame University Press, 2006.

Brito, A. Barahona de, et al. *The Politics of Memory: Transitional Justice in Democratizing Societies*. Oxford: Oxford University Press, 2001.

Brookes, Peter T. R. "Strategic Realism: The Future of U.S.-Sino Security Relations." *Strategic Review* (Summer 1999): 53–56.

Brownell, Susan. *Beijing's Games: What the Olympics Mean to China*. New York: Rowman & Littlefield, 2008.

Bruland, Peter, and Michael Horowitz. "Research Report on the Use of Identity Concepts in Comparative Politics." Harvard Identity Project, Harvard University, 2003.

Burgess, Heidi, Guy Burgess, Tanya Glaser, and Mariya Yevsyukova. *Transformative Approaches to Conflict*. University of Colorado Conflict Research Consortium, http://www.colorado.edu/conflict/transform/index.html.

Burton, John W. *Conflict Resolution: Its Language and Processes*. Lanham, MD: Scarecrow Press, 1996.

Buruma, Ian. "The Joys and Perils of Victimhood." *New York Review of Books*, April 8, 1999.

Callahan, William A. *China: The Pessoptimist Nation*. Oxford: Oxford University Press, 2010.

Callahan, William A. "History, Identity and Security: Producing and Consuming Nationalism in China." *Critical Asian Studies* 38, no. 2 (2006): 179–208.

Callahan, William A. "National Insecurities: Humiliation, Salvation, and Chinese Nationalism." *Alternatives* 29 (2004): 199–218.

CCCPC (Central Committee of the Communist Party of China). "Aiguo zhuyi jiaoyu shishi gangyao" [Outline on the implementation of patriotic education]. *Renmin Ribao* [People's Daily], September 6, 1994.

CCCPC. "Guanyu chongfeng liyong wenwu jinxing aiguozhuyi he geming chuantong jiaoyu de tongzhi" [Notice about conducting education of patriotism and revolutionary tradition by exploiting extensively cultural relics]. Beijing: Government Printing Office, 1991.

CCCPC. "Guanyu jiaqiang aiguozhuyi jiaoyu jidi gongzuo de yijiang" [Opinions on strengthening and improving the work of patriotic education bases]. *Renmin Ribao*, October 3, 2004.

CCCPC. "Guanyu jingyibu jiaqiang he gaijing weichengnianren sixiang daode jianshe de ruoguan yijiang" [Proposals of the CCCPC and the State Council on further strengthening and improving ideological and moral education of minors]. Beijing: Government Printing Office, 2004.

Chang, Iris. *The Rape of Nanking: The Forgotten Holocaust of World War II*. New York: Basic Books, 1997.

Chen, Guo-ming, and Ringo Ma. *Chinese Conflict Management and Resolution*. Westport, CT: Ablex, 2000.

Chen, Jian. "The China Challenge in the Twenty-First Century." Peaceworks no. 21. Washington, DC: U.S. Institute of Peace, 1998.

Chen, Jie. "The Impact of Reform on the Party and Ideology in China." *Journal of Contemporary China* 9 (1995): 22–34.

Chiang, Kai-shek. *China's Destiny*. Translated by Wang Chung-hui. New York: Macmillan, 1947. Reprint, New York: Da Capo Press, 1976.

Christensen, Thomas J. "Chinese Realpolitik: Reading Beijing's World-View." *Foreign Affairs* 75, no. 5 (1996).

Christie, Kenneth. *The South African Truth Commission*. New York: St. Martin's Press, 2000.

Clinton, Bill. *Public Papers of the Presidents of the United States, William J. Clinton, Book* 2. Washington, DC: National Archives and Records Administration, 1999.

Coble, Parks M. "China's 'New Remembering' of the Anti-Japanese War of Resistance, 1937–1945." *China Quarterly* 190 (2007): 394–410.

Cohen, Paul A. "Remembering and Forgetting: National Humiliation in Twentieth-Century China." *Twentieth-Century China* 27, no. 2 (2002): 1–39.

Cohen, Paul A. *Speaking to History: The Story of King Goujian in Twentieth-Century China*. Berkeley: University of California Press, 2009.

Cohen, Raymond. *Negotiating Across Cultures: Communication Obstacles in International Diplomacy*. Washington, DC: U.S. Institute of Peace Press, 1991.

Cole, Elizabeth, and Judy Barsalou. *Unite or Divide? The Challenges of Teaching History in Societies Emerging from Violent Conflict*. Special Report no. 163. Washington, DC: U.S. Institute of Peace, 2006.

Cummings, Lucy M. "PRC Foreign Policy Responsiveness to Domestic Ethical Sentiment." PhD diss., Johns Hopkins University, 2001.

Deng, Xiaoping. *Selected Works of Deng Xiaoping*. Vol. 3. Translated by *People's Daily*. Beijing: Foreign Language Press, 1994.

Denton, Kirk A. "Heroic Resistance and Victims of Atrocity: Negotiating the Memory of Japanese Imperialism in Chinese Museums." *Japan Focus*, October 17, 2007.

Dikötter, Frank. *The Discourse of Race in Modern China*. Stanford, CA: Stanford University Press, 1992.

Ding, X. L. *The Decline of Communism in China: Legitimacy Crisis, 1977–1989*. Cambridge: Cambridge University Press, 1995.

Duara, Presenjit. "De-constructing the Chinese Nation." In *Chinese Nationalism*, edited by Jonathan Unger, pp. 31–55. Armonk, NY: M. E. Sharpe, 1996.

Ebrey, Patricia Buckley. *The Cambridge Illustrated History of China*. Cambridge: Cambridge University Press, 1996.

Economy, Elizabeth C., and Adam Segal. "China's Olympic Nightmare: What the Games Mean for Beijing's Future." *Foreign Affairs* 87, no. 4 (2008): 47–56.

Eller, Jack David. *From Culture to Ethnicity to Conflict: An Anthropological Perspective on International Ethnic Conflict*. Ann Arbor: University of Michigan Press, 1999.

Evans, Richard J. "Redesigning the Past: History in Political Transitions." *Journal of Contemporary History* 38, no. 1 (2003): 5–12.

Fairbank, John King, and Merle Goldman. *China: A New History*. Cambridge, MA: Harvard University Press, 2006.

Fairbank, John K., and Kwang-Ching Liu, ed. *The Cambridge History of China*. Vol. 2, *Late Ch'ing, 1800–1911*, part 2. Cambridge: Cambridge University Press, 1980.

Farrer, James. "Nationalism Pits Shanghai Against Its Global Ambition." *Yale Global*, April 29, 2005.

Fitzgerald, John. *Awakening China: Politics, Culture, and Class in the Nationalist Revolution*. Stanford, CA: Stanford University Press, 1996.

Fitzgerald, John. "The Nationless State." In *Chinese Nationalism*, edited by Jonathan Unger, pp. 56–85. Armonk, NY: M. E. Sharpe, 2007.

Fukuyama, Francis. "The New Nationalism and the Strategic Architecture of Northeast Asia." *Asia Policy* 3 (2007): 38–41.

Galtung, Johan. "The Construction of National Identities for Cosmic Drama: Chosenness-Myths-Trauma (CMT) Syndromes and Cultural Pathologies." In *Handcuffed to History*, edited by P. Udayakumar, pp. 61–81. Westport, CT: Praeger, 2001.

Galtung, Johan. *Globe Projections of Deep-Rooted U.S. Pathologies*. Occasional Paper no. 11. Fairfax, VA: Institute for Conflict Analysis and Resolution, 1996.

Galtung, Johan. *Peace by Peaceful Means*. London: Sage, 1996.

George, Alexander. "The Causal Nexus Between Cognitive Beliefs and Decision-Making Behavior." In *Psychological Models in International Politics*, edited by L. Falkowski, pp. 95–124. Boulder, CO: Westview Press, 1979.

Gibson, James L. *Overcoming Apartheid: Can Truth Reconcile a Divided Nation?* New York: Russell Sage Foundation, 2004.

Gilpin, Robert. *War and Change in World Politics.* Cambridge: Cambridge University Press, 1981.

Goldstein, Judith, and Robert O. Keohane. "Ideas and Foreign Policy: An Analytical Framework." In *Ideas and Foreign Policy: Beliefs, Institutions, and Political Change*, edited by Judith Goldstein and Robert O. Keohane, pp. 3–30. Ithaca, NY: Cornell University Press, 1993.

Gong, Gerrit W., ed. *Memory and History in East and Southeast Asia.* Washington, DC: CSIS Press, 2001.

Gries, Peter Hays. *China's New Nationalism: Pride, Politics, and Diplomacy.* Berkeley: University of California Press, 2004.

Gries, Peter Hays. "Face Nationalism: Power and Passion in Chinese Anti-Foreignism." PhD diss., University of California, Berkeley, 1999.

Gries, Peter Hays, and Peng Kaiping. "Culture Clash? Apologies East and West." *Journal of Contemporary China* 11, no. 30 (2002): 173–78.

Guo, Baogang. "Political Legitimacy and China's Transition." *Journal of Chinese Political Science* 8, nos. 1–2 (2003): 1–25.

Guo, Yingjie. "Patriotic Villains and Patriotic Heroes: Chinese Literary Nationalism in the 1990s." In *Nationalism and Ethnoregional Identities in China*, edited by William Safran, pp. 163–88. London: Routledge, 1998.

Halbwachs, Maurice. *On Collective Memory.* Edited and translated by Lewis A. Coser. Chicago: University of Chicago Press, 1992.

Hamada, Tomoko. "Constructing a National Memory: A Comparative Analysis of Middle-School History Textbooks from Japan and the PRC." *American Asian Review* 21, no. 4 (2003): 109–45.

Hamrin, Carol Lee, and Zheng Wang. "The Floating Island: Change of Paradigm on the Taiwan Question." *Journal of Contemporary China* 13 (2004): 339–49.

Hanes, W. Travis, III and Frank Sanello. *The Opium Wars: The Addiction of One Empire and the Corruption of Another.* Naperville, IL: Sourcebooks, 2002.

Harrison, James P. "Communist Interpretations of the Chinese Peasant Wars." *The China Quarterly* 24 (1965): 92–118.

Harrison, James P. *The Long March to Power: A Political History of the Chinese Communist Party, 1921–1972.* London: Praeger, 1972.

Hein, Laura, and Mark Selden. "The Lessons of War, Global Power, and Social Change." In *Censoring History: Citizenship and Memory in Japan, Germany, and the United States*, edited by Laura Hein and Mark Selden, pp. 3–52. Armonk, NY: M. E. Sharpe, 2000.

Higher Education Press. *Zhongguo jixiandaishi: 1840–1949* [Higher education "95" national key textbook, Chinese modern and contemporary history, 1840–1949]. Beijing: Gaodeng Jiaoyu Chubanshe, 2001.

Horvat, Andrew. "Overcoming the Negative Legacy of the Past: Why Europe Is a Positive Example for East Asia." *Brown Journal of World Affairs* 11 (Summer–Fall 2004): 137–48.

Houlihan, Barrie, and Mick Green. *Comparative Elite Sport Development: Systems, Structures and Public Policy*. Oxford: Butterworth-Heinemann, 2007.

Hsu, Immanuel C. Y. *China's Entrance into the Family of Nations: The Diplomatic Phase, 1858–1880*. Cambridge, MA: Harvard University Press, 1960.

Hsu, Immanuel C. Y. *The Rise of Modern China*. New York: Oxford University Press, 1990.

Hu, Jintao. "Report at the 17th CCP National Congress." Beijing, October 24, 2007.

Hu, Ping. "Dui lishi xu xinhuai qianjing." In *Hu Ping geren wenji* [Selected works of Hu Ping], 2003. http://members.lycos.co.uk/chinatown/author/H/HuPin/HuPin137.txt.

Huang, Grace. "Chiang Kai-shek's Politics of Shame and Humiliation, 1928–34." Paper presented at the Institut Barcelona D'Estudis Internacional (IBEI), Barcelona, Spain, June 11, 2009.

Huntington, Samuel P. *The Clash of Civilizations and the Remaking of World Order*. New York: Simon & Schuster, 1996.

Hutchinson, John, and Anthony D. Smith, eds. *Ethnicity*. Oxford: Oxford University Press, 1996.

Ienaga, Saburo. "The Glorification of War in Japanese Education." *International Security* 18, no. 3 (1994): 113–33.

Jabri, Vivienne. *Discourses on Violence: Conflict Analysis Reconsidered*. Manchester, England: Manchester University Press, 1996.

Jedlicki, Jerzy. "Historical Memory as a Source of Conflicts in Eastern Europe." *Communist and Post-Communist Studies* 32 (September 1999): 225–32.

Jiang, Tingfu. *Zhongguo jindaishi* [Modern history of China]. Changsha: Shangwu, 1938. Reprint, Shanghai: Shanghai Guji Chubanshe, 2001.

Jiang, Zemin. "Aiguo zhuyi he woguo zhishi fenzi de shiming" [Patriotism and the mission of the Chinese intellectuals; speech at a report meeting held by Youth in the Capital to commemorate the May 4th Movement]. *Renmin Ribao*, May 4, 1990.

Jiang, Zemin. "Jiang Zemin zongshuji zhixin Li Tieying He Dongchang qiangdiao jinxing zhongguo jinxiangdaishi he guoqing jiaoyu" [General Secretary Jiang Zemin's letter to Li Tieying and He Dongchang stressed to conduct education on Chinese modern and contemporary history]. *Renmin Ribao*, June 1, 1991.

Jiang, Zemin. "Report at the 15th CCP National Congress." Beijing, September 12, 1997.

Jiang, Zemin. "Report at the 16th CCP National Congress." Beijing, November 14, 2002.

Jiang, Zemin. "Speech at the Meeting Celebrating the 80th Anniversary of the Founding of the Communist Party of China." *Renmin Ribao*, July 1, 1991.

Jiang, Zemin. "Speech at the 6th Plenary Session of the 14th CCP National Congress." *Renmin Ribao*, October 10, 1996.

Johnston, Alistair Iain. *Cultural Realism: Strategic Culture and Grand Strategy in Chinese History*. Princeton, NJ: Princeton University Press, 1995.

Johnston, Alistair Iain. "Is China a Status Quo Power?" *International Security* 27, no. 4 (2003): 5–56.

Kammen, Michael. *The Mystic Chords of Memory*. New York: Vintage Books, 1993.

Kanji, Nishio, et al., eds. *Atarashii rekishi kyōkasho* [New history textbook]. Tokyo: Fusosha, 2005.

Kataoka, Tetsuya. *Resistance and Revolution in China: The Communists and the Second United Front*. Berkeley: University of California Press, 1974.

Katzenstein, Peter J. "Alternative Perspectives on National Security." In *The Culture of National Security: Norms and Identity in World Politics*, edited by Peter J. Katzenstein, pp. 1–32. New York: Columbia University Press, 1996.

Kaufman, Stuart J. *Modern Hatreds: The Symbolic Politics of Ethnic War*. Ithaca, NY: Cornell University Press, 2001.

Kellas, James G. *The Politics of Nationalism and Ethnicity*. New York: Macmillan, 1998.

Kennedy, Scott, and Michael O'Hanlon. "Time to Shift Gears on China Policy." *Journal of East Asian Affairs* 10, no. 1 (1996): 45–73.

Khong, Yuen Foong. *Analogies at War: Korea, Munich, Dien Bien Phu, and the Vietnam Decisions of 1965*. Princeton, NJ: Princeton University Press, 1992.

Kim, Samuel S. "The Evolving Asian System: Three Transformations." In *International Relations of Asia*, edited by David Shambaugh and Michael Yahuda, pp. 35–56. Lanham, MD: Rowman & Littlefield, 2008.

Kohn, Hans. "The Nature of Nationalism." *American Political Science Review* 33, no. 6 (1939): 1001–21.

Lederach, John Paul. *Building Peace: Sustainable Reconciliation in Divided Societies*. Washington, DC: U.S. Institute of Peace Press, 1997.

Lee, Myon-Woo. "Textbook Conflicts and Korea-Japan Relations." *Journal of East Asian Affairs* 15, no. 2 (Fall–Winter 2001): 421–46.

Legro, Jeffrey W. "What China Will Want: The Future Intentions of a Rising Power." *Perspectives on Politics* 5, no. 3 (2007): 515–34.

Levenson, Joseph R. *Confucian China and Its Modern Fate: A Trilogy*. Berkeley: University of California Press, 1968.

Li, Hongshan. "China Talks Back: Anti-Americanism or Nationalism? A Review of Recent 'Anti-American' Books in China." *Journal of Contemporary China* 6, no. 14 (1997): 153–60.

Liang, Qichao, "Wuxu Zhengbian Ji" [An account of the 1898 coup]. In *Yinbingshi Heji* [Collected works of Yinbingshi], Vol. 6, pp. 1–157. Shanghai: Zhonghua Shuju, 1936.

Lind, Jennifer M. "Regime Type and National Remembrance." EAI Fellows Program Working Paper Series no. 22. Seoul: East Asia Institute, 2009.

Liu, Lydia. *The Clash of Empires: The Invention of China in Modern World Making.* Cambridge, MA: Harvard University Press, 2004.

Lovell, Julia. "It's Just History: Patriotic Education in the PRC." *China Beat*, April 22, 2009. http://thechinabeat.blogspot.com/2009/04/its-just-history-patriotic-education-in.html.

Lowenthal, David. *The Past Is a Foreign Country*. Cambridge: Cambridge University Press, 1985.

Lu, Xun. *Nahan* [*Call to Arms*]. In *Lu Xun's Vision of Reality*, translated by W. Lyell. Berkeley: University of California Press, 1976.

Ma, Licheng. "Dui ri guanxi xin siwei" [New thinking on Sino-Japanese relations]. *Zhanlue yu Guanli* [Strategy and Management] 6 (2002).

Mao, Zedong. "The Chinese People Have Stood Up!" *Renmin Ribao*, September 22, 1949.

Mao, Zedong. *Selected Works of Mao Tse-tung*. Vol. 2. Beijing: Foreign Languages Press, 1967.

Markovits, Andrei S., and Simon Reich. *The German Predicament*. Ithaca, NY: Cornell University Press, 1997.

McBride, Ian, ed. *History and Memory in Modern Ireland*. Cambridge: Cambridge University Press, 2001.

Mearsheimer, John. *The Tragedy of Great Power Politics*. New York: W. W. Norton, 2001.

Mercer, Jonathan. "Anarchy and Identity." *International Organization* 49, no. 2 (1995): 229–52.

Merkel-Hess, Kate, Kenneth L. Pomeranz, Jeffrey N. Wasserstrom, and Jonathan D. Spence. *China in 2008: A Year of Great Significance*. New York: Rowman & Littlefield, 2009.

Merridale, Catherine. "Redesigning History in Contemporary Russia." *Journal of Contemporary History* 38, no. 1 (2003): 13–28.

Miller, H. Lyman. "The Road to the 16th Party Congress." *China Leadership Monitor*, no. 1 (2002): 1–10.

Ministry of Education [China]. *Lishi jiaoxue dagang* [Teaching guideline for history education]. Beijing: Renmin Jiaoyu Chubanshe, 2002.

Mitter, Rana. *A Bitter Revolution*. Oxford: Oxford University Press, 2004.

Morse, Hosea Ballou. *The International Relations of the Chinese Empire*. Vol. 1. London: Longmans Green, 1910.

Muppidi, Himadeep. "Postcoloniality and the Production of International Insecurity." In *Cultures of Insecurity*, edited by Jutta Weldes, Mark Laffey, Hugh Gusterson, and Raymond Duvall, pp. 119–46. Minneapolis: University of Minnesota Press, 1999.

National Education Council [China]. "Zhongxiaoxue jiaqiang jindai xiandaishi he guoqing jiaoyu de zongti gangyao" [General outline on strengthening education on Chinese modern and contemporary history and national conditions]. Beijing: Government Printing Office, 1991.

Pei, Minxin. "The Paradoxes of American Nationalism." *Foreign Policy* 136 (2003): 30–37.

Pennebaker, J. W. *Collective Memory of Political Events*. Mahwah, NJ: Erlbaum, 1997.

PEP (People's Education Press). *Chuji zhongxue jiaokeshu zhongguo gudaishi* [Middle school textbook Chinese ancient history]. Beijing: Renmin Jiaoyu Chubanshe, 1992.

PEP. *Chuji zhongxue jiaokeshu zhongguo lishi* [Middle school textbook Chinese history]. Beijing: Renmin Jiaoyu Chubanshe, 1992.

PEP. *Gaoji zhongxue jiaokeshu zhongguo jinxiandaishi* [High school textbook Chinese modern and contemporary history]. 2 vols. Beijing: Renmin Jiaoyu Chubanshe, 1992.

PEP. *Putong gaozhong kecheng biaozhun shiyan jiaokeshu lishi* [Normal high school standard textbook history]. Vol. 1. Beijing: Renmin Jiaoyu Chubanshe, 2007.

PEP. *Quanrizhi putong gaoji zhongxue jiaokeshu zhongguo jinxiandaishi* [Full-time standard high school textbook Chinese modern and contemporary history]. 2 vols. Beijing: Renmin Jiaoyu Chubanshe, 2003.

Podeh, Elie. "History and Memory in the Israeli Educational System: The Portrayal of the Arab-Israeli Conflict in History Textbooks, 1948–2000." *History and Memory* 12 (2000): 65–100.

Putnam, L., and M. Holmer. "Framing, Reframing, and Issue Development." In *Communication and Negotiation*, edited by L. Putnam and M. E. Roloff, pp. 128–55. Newbury Park, CA: Sage, 1992.

Pye, Lucian W. *International Relations in Asia: Culture, Nation and State*. Washington, DC: Sigur Center for Asian Studies, 1998.

Pyle, Kenneth B. "Nationalism in East Asia." *Asia Policy* 3 (2007): 29–37.

Pyle, Kenneth B. "Reading the New Era in Asia: The Use of History and Culture in the Making of Foreign Policy." *Asia Policy* 3 (2007): 1–11.

Record, J., and W. Andrew Terrill. *Iraq and Vietnam: Differences, Similarities and Insights*. Carlisle, PA: Strategic Studies Institute, 2004.

Renwick, Neil, and Cao Qing. "Chinese Political Discourse Towards the 21st Century: Victimhood, Identity and Political Power." *East Asia* 17, no. 4 (1999): 111–43.

Rose, Caroline. *Interpreting History in Sino-Japanese Relations: A Case Study in Political Decision-Making*. London: Routledge, 1998.

Roudometof, Victor. *Collective Memory, National Identity, and Ethnic Conflict: Greece, Bulgaria and the Macedonian Question*. Westport, CT: Praeger, 2002.

Saunders, Harold H. "Sustained Dialogue in Managing Intractable Conflict." *Negotiation Journal* 19, no. 1 (2003): 85–95.

Schoppa, Keith. *Revolution and Its Past: Identities and Change in Modern Chinese History*. 2nd ed. Upper Saddle River, NJ: Pearson Prentice Hall, 2006.

Shambaugh, David. "The United States and China: A New Cold War?" *Current History* 94, no. 593 (1995): 241–47.

Shaules, Joseph. *Deep Culture: The Hidden Challenges of Global Living*. Clevedon, England: Multilingual Matters, 2007.

Shen, Simon. "Nationalism or Nationalist Foreign Policy? Contemporary Chinese Nationalism and Its Role in Shaping Chinese Foreign Policy in Response to the Belgrade Embassy Bombing." *Politics* 24, no. 2 (2004): 122–30.

Shi, Yinhong. "Zhongri jiejing yu waijiao geming" [Japan-China rapprochement and diplomatic revolution]. *Zhanlue yu Guanli* [Strategy and Management], 2003.

Shirk, Susan L. *China: Fragile Superpower*. New York: Oxford University Press, 2007.

Shulsky, Abram N. *Deterrence Theory and Chinese Behavior*. Arlington, VA: Rand, 2000.

Smith, Anthony D. *The Ethnic Origins of Nations*. Oxford, England: Blackwell, 1986.

Smith, Anthony D. *Myths and Memories of the Nation*. Oxford: Oxford University Press, 1999.

Soh, Chunghee Sarah. "Politics of the Victim/Victor Complex: Interpreting South Korea's National Furor over Japanese History Textbooks." *American Asian Review* 21, no. 4 (2003): 145–79.

Song, Qiang, Zhang Zangzang, and Qiao Bian. *Zhongguo keyi shuo bu: Lengzhan hou shidai de zhengzhi yu qinggan jueze* [China can say no: Political and emotional choices in the post–Cold War era]. Beijing: Zhonghua Gongshang Lianhe Chubanshe, 1996.

Spence, Jonathan D. *The Search for Modern China*. New York: W. W. Norton, 1990.

Sullivan, Roger W. "Discarding the China Card." *Foreign Policy* 86 (1992): 3–23.

Tajfel, Henri. *Human Groups and Social Categories: Studies in Social Psychology*. Cambridge: Cambridge University Press, 1981.

Tajfel, H., and J. C. Turner. "The Social Identity Theory of Intergroup Behavior." In *Psychology of Intergroup Relations*, edited by S. Worchel and L. W. Austin, pp. 7–24. Chicago: Nelson-Hall, 1986.

Tamura, Eileen H, et al. *China: Understanding Its Past*. Honolulu: University of Hawaii Press, 1997.

Teng, Suyu, and John Fairbank. *China's Response to the West*. Cambridge, MA: Harvard University Press, 1954. Reprinted in Mark A. Kishlansky, ed., *Sources of World History*, vol. 2. New York: HarperCollins College, 1995.

T. H. R. "The Uses of the Past." *Hedgehog Review* 9, no. 2 (2007): 1–6.

Thurston, Anne F. "Community and Isolation: Memory and Forgetting." In *Memory and History in East and Southeast Asia*, edited by G. Gong, pp. 149–72. Washington, DC: CSIS Press, 2001.

Tidwell, A. C. *Conflict Resolved? A Critical Assessment of Conflict Resolution.* New York: Pinter, 1998.

Tong, Zeng. *Zuihou yidao fangxian* [The last frontier]. Beijing: China Social Science Press, 2003.

Townsend, James. "Chinese Nationalism." In *Chinese Nationalism*, edited by Jonathan Unger, pp. 1–30. Armonk, NY: M. E. Sharpe, 1996.

Unger, Jonathan, ed. *Using the Past to Serve the Present: Historiography and Politics in Contemporary China.* Armonk, NY: M. E. Sharpe, 1993.

Volkan, Vamik D. *Bloodlines: From Ethnic Pride to Ethnic Terrorism.* New York: Farrar, Straus & Giroux, 1997.

Volkan, Vamik D. "Large Group Identity and Chosen Trauma." *Psychoanalysis Downunder* 6 (2005): 1–32.

Volkan, Vamik D. *The Need to Have Enemies and Allies: From Clinical Practice to International Relationships.* Northvale, NJ: Jason Aronson, 1988.

von Falkenhausen, Lothar. "The Waning of the Bronze Age: Material Culture and Social Developments, 770–481 b.c." In *The Cambridge History of Ancient China: From the Origins of Civilization to 221 B.C.*, edited by Michael Loewe and Edward L. Shaughnessy, pp. 450–544. Cambridge: Cambridge University Press, 1999.

Wade, Geoff. "The Zheng He Voyages: A Reassessment." ARI Working Paper no. 31. Singapore: Asia Research Institute (October 2004): 1–27.

Wang, Dong. *China's Unequal Treaties: Narrating National History.* Lanham, MD: Lexington Books, 2005.

Wang, Jianwei. *Limited Adversaries: Post–Cold War Sino-American Mutual Images.* New York: Oxford University Press, 1999.

Wasserstrom, Jeffrey N. "Asia's Textbook Case." *Foreign Policy* 152 (2006): 80–82.

Wasserstrom, Jeffrey N. *China's Brave New World, and Other Tales of Global Times.* Bloomington: Indiana University Press, 2007.

Weber, Max. *Essays in Sociology.* Edited by H. H. Gerth and C. Wright Mills. New York: Oxford University Press, 1946.

White, Tyrene. "Postrevolutionary Mobilization in China: The One-Child Policy Reconsidered." *World Politics* 43, no. 1 (1990): 53–76.

Wireman, Billy. "The People's Republic of China Turns 50." *Vital Speeches of the Day*, July 15, 2000.

Xu, Guoqi. *China and the Great War: China's Pursuit of a New National Identity and Internationalization.* Cambridge: Cambridge University Press, 2005.

Xu, Guoqi. "Internationalism, Nationalism, National Identity: China from 1895 to 1919." In *Chinese Nationalism in Perspective*, edited by George Wei and Xiaoyun Liu, pp. 101–20. Santa Barbara, CA: Greenwood Press, 2001.

Xu, Guoqi. *Olympic Dreams: China and Sports, 1895–2008*. Cambridge, MA: Harvard University Press, 2008.

Xu, Jilin. "Historical Memories of May Fourth: Patriotism, but of What Kind?" Translated by Duncan M. Campbell. *China Heritage Quarterly*, no. 17 (2009).

Yan, Xuetong. "The Rise of China in Chinese Eyes." *Journal of Contemporary China* 10, no. 26 (2001): 33–39.

Yan, Xuetong. *Zhongguo guojia liyi fenxi* [Analysis of China's national interests]. Tianjin: Tianjin People's Press, 1997.

Yang, Guobin. "A Civil Society Emerges from the Earthquake Rubble." *Yale Global*, June 5, 2008.

Yang, Jui-Sung. "Imaging National Humiliation: 'Sick Man of East Asia' in the Modem Chinese Intellectual and Cultural History." *Journal of History* (Zheng zhi da xue li shi xue bao) 23 (2005): 1–44.

Yee, Albert. "Semantic Ambiguity and Joint Deflections in the Hainan Negotiations." *China: An International Journal* 2 (2004): 53–82.

Yick, Joseph. *Making of Urban Revolution in China: The CCP-GMD Struggle for Beiping-Tianjin, 1945–1949*. New York: M. E. Sharpe, 1995.

Yoshida, Takashi. "Advancing or Obstructing Reconciliation? Changes in History Education and Disputes over History Textbooks in Japan." In *Teaching the Violent Past,* edited by Elizabeth Cole, pp. 51–80. New York: Rowman & Littlefield, 2007.

Yuan, Weishi. "Xiandaihua yu lishi jiaokeshu" [Modernization and history textbooks]. *Bingdian*, January 11, 2006.

Zajda, Joseph, and Rea Zajda. "The Politics of Rewriting History: New History Textbooks and Curriculum Materials in Russia." *International Review of Education* 49, no. 3/4 (2003): 363–84.

Zerubavel, Yael. *Recovered Roots: Collective Memory and the Making of Israeli National Tradition*. Chicago: University of Chicago Press, 1995.

Zhang, Ming. "The New Thinking of Sino-U.S. Relations: An Interview Note." *Journal of Contemporary China* 6, no. 14 (1997): 117–23.

Zhao, Dingxin. "An Angle on Nationalism in China Today: Attitudes among Beijing Students after Belgrade 1999." *China Quarterly* 172 (2002): 49–69.

Zhao, Suisheng. *A Nation-State by Construction: Dynamics of Modern Chinese Nationalism*. Stanford, CA: Stanford University Press, 2004.

Zhao, Suisheng. "A State-Led Nationalism: The Patriotic Education Campaign in Post-Tiananmen China." *Communist and Post-Communist Studies* 31, no. 3 (1998): 287–302.

Zhu, Wenli. "How Chinese See America." Paper presented at "China–U.S. Substantial China Dialogue," Beijing, October 31–November 2, 2000.

Zong, Hairen. "Zhu Rongji in 1999 (1)." *Chinese Law & Government* 35, no. 1 (2002): 1–73.

Zong, Hairen. "Zhu Rongji in 1999 (2)." *Chinese Law & Government* 35, no. 2 (2002): 1–91.

INDEX

I

O

P

T

U

V

W

X

Y

Z

Printed in the USA
CPSIA information can be obtained
at www.ICGtesting.com
JSHW010954310823
47579JS00012B/674